VOICES

OF THE CHESAPEAKE BAY

by
Michael Buckley

With photography by
David W. Harp

I AM CERTAIN THAT AFTER THE DUST OF CENTURIES HAS PASSED OVER OUR CITIES, WE, TOO, WILL BE REMEMBERED NOT FOR VICTORIES OR DEFEATS IN BATTLE OR IN POLITICS, BUT FOR OUR CONTRIBUTION TO THE HUMAN SPIRIT.
— *John F. Kennedy*

Dedication

This book is dedicated to my family, especially to my mother
who made all this possible.

Table of Contents

John Wennersten, Author, *Chesapeake: An Environmental History*
Vince Leggett, Blacks of the Chesapeake Foundation

Chapter Four · 85
Chesapeake Bay Ecosystems

Pat Vojtech, Author, *Chesapeake Wildlife: Stories of Survival & Loss*
Dr. Robert and A. J. Lippson, Authors, *Life in the Chesapeake*
Dr. Laura Murray, Scientist/Educator, Horn Point Laboratory
Dr. Tom Miller, Fisheries Ecologist, Chesapeake Biological Laboratory
Bill Goldsborough, Senior Scientist, Chesapeake Bay Foundation
Dr. Carole Baldwin, Marine Biologist/Author, Smithsonian National Museum of Natural History

Chapter Five · 125
Watermen

Earl White, First Mate, Skipjack *Stanley Norman*
Captain Dallas and Kaki Bradshaw, Smith and Tangier Islanders
David "Bunkie" Miller and Marybelle Miller with Ed Klein, Musicians, Tilghman Island
Larry Simns, President, Maryland Watermen's Association
Mick Blackistone, Executive Director, Crab Restoration Around the Bay (CRAB)
Captain Ed Farley, Skipjack *H.M. Krentz*

Acknowledgments

My first thanks are to Marci Andrews and Lenny Rudow who both believed that the *Voices of the Chesapeake Bay* interviews would make a good read, regardless of the challenges of translating interviews into printed words. Many thanks also to Donna McGee, Lorrie Castenada, and Christine Kennedy for graciously helping to transcribe the audio interviews.

My heartfelt gratitude to Dick Franyo, Don Baugh, and Mark Wasserman for igniting my spirit and, perhaps unwittingly, being role models in my life. To my colleagues at radio station 103.1 WRNR: Bob Waugh, Alex Cortright, Rob Timm, Judy Buddensick and the rest of the RNR crew for their support of the *Voices of the Chesapeake Bay* series over the past seven years. On behalf of everyone who listens, reads and yearns to know more about this amazing natural wonder, thanks for keeping the *Voices* project alive. To Brian Henley and everyone at *The Capital,* thanks for publishing *The Music Box,* my weekly column on the national music scene.

Sincere thanks to David O'Neill, Melanie Teems and everyone at the Chesapeake Bay Trust, Maryland State Arts Council, the Boatyard Bar & Grill for sponsorships and assistance over the years, and the Keith Campbell Foundation for the Environment, Verna Harrison, and Julie Trask. Kudos to Vince Lupo, Dave Gendell at *Spinsheet,* MD State Archives, Jeff Place at Smithsonian Folkways, Harry Merrick and Merrick Towel Communications (web and graphics assistance), Joe Compton, Jackie Fletcher, and www.AmericanHistoricalTheatre.com Thanks to Christopher Conner at UMCES, Barbara Escher at the Baltimore School of Massage, musician Deanna Dove, Ellen Flattery at MPT, Kessler Burnett at *Chesapeake Life,* Lisa Rowe, Steve Kingston and WINX-FM, Fred Hickman and Christine Rozycki.

Special thanks to Chesapeake champions Keith Campbell and photographer David Harp for making the photographs for this book possible. Check out Dave's epic landscape photography at www.ChesapeakePhotos.com.

Thanks to my family on both coasts and particularly William and Pamela Sommerfield who have given me unwavering support over the years through their spirit, cultural values, ethics and our work together in creating the American Historical Theatre. It's such a blessing to spend this time together, through all the victories and the struggles.

Finally, all my love and thanks to Donna McGee and her family for making me feel at home in their lives.

<u>Prologue</u>

Lifelong Learning

Many people travel across the Chesapeake Bay Bridge and only see a big, flat body of water. It is my hope that *Voices of the Chesapeake Bay* will help them see deep into that water, and glimpse into the lives of the people living in and around the bay. These interviews present knowledgeable people with amazing stories that enhance our understanding of the world around us and allow us to see things we may not have recognized before. By listening to these stories we can begin to understand the diversity of our world and how we play a part in an ecosystem that must be kept in balance.

The *Voices of the Chesapeake Bay* interviews also give us a chance to see the region from many different points of view. Doing these interviews has granted me the opportunity to continue on a path of lifelong learning, a process which is vital to our development as complete human beings, and this book's goal is to provide the same opportunity to others. To help us all go back and re-learn what we already know with fresh eyes, equipped with the advantage of knowledge, age and experience. The *Voices* interviews allow us to see life through a variety of perspectives, each a snapshot of a stretch of time. This loose collection of over 50 edited audio interviews provides the opportunity to look in on our neighbors, get to know a bit about their lives, and be inspired by their accomplishments.

1

Bay Beginnings

These are the facts. The Chesapeake Bay is the largest of 130 estuaries in the United States. An estuary is a mixing bowl, where freshwater and saltwater combine. This mixing of warm, brackish, relatively shallow water offers a great environment in which things can grow.

The Chesapeake Bay is approximately 200 miles long, four miles wide near Aberdeen and 35 miles wide at the mouth of the Potomac River. Saltwater makes up 50 percent of the water in the bay, and floods in from the Atlantic Ocean. More than 150 rivers and streams drain freshwater into the Chesapeake, including the great Susquehanna, which provides 50 percent of the freshwater in this estuary. Elaborate systems of underground aquifers also contribute to the 18 trillion gallons of water in the bay. The Chesapeake is a watershed of 64,000 square miles including six states: Delaware, Maryland, New York, Pennsylvania, Virginia, and West Virginia, plus the District of Columbia. From these facts we can begin to understand just how complex and vast the bay is. But it's just a beginning.

Dr. Peter Kranz, Paleontologist/Founder, The Dinosaur Fund

500,000,000 to 65,000,000 BC

One day during my radio show, I received a telephone call from a listener suggesting a good candidate for a Voices *interview, Dr. Peter Kranz. Dr. Kranz is the founder of the Dinosaur Fund, an organization that presents opportunities to learn about dinosaurs from the Washington, D.C. area. In other words, he takes people on field expeditions around Washington to dig for fossils.*

I found Dr. Kranz during the winter of 2006, moonlighting as a biology teacher at an elementary school for gifted students in a neighborhood near George Washington University. Between his classes I was invited to sit at a very small desk, with Dr. Kranz across from me at the teacher's desk. Talk about going back to school! Just like the smartest kid in the class, I proceeded to grill Dr. Krantz about the prehistory of the Chesapeake Bay region.

"Some half a billion years ago, there was a land mass that represented eastern North America and what we call the Proto-Atlantic Ocean or the Iapetus Sea," Dr. Kranz explained. "Conditions were very much like they are in the Bahamas today, sort of coral atolls and coral reefs and warm, subtropical conditions. Somewhere during the middle part of Paleozoic time, between 300 and 400 million years ago, the plates of the earth began to move and change their orientation. The Proto-Atlantic Ocean disappeared about 200 million years ago, more or less, and a giant super continent called Pangaea formed. In other words, you could stand with one foot in Europe and one foot in North America and there was no ocean between them. It was just one big continent. And it was fairly hot and dry, for the most part.

Around 200 million years ago, the whole thing began to split up again and the modern Atlantic Ocean began to form. It was like an Atlantic River at that point, very small but continuing to widen. Not all areas became the Atlantic Ocean. Some of the cracks filled up with lakes, and this string of lakes ran from Nova Scotia down through Pennsylvania, all the way through Maryland and Virginia, through Gettysburg, Thurmont, on down into Leesburg, Manassas, Culpepper, and then on down to Richmond and North Carolina. It was what everybody thinks of as classical dinosaur environment–somewhat tropical, with volcanoes all over the place."

A tropical climate with volcanoes in the Mid-Atlantic? Sounds like global warming isn't such a new phenomenon. Dr. Kranz described a landscape much different from the Chesapeake region we know today. As the Atlantic Ocean continued to widen the Appalachian Mountains wore away, and their sand, clay, and gravel formed a shoreline that would cover the belt between Interstate 95 and the Baltimore/Washington Parkway. This shoreline ran from present-day Elkton, Maryland, down into Virginia, along the eastern and western shores of the Potomac River, and up toward the Chesapeake Bay near Gibson Island and Bohemia Mills.

"You find fossils in those coastal deposits of sand and clay washed away from the Appalachian Mountains, from the dinosaur age ranging from approximately 120 million years ago to about 65 million years ago. In other words, the end of the age of dinosaurs.

The youngest deposits are marine, coming from the ocean. And those are found primarily out towards Bowie and up toward Gibson Island. The most complete fossil skeleton that we have from the dinosaur times in this area is a mosasaur, which looks like a giant lizard-alligator type thing. It's a close relative of today's Komodo Dragon, which you can see at the zoo.

Dinosaurs that have been found in this area represent

every kind you can think of. The names of the dinosaurs are unfamiliar because the dinosaurs here are not the same dinosaurs that are found in the western United States or elsewhere in the world. We have large, plant-eating dinosaurs like brontosaurus. The local version is called Astrodon johnstoni, which happens to be the state dinosaur of Maryland. It became state dinosaur in 1998. It has a long neck and a long tail. Some of them might have been 50 to 60 feet tall and as long as 100 feet. The original specimen was found in November of 1858 in Muirkirk, which is just south of Laurel. It became the official state dinosaur because the first specimen was found here. And my research shows it was actually presented to the Maryland Academy of Sciences 15 days before the one that's usually considered the first dinosaur from North America, the Hadrosaurus foulkii, from New Jersey. So in a sense, Maryland can claim to have the first dinosaur from North America."

Dr. Stephen Godfrey, Curator of Paleontology, Calvert Marine Museum

65,000,000 to 10,000,000 BC

When it comes to prehistoric times, people in the Chesapeake Bay region tend to think of Calvert Cliffs and hunting for sharks' teeth. Calvert Cliffs is a 30 mile stretch along the Chesapeake Bay in Southern Maryland, 14 miles south of Price Frederick. This deposit is far more recent than the period Dr. Krantz discussed, and was formed about 15 million years ago when Southern Maryland was covered by a warm, shallow sea. More than 600 species of fossils have been identified from these cliffs, the most common being the teeth of various species of shark.

Calvert Cliffs State Park is operated and maintained by the Friends of Calvert Cliffs State Park and the State Forest and Park Service. The park offers public trails that lead to the cliffs. Due to erosion access to the actual cliffs is prohibited, but the beaches below are fair game. Visitors can keep any fossils and sharks' teeth they find there.

To learn more about Chesapeake prehistory and Calvert Cliffs, I placed a call to the Calvert Marine Museum, in Solomons Island, Maryland, which collects, preserves, and interprets Miocene-era fossils that erode from the cliffs. I was referred to Dr. Stephen Godfrey, the museum's Curator of Paleontology.

Dr. Stephen Godfrey is a native of Canada. He caught the collecting bug as a child, bringing home animal skeletons for his bedroom museum. Following a post-doctoral fellowship at the University of Toronto, he moved to Drumheller, (the "Dinosaur Capital" of Canada,) and then on to Sydney, Australia. Dr. Godfrey became a specialist at recreating missing bones for skeletal dinosaur displays in many of the world's most prestigious natural history museums. In 1998, he became Curator *of Paleontology at the Calvert Marine Museum. As we sat in his fossil-filled office in the winter of 2006, I asked Dr. Godfrey about his fascination with the early history of our planet and the Chesapeake Bay region.*

"I decided to go into paleontology because I was raised in a Young Earth Creationist family," Dr. Godfrey said. "My expectation, and what I was taught growing up, was that the earth and the universe were approximately 6,000 years old. Of course, you know that is diametrically opposed to consensus in science and certainly evolutionary theory—the earth being approximately four or five billion years old and earth and life having evolved on earth through that period. Within Christianity there is the full spectrum of belief. There are Christians who believe that the Genesis account should be taken literally. I also actually believe that it should be taken literally. But in addition to be taken literally, it should be accurate scientifically for all people at all times. Young Earth Creationists take that literal account, which describes a young earth cosmology, and they believe that to be scientifically accurate as well, which I no longer believe it to be. But that was the environment in which I grew up, as opposed to Christians who accept the scientific consensus that the earth and universe are much older.

Having grown up in an environment in which the earth is only 6,000 to 10,000 years old we viewed the opposing philosophy, evolutionary theory, as denying the existence of God. It was very troubling to me that there was this other branch of knowledge–science, biology, paleontology–that was so at odds with what the Bible purported to claim, to preach, to teach. We had been taught and believed that God had created everything that there is, all species, essentially instantaneously as in the description in Genesis. So in my third year at Bishop's University I decided to find out for myself if the claims that were being made by scientists, specifically paleontologists, were real–if the fossil record was true, was accurate, was reliable, or if paleontologists were creating this false doctrine. If they were sort of just fiddling with the evidence to make it appear as though animals had changed through time. I wanted to find out for myself, and that was really what motivated me to study paleontology.

I don't think there's any doubt now that a meteorite impact contributed to the final extinction at what's called the cretaceous tertiary boundary about 65 million years ago. There's good evidence of this under the Yucatan Peninsula, where they've actually mapped out where one of these impacts occurred. Obviously the crater site has now been covered with sediment, but they can still map the sea floor and the sediments that lie below the sea floor to show the perimeter of this gigantic crater and the devastation that it created. The Decan Traps, the vast volcanic beds in India, is one of the largest accumulations of lava anywhere on earth. That happened at about the same time. I'm not a geologist, so I'm reluctant to say that there's a direct correlation of one with the other. But I think that there's good evidence that both are related to the demise of a world that was filled with creatures, some of which were very unlike animals that are living today. That happened 65 million years ago.

There was another impact about 35 million years ago where the mouth of the Chesapeake Bay is today. They've mapped the contour of what's called the Exmore Crater, just north of Norfolk. The Chesapeake didn't exist at that time, it was just the Atlantic Ocean. The Delmarva Peninsula did not exist at that time, either. That's a more recent geologic phenomenon.

My mandate at the Calvert Marine Museum is simply to collect, preserve, and interpret the fossils along the Chesapeake Bay, specifically Calvert Cliffs, which comprises sea cliffs that range in height from a few feet up to about 125 feet high. The age of the sediments ranges from about 20 down to about 10 million years old. These are sediments that accumulated for the most part in shallow marine areas. As rivers were flowing from the Appalachian Mountains into the Atlantic Ocean, they were carrying with them sediments that accumulated in this part of Southern Maryland. The global climate was warmer then. There was less ice at the South Pole, there was no ice at the North Pole. If you melt the ice you have global warming, you raise the level of the ocean; so this part of the world was flooded. That's why Calvert Cliffs is so important. As the cliffs erode, the skeletons and fossil shells fall down on the beach and we're able to collect and study them. A lot of what we do is a little bit like CSI, but it's CSI paleontology. It's detective work. We're left with clues about what the animals looked like, about their behavior, and from that we try to piece together what happened here in Southern Maryland prehistorically. We can then compare the fossilized remains of those animals to ones that are living today. We can look back in time to see how plants and animals have changed through time. That's the principal evidence for evolution that we now have. It's the fossil record.

Since it was a shallow marine seascape we're finding examples of animals that would have lived in that environment, and from time to time we're finding the remains of animals that didn't typically live in that environment. For example, we find the remains of camels, tapiers, rhinos, peccaries, and a unique North American example of a mastodon elephant. These terrestrial animals were living in the Washington area up in the Piedmont Mountains. During storms, if they drowned, you can imagine a carcass bloating and then floating out to sea. As the carcass then decomposes it's dismembered by scavengers feeding on it. The bones are scattered over the bottom. More sediment comes in, piles up on top of those bones, and they have a good chance of becoming fossilized as opposed to dissolving or disintegrating.

From time to time we find feces fossilized as well; Paleontologists have named fossilized excrement 'coprolite.' Remarkable items can be preserved in coprolites. We have two coprolites from Calvert Cliffs that preserve feathers. So an animal, like a Miocene crocodile, could have eaten a bird. The feathers were difficult to digest and passed through the system of this animal, and then those feces were fossilized. We've had the extreme good fortune of being able to find those. Calvert Cliffs is the only place in the world where fossilized feces have been found with preserved feathers in them.

We've also taken out a lot of whale and dolphin skulls. All the whales that have been found at Calvert Cliffs so far are members of an extinct family of whales, cetotheres, the precursors to the largest ever living animals, the rorquals, which include the blue whale, fin whale, sai whale, and minke whale. Those whales would have ranged from 10 to 25 feet in length. They were large animals in their own right, but small when compared to the largest of the filter-feeding whales. The southern blue whale can be in excess of 100 feet long. You're talking about incredibly big animals. People think that dinosaurs were the largest, and they were certainly the largest terrestrial animals. But in looking at all of life, by far the blue whale outstrips them all.

The dolphins that we find are often members of families that are entirely extinct, but we do find members of families that are still living. One of the exciting dolphins that I'm currently working on as a research project with a member of the Smithsonian staff, Dave Bohaska, is the most primitive representative of a family of dolphins that is living today, the Ganges River dolphin. They're limited now to freshwater rivers in India, Pakistan, Nepal, and Bangladesh. If it were not for the fossil record we would know nothing of what the ancestors of the living animals looked like, nor would we know about where they lived in prehistoric times. During the Miocene the platinistidae family–which today is endangered–was much more anatomically diverse and geographically widespread. We know that because we find their fossils preserved in Calvert Cliffs, this portal to the Miocene Epic. It's all interconnected. It's a point, a page from the history book that we're able to look at."

John Page Williams, Senior Naturalist, Chesapeake Bay Foundation

20,000 BC

The Chesapeake Bay Foundation (CBF) was formed in 1967 by a group of concerned citizens who wanted to educate others about becoming good stewards of this amazing natural resource we call the Chesapeake. CBF has over 100,000 members, and is led by a group of highly trained scientists, educators, and other specialists working in partnership with government, business, and citizens to preserve and protect the bay.

John Page Williams is the foundation's Senior Naturalist. John Page has served CBF since 1973 as a field educator, program administrator, fundraiser, and staff writer. He also runs educational field trips by canoe, outboard skiff, and workboat, on every river system in the bay. John Page is the lead CBF staffer in a partnership with the Conservation Fund and the National Geographic Society, working to develop the new Captain John Smith Chesapeake National Historic Water Trail. He also works with fishermen and boaters to improve water quality and restore the ecosystem's health. He has written two important books, Chesapeake Bay in Small Boats *and* Chesapeake Almanac.

Robin and I met with John Page in the spring of 2000 to learn how this great estuary was created. This was the first Voices of the Chesapeake Bay *interview, and it lit a spark that lifted the whole project.*

"Twenty thousand years ago the earth was a lot drier and colder and a tremendous amount of water was tied up in the polar ice caps. The North Pole glacier extended all the way into what's now north-central Pennsylvania, and as the earth started warming, a river developed. It was a big river

that ran off the icecap, south and east down to the Atlantic. As the earth continued to warm and rainfall increased, the river started carrying more and more water.

Sea level rose from the melting of the ice caps, and the ocean began to back up into the valley floor of the river. Gradually it backed up 195 to 200 miles. All the way to what we now call Smith's Falls, just above Port Deposit, Maryland. It also backed up 100 miles on the Potomac River. It backed up close to 80 miles on the Rappahannock, I guess about 80 miles on the James, and then up into the Choptank and the Patuxent, until it took the shape it does today.

The Native Americans named the big river Susquehanna. It comes from all the way up in south-central New York State–Binghamton, Corning, Elmira, even Cooperstown. We generally think of Cooperstown as the head of the watershed. From Havre de Grace up to Binghamton is, I think, a little over 300 river miles.

For some reason the Native Americans decided they should change the river's name where it hit tide, up there where it widens out into the Susquehanna Flats... they changed its name to Chesapeake, which means 'great shellfish bay.' What's funny is they didn't make the same distinction on the Potomac, so the tidal Potomac is still the Potomac, the tidal Rappahannock is still the Rappahannock. It's the same with the James and all the others. For some reason, they made a distinction between the Susquehanna River and the Chesapeake Bay.

Rivers generally get measured by geologists by how much freshwater they flow. By that measure the Susquehanna is the largest river on the Atlantic Coast by a factor of a little bit more than two. It is slightly larger than the Connecticut and the Hudson put together.

The Potomac, by that measure, is the eighth largest river on the Atlantic Coast. But this is all part of the Susquehanna system. If you measure the whole thing together, what you're looking at is a river system that's about four times as large as the Connecticut or the Hudson in terms of how much freshwater comes into it. The truth is, if you think about the Susquehanna in this way, and you think about the Bay as being the tidal Susquehanna, then all these other rivers are part of that one river."

Now that we had a basic understanding of the early geological formation of the Chesapeake Bay Region, we decided to learn about a few of the animals that lived here during those prehistoric times, and continue to exist today. I'd heard something about an ancient fish that grows up to 12 feet long, and also of the mysterious horseshoe crab. Our friend and program partner Dr. Robin Jung suggested that amphibians such as frogs and salamanders also remained from those ancient days. So the Voices *project next looked into the lives of some of these earliest bay creatures.*

Dr. Andrew Lazur, Sturgeon Enhancement Program

Horn Point Laboratory, on the Eastern Shore near Cambridge, part of the University of Maryland Center for Environmental Science (UMCES), is dedicated to preserving one of the oldest Chesapeake Bay species. The lab's Sturgeon Enhancement Program is studying the reproductive habits of the bay's severely depleted sturgeon population, and finding ways of bringing it back from the brink of extinction.

The world-wide demand for sturgeon eggs–caviar–caused the fish to be over-harvested. Taking sturgeon out of the bay is banned now, and the scientists at Horn Point Laboratory are finding inventive ways to repopulate the bay with this fascinating and ancient species.

The lab's hatchery is made up of five wet labs full of large and small fish tanks, and two dry labs where researchers perform water-quality analysis and fish necropsy. The lab also has an environmental control room, which allows scientists to control light periods and water temperatures in order to condition fish to spawn at any time of year.

Dr. Andrew Lazur, Associate Professor, Aquaculture Specialist for UMCES, leads the Sturgeon Enhancement Program. In 2006, I interviewed him at the laboratory while observing a six-foot sturgeon circling in a tank just below.

"Sturgeon do have that Jurassic look because they are a Jurassic species. They have the finage and the external scales called scoots, just like a turtle. They date back 100 million years to the Jurassic period, so they're one of several species that have survived what the dinosaurs went through, which is really amazing. There are only a few species of Jurassic fish. You have the gar, the bowfin, and the ciliocamph, which is found on the coast of Africa offshore.

There are 28 species of sturgeon worldwide. They tend to be what we call temperate species, found in cooler climates.

They're certainly not tropical. Probably the southernmost species that you'll find is the Gulf of Mexico sturgeon, which is
very similar to the Atlantic sturgeon.

When you look at the most important species worldwide
today, and for the last 100 years, it's probably the beluga
sturgeon in Russia, captured in the Black and Caspian seas.
It was harvested, and is still harvested to some extent, for its
highly prized caviar. It's a large egg. And then it's processed
via salting, etc., into caviar. So our species of sturgeon on the
East Coast, both the Atlantic sturgeon and the short-nosed
sturgeon, were harvested for their caviar and meat. In fact,
we have historical records that they found scoots in Indian
mounds, so we know that sturgeon were also harvested by
Native Americans. In the 1800's in particular, sturgeon was
harvested primarily for its caviar, processed, and then shipped
to Europe.

Sturgeons are bottom feeders. Their mouth is designed
almost like a tube and it can grab small crustaceans, soft-
shell clams or benthic organisms (animals that live either on
the bottom or in the mud) such as insect larvae. Sturgeons
are more carnivore than omnivore. They slant toward small
animals. They can eat small fish, but the way their mouth is
shaped it's really for slow-moving prey. It's not like a preda-
cious fish such as striped bass, where the mouth is right there,
in front and open, to chase prey. Sturgeon just kind of forage
along on the bottom and their elongated snout allows them to
root up things. Their downward-pointing mouth is such that
they can actually suck things up almost like a vacuum cleaner,
and crush them. So if it's a clam, they can break that shell and
then get to the insides.

Atlantic sturgeon are not federally protected under the
Endangered Species Act. The The Atlantic States Marine Fisheries Commission (ASMFC) which is a consortium of the 13 Atlantic states, regulates the fishery of Atlantic sturgeon. I think
it was in 1997, the Atlantic States Marine Fisheries Commission passed a moratorium on fishing all Atlantic sturgeon, and
there is currently no recreational or commercial catching of

them. In that sense they are protected. The short-nosed sturgeon, however, is federally protected. In fact, if anybody was to catch a short-nosed sturgeon they'd have to release it immediately. You can tell pretty easily between the two because short-nosed tend to be a lot smaller in size. They reach maybe 80 pounds at their maximum, whereas an Atlantic sturgeon historically was over 1,000 pounds in size and 14 feet long. So it's a huge fish.

Sturgeon are interesting because they're an anadromous species, meaning they spend their adult lifecycle in the marine environment and then migrate or "run" up freshwater rivers to spawn, similar to striped bass. Fortunately, in the Chesapeake Bay there are no dams blocking access to their habitat. Their preferred habitat is the harder bottom, not necessarily rock, but rock does work for spawning. The geology of the bottom has really changed, influencing the spawning of Atlantic sturgeon. In fact, when we think about Atlantic sturgeon and we look at all the surveys that go on, there have only been two documented spawns of Atlantic sturgeon in the last 40 years in the Chesapeake Bay. That's pretty phenomenal. That's not to say there aren't more spawns going on, which is probably the case. We certainly hope it's the case. But there have only been two situations where young of the year have been sighted, which would verify that there was a spawn.

What you're seeing here at Horn Point is basically a hatchery. We have the "brood" or adult tanks, and larval rearing systems and tanks. We can extract eggs, and fertilize them. We can check the motility rate of the sperm to know that they're active and viable. We also can do samples of the eggs as they are fertilized and develop. We put those eggs in a specialized hatching jar with aerated, flowing water, which keeps the eggs buoyant and at the right temperature.

Once they hatch out we put them in small larval tanks. We can crowd a lot of small larvae in one small tank. So our goal is to spawn the fish, then do test-releases to try to answer a multitude of questions: What's the ideal size of sturgeon to stock? What's the ideal time of year to stock these fish? Where do we stock in the bay? Do we target just certain rivers or can we release fish throughout the bay? We can learn how successful stocking is by inserting radio tags or other types of tags and tracking these animals. And ultimately, we want to track these animals 10 or 15 years, so when these young become adults we know what kind of contribution they're making back to the reproductive pool. But you can see that's a long-term process. It's not a one year project. We're talking about two decades of work just to see what sort of effect our restoration program will have on the species.

Sturgeon is an ideal species to do restoration work with because there is no commercial or recreational catch. So we know the animals that we release will not be impacted by the fisheries. Several billion young salmon are released every year by hatcheries, and while they may be making a contribution to the numbers, they're also still harvested both recreationally and commercially. You need to know the animal and the environment really well to develop a sustainable population, a managed population.

Sturgeon have been harvested for many reasons. Their swim bladder, a huge organ within the sturgeon, was used for isinglass, which was once used as a fine filter for making wines. In colonial times, isinglass was stretched and hardened for use as early glass. Native Americans counted sturgeon as a food source, as did Colonial Americans, who harvested it for its caviar. For a brief time caviar was second only to tobacco as a colonial cash crop. The resource was quickly exhausted because the few large females in the sturgeon population were targeted for their roe, damaging the species' ability to reproduce. The fishery peaked in about 1905, declined since then, and has been essentially flat for about 100 years.

There was a study done in 1996 by my colleague Dave Secore and Maryland DNR and Fish and Wildlife Service. They released 3,300 Atlantic sturgeon into the Nanticoke River. They tracked them for three years and had a 14-percent recapture rate, which is fantastic for a fish restoration project. It showed that the animals were doing well. So that's a glimmer of hope for us to hang our hat on—certainly, these animals can survive."

Photo courtesy of U.S Geological Survey Patuxtent Wildlife
Research Center

Dr. Robin Jung, Biologist, U.S.G.S. Patuxent Wildlife Research Center

While Andy Lazur worked to save the sturgeon, our good friend and partner, Dr. Robin Jung, was doing amazing research further inland on some of our planet's oldest living creatures: salamanders and frogs.

In the early 1990's, Robin had been reading about the drastic decline of the amphibian population and a project conducted by a group of Minnesota school children on the malformations they were finding on local frogs. Robin had been studying bird behavior, but decided to switch her research to amphibians to try to determine what was causing their declines.

Robin began her work in Wisconsin, studying the effects of polychlorinated biphenyls (PCBs), dioxin, and acid rain issues on amphibians. She moved to Annapolis in 1998 to take a wildlife biologist job at the U.S. Geological Survey Patuxent Wildlife Research Center in Laurel, Maryland. At the center she monitors different groups of amphibians, looking at the effects that landscape changes, land use, water quality, and other environmental factors have on amphibian populations.

In spring of 2003, Robin and I trucked out to visit a vernal pool site called Laura's Pond, on a U.S. Department of Agricultural property in the Beltsville Agricultural Research Center. On the way she told me about how these primitive creatures evolved from fish. The fossil record states that first there were fish (about 500 million years ago), then amphibians (around 400 million years ago), then reptiles, mammals, and birds.

When we think of amphibians we think of frogs, toads, salamanders, and newts. Judging from the sound of it, we were surrounded by all four at Laura's Pond. It was spring and the time was right for these creatures to come to the pond in search of mates. The pond was surrounded by a short synthetic cloth fence about a foot high, just enough to stop the salamanders in their tracks. All around the fence were pieces of plywood that the creatures would crawl under to stay moist and out of the sun. As we ventured onto the site, Robin explained her fascination.

"Amphibians have been on earth for 400 million years, before the dinosaurs and everything. Although very different from the amphibians we have now they were the first vertebrates to come on land. They evolved out of fish. The first amphibians were really large. Ichthyostega was quite a large amphibian, several feet long.

These vernal pools are called vernal because usually they fill up with spring rains or snow melt. This one is more of a permanent pond. I've never seen it completely dry up but it's definitely used by hundreds of spotted salamanders and wood frogs.

Ahh, salamanders everywhere! Aren't they beautiful? This pond has been studied for about five years now. Dr Laura Mazanti put a drift fence around it with cover boards on either side of the fence. It's a silt fence about one foot tall, made out of plastic, completely surrounding the pond. Then on either side of the fence we have these two-by-four-foot boards. When the salamander or wood frog tries to come to the pond and can't get in, instead, they go under the boards and hide there. That's when we turn over the boards, find them underneath and measure them. Gosh, look at all of them! With the spotted salamanders we take pictures of every individual and count the spots, because they have unique numbers and patterns. So by photograph identification we can tell exactly who is coming into the pond every year.

We also count egg masses at many ponds, to get an idea of how many amphibians came there. There's a one-to-one relationship so if you count 300 egg masses in a pond you know that there were 300 females that came there to breed.

The purpose of the study is to look at long-term changes in the population of spotted salamanders coming to breed at this site. Spotted salamanders are six to eight inch salamanders that are black with bright yellow spots. They're beautiful salamanders and they spend most of their lifetime underground. Ninety-five percent of their life they're underground in the woods using old mouse burrows, but during the early spring on wet rainy nights, they migrate to vernal pools to breed. It's kind of like a big orgy. The males come first and lay their spermatophores, their sperm packets. We'll see some of those out in the water. Then the females come. The males and females all congregate together in what's called a liebespeil, a kind of a love fest. We won't be able to see that now because it's daytime, but if we're out here on a wet rainy night you can see it happening.

We want to keep the woods around these vernal pools. A lot of salamanders and frogs get squished on roads that have a lot of traffic on them. If there's a highway where there are more than 26 cars per minute, up to 100 percent of the frogs and salamanders crossing could get squashed. If they do make it to the ponds, their eggs will hatch into little tadpoles in a couple of weeks. It depends on the temperature. If it's really warm they'll develop faster. Spotted salamander eggs, some are clear. They're very solid looking. There's a big jelly coat around the eggs. Some of them become white. They're almost white day-glow. Some of them turn green because algae start growing in the jelly of the egg masses. And it's a really neat example of a symbiotic relationship, because the algae produce oxygen for the developing embryos and the salamander jelly provides a kind of medium and nutrition for the algae. It's a give and take thing.

We actually have more salamander species in Maryland than frogs and toads. We've got some really interesting salamanders here. The spotted salamander, of course, and we have big tiger salamanders on the eastern shore. They can get up to 10 inches or so. There are also a lot of salamanders that breed in streams in Maryland. Two-lined salamanders are very common. If you go to any rocky stream around here and turn over rocks in the stream you'll probably find them. They're brown with two yellow stripes down their back. We also have redback salamanders. These are actually a terrestrial salamander. You'll find them under rocks and logs just in the woods. They lay their eggs on land, and redback salamanders don't actually need water. They need moist places but instead of hatching into a tadpole or a larva that has gills, all the development happens in the egg and they hatch out as miniature salamanders. They go egg, mini-salamander, salamander. You might not believe it, but if you were to take an acre of deciduous forest in the eastern United States and weigh all the birds in that acre or all the mammals in the acre, the salamanders and amphibians would actually weigh more. They're extremely abundant, and therefore very important in food webs and ecosystem processes.

There are a lot of things that eat amphibians: raccoons, opossums, birds. For example, at Laura's Pond we've seen turtles chowing down on tadpoles. We've seen herons gobbling up frogs. There are some amphibians that animals don't eat. For example, the red spotted newt has this bright orange terrestrial juvenile stage that's warning coloration. They actually have poisonous glands in their skin, so if something eats them they'll get sick. The monarch butterfly is the same way. It's got this bright orange warning coloration.

Amphibians also are important predators on things that we don't like, like mosquitoes and invertebrates. A bullfrog can eat about 6,000 insects in a night. That's a lot of mosquitoes, so they can really help control insect populations."

If you look at them head-on, it does look like they have a smile on their face. And some salamanders are quite modest. Some males, when you pick them up they'll take their hind legs and cover over their cloacae area. It's so funny. They do smile!"

2

Native People of the Chesapeake Bay

Mervin Savoy, Tribal Chairwoman, Piscataway Canoy and Sub-tribes

What was it like here in Chesapeake country before European settlers set foot in the area? We know that the region was bountiful, teaming with life. Stories passed down through many generations of Native Americans give us a glimpse into the not-so-distant past. Passing an oral history from one person to the next was once the essence of communication in a much smaller world. Native Americans who lived in the Chesapeake region continue, to this day, to help us envision what the world was like before human domination. During a time when man was simply another species.

One of our earliest Voices interviews in 2000 was with Mervin Savoy, Tribal Chairwoman for the Piscataway Canoy and Sub-tribes. The Piscataway Canoy and Sub-tribes are the indigenous peoples of Maryland's western shore. Mervin has dedicated her life to preserving the legacy of her tribe. Through Mervin's eyes we can begin to imagine a lifestyle of connection to all things great and small. The ability to feel and understand ourselves as simply a part of nature–something that has been largely lost in the modern world. We wanted to learn more about that way of life and Mervin was the perfect person to answer our questions. She illuminated the customs *of another time, creating pictures in our minds of a very different world from what we see and experience today.*

"I was born in the month of frogs. You know when that is? That's March. The Piscataway Canoy have resided in Maryland for over 12,000 years. We were here before Columbus decided to get lost. Native Peoples believe we've always been here. We don't believe the Bering Strait theory. If we followed game from Asia to here, why couldn't we have followed it from America to Asia? The trail went both ways, right? Nothing to say you couldn't go north. You had to go south all the time? We've always been here. This is the land where we were meant to be.

You'd be surprised at the types of animals we had here years ago. People don't realize. There were elk in Southern Maryland. There were wolves here. There were mastodons here. One of the largest dinosaur burial grounds in the United States is right here in Maryland, in Largo. Green alligators lived in Maryland. Oh, God, the sharks that were in the Potomac River! Whales, dolphins, barracudas, sturgeons–300 pound sturgeons in the Potomac River. Oh, Mother Nature had a rough day that day, because that's one of the ugliest fish out there.

Did you see where the largest tiger sharks found were right here in Maryland at Point Lookout? Humongous teeth! We had forest buffalo here. Not the buffalo you see in the western plains, but a smaller type of buffalo lived right here in Maryland. The last wild buffalo killed here was in 1704, in Largo. That wasn't that long ago.

In the old days Native People prayed for everybody. I mean your whole day was taken up in prayer. If you survived the night, when you got up you said a prayer of thanksgiving. If you went on a hunt, you asked forgiveness for taking the life of a living creature. If you cut down trees, you asked forgiveness for cutting down a tree, because you're taking the life of a living thing. Everything but rocks needs sun and water to nurture, to survive–animals, bugs, trees, poison ivy, mosquitoes. You know, they can't survive without all these elements that human beings also need to survive. So it's all living things, whether people see that or not. They call it the animalism religion. It had nothing to do with that. If animals didn't survive or live, how would you survive?

Of course, tribes did not have land grants or fences. They had territorial boundaries, and you knew where. It was inherited rights; even today, inherited rights. Our people didn't know about paper, didn't have deeds. The land belonged to all the people. No one person owned property. It was owned by the whole tribe.

Clans had certain territorial rights. And you had certain times of the year when certain clans got together with neighboring clans of the same type and went hunting and fishing or spring foraging, or whatever they were doing. That was the time that people got together and usually young people were paired up by the grandparents with whom they were going to marry.

Ninety-five percent of all North American tribes are matrilineal. There's no such thing as a hereditary chief. That doesn't happen. People select their leaders. Usually it's the women of the tribes who do this, and you inherit through your mother's bloodline. Your father brings nothing to the table. He is your biological father and that is it. In the old days, he didn't teach you anything. He did not support you in any way. When he married your mother he moved into her house, onto her property. He took care of his sister's children. Your mother's brothers took care of you. That's what makes it a matrilineal society. My father is Deer Clan, my mother is Turtle Clan. My father can't teach me anything about my mother's people. I belong to my mother's family, not my father's family. The female wolf is always the alpha. The male is always subservient to her.

In the old days, all seven clans lived in a village. But you had villages throughout your territory. Without these seven family units in the village, it didn't survive. You had hunters, you had farmers, you had builders, you had fishermen. These were jobs that each clan was assigned to do. You inherited that. The Bear Clan were the warriors. They didn't want to be fishermen. They didn't have to be hunters. They didn't have to build the houses or canoes. Their job was to be warriors. The Wolf Clan, they were your sentries. They'd police. They made sure the territory was safe. If someone came in your territory, they knew it. The word went out. When you went to war the Bear Clan was the first on the defense lines.

When it came time to be the shamans or medicine men your had the Turtle Clans, your priests and religious people. The Deer Clans they were the ones who made sure there was food for everybody. The Beaver Clan, they built houses and canoes. Look at what they do. The Turkey Clan, they were called 'squawkers.' Still got some. When it was time for the grand councils or their regular council meetings, they would go from house to house and find out what the complaints were, what the concerns were. And they were able to bring it to the council and discuss what was going on in the village, who had a problem. And look at our today's modern society. Who is that? That's the Senate and Congress. They're supposed to be the voice of the people. We have modernized systems in the 21st century, but our people have been doing it for thousands of years.

One of the things we didn't do, which your folks have a problem with, is you all like beachfront property. We know to get away from the water because water has a way of going at certain seasons or at the moon. We knew not to build on the water. We built up away from the water. That way our houses didn't wash away. Lasted for 70 to 100 years. Europeans wanted waterfront property and they built on the water, not thinking different seasons, cycles of the moon.

Freshwater was very important for every aspect. You were close enough to do your foraging for water plants or marsh plants. You were able to go fishing or hunting because everything comes to the water to drink. Plus you bathe everyday and if you went hunting or fishing or worked in the fields then of course you bathed twice a day.

Maryland, we had everything. We had the Atlantic Ocean.

We had the Chesapeake Bay. We had the rivers. We had a mountainous region. We had a desert region. We had the Piedmont. What did we need to leave for? The woods were teaming with different kinds of animals. There were all kinds of seafood. The soil was so rich you could plant anything. What did we need to go anywhere for? This was one of the reasons our people refused to go west... Why?"

Bob Gajdys, Mohawk Elder, Former US Commissioner of Indian Affairs

Bob Gajdys, a Mohawk Indian originally from Upstate New York, is a well-respected Native American elder. He was chosen by President Richard Nixon in the 1970's to serve as a Commissioner of Indian Affairs. Bob now lives in Prince Frederick, Maryland, where he has worked with a group to create an authentic Indian village at Jefferson Patterson Park. This is a place where people can come to get a feeling for what Indian life was like in the early 1600's. In late 2006, I asked Bob Gajdys about Native American spirituality and how he experiences the world through the ancient ways of his people.

"I happen to be a traditionalist, meaning that I carry on a lot of the customs and traditions that have been passed on from generation to generation. Before coming here this morning I needed to cleanse myself and I did a smoke ceremony as the sun came up. I have a combination of tobacco and sweet grass that I use, but you can use any form of tobacco. We do not use peyote; we do not use marijuana. In fact just the opposite. There cannot be drugs. Sage is looked at as one of the things to cleanse. It varies by tribe and it varies by tradition. It varies by what is available.

As a traditionalist I also believe in Mother Earth. The air, the sky, and all creatures are my brothers and sisters. That tree right there has a spirit. If I were to cut a tree down I would pray to the spirit of the tree and tell it why I have to cut it down. Back during World War II we didn't have much on the farms. We belonged to the ration program and so on. So I used to trap. Every time I trapped my brother or sister I prayed to them and thanked them for allowing me to do it, and told them what I was going to do. And these customs are the same throughout a lot of the Indian world today. For Native people who believe in Mother Earth spirituality, their life has to be in balance with everything around them. There has to be a relationship with you and everything in the world around you because you're only part of this world. And if you get out of balance for whatever reason, it can be an illness, it can be something psychological–or maybe even because the Redskins lost–then you need to get back into balance.

I do a lot of teaching. Tomorrow I'm teaching at an elementary school outside of Prince Frederick to about 150 fourth graders. I take a lot of my stuff that I've accumulated, my regalia and so on, and I talk to the kids. I have collected things like moccasins, pipes, and beadwork. I show them my medicine. Amongst my people when you get married your wife gives you something that is in part of your medicine, and you give something to her. My wife gave me this carved eagle from an antler done by Stan Hill, who is a Mohawk of international fame. He's no longer with us. Grandfather took him away last year. I gave my wife two straw dolls. And that's her spirit.

One of the things that I did as a traditionalist, not all Native People do this, is that when you're around 12 or 13 years old you have an "awakening" or a "spirit quest," which usually means that you go through a period of cleansing. There are cleansing ceremonies. Then you go into the wilderness or it could be out on the water. In my case it was up in the Adirondacks. I spent two days in the wilderness without food, just water. You try to get vision and hopefully the Grandfather will give you some sign of what's going to be important in your life and what it's going to mean. You bring that sign back if you're fortunate enough to get one. Sometimes the matriarchs and the elders will tell you what it means if you're not aware of it yourself. What I saw after two days, I saw the animals and creatures, the brothers and sisters all around me. And I came away with a very humble feeling that I was so small and insignificant a part of the whole. But I was an important part of the whole because all of nature responded to me while I was there. Everything from the ant to the eagle was all around. And then I had a vision of the hawks and the eagles talking to me...very strong, very strong."

As Bob was leaving the interview, he told me that he had seen a family of deer that morning. A five-point buck, his significant other, and a pair of fawns. Bob told me he had talked to the deer, as is the native custom, and told them thanks. He added that I might have thought him a little crazy if he had shared this when he had arrived for the interview. I reassured Bob that I had an open mind and appreciated his respect for the animals.

After he left, I went for a walk in a nearby park along the riverbank. At the trail's end I noticed two trees bowing toward the water because of erosion. Closer inspection revealed a long plank lying across the two trees, about eight feet above the beach. Somebody had placed the board to sit on, and enjoy the view of the water. As I came closer, I saw someone had left a sign on the plank. Was it for me? I took it as such. Someone had spread a pool of sand on the plank, making an oblong circle. Within the sand was a symbol made of stones: a four-inch cross pointing in the four cardinal directions. The south point on the circle was an oyster shell. In the sand, written by someone's finger, was the message "Keep Your Hopes Up."

I thought about that message, as I slowly walked down the path in the direction from which I had come. More perfect words had never been spoken. As I walked along I heard a scratching sound, and I thought, "Why would someone be raking leaves in such a great big park?" I rounded a bend and there he was–a five-point buck. I took a few more steps and, sure enough, there was a whole family of deer just like the one Bob had described to me.

If we are willing to listen and look carefully, signs are all around us. This is one of the things that Bob Gajdys tries to tell us, one of the beliefs that has been passed from person to person for thousands of years. As I watched the deer, I heard another rustling sound. High in an oak, a great owl swooped up and perched in full view. I felt at home in the woods with these creatures and told them "thank you," before continuing on home.

Daniel Firehawk Abbott, Nanticoke descendant

At a National Geographic Society conference celebrating the Native Americans of the Chesapeake region in late 2006, I happened upon an Indian man surrounded by a small crowd demonstrating the uses of traditional tools. Daniel "Firehawk" Abbott is a descendant of the Nanticoke people of Maryland's Eastern Shore. He grew up in Lower Dorchester County, a wild and enchanted region of huge, beautiful, open marshlands, teaming with wildlife.

Firehawk, a graduate of the University of Maryland, has devoted his life to researching Mid-Atlantic Indian culture. His studies include the development and fabrication of prehistoric clothing, tools, and architecture. Firehawk regularly demonstrates these wares and customs at historic sites and schools in the region. About a month after the National Geographic conference, I had the pleasure of visiting with Firehawk at his Eastern Shore home near Denton, in the tiny farming enclave of Greensboro, Maryland, on the Upper Choptank River. We sat in his living room, surrounded by historically accurate recreations of stone and bone Indian tools and weapons. There were bows and arrows, javelins, and tomahawks used for hunting, protection, and survival.

"I was born and raised in Cambridge, Maryland, which is a mite south of here," said Firehawk. "If you're talking about my culture, it's English and American Indian. I found out the American Indian part through my grandfather. He was a Lower Shore waterman, as his father and his father had been before him, in Robins, Maryland. It's just miles and miles of grasses and pine-studded islands. They call it 'the big water.' It's a place my ancestors went to and harvested regularly. It's a beautiful spot, it really is.

My grandfather's name was Parks Abbott. A lot of people knew him. He used to build 60 foot dovetail workboats. I don't think they're found anywhere else in the Bay. They have a fantail on them that juts out at the stern. And we used to go out when I was young. He had an old Chrysler engine in his workboat. That thing was huge and it made a lot of noise. He had a shifter transmission hooked in the engine and we'd go cruising out the creeks. He'd be shifting and when he hit the open water he'd shift that thing, man. Hah! He'd rev her up and slam her into gear and the whole bow would lift up out of the water. He didn't even have a clutch on that thing. We'd slam into the waves and we'd just cruise on out.

He'd crab. He'd run drags, set out pots, and run trotlines for crabs in the summer. Then he'd tong oysters in the winter and trap muskrat. I was raised on that. There aren't as many around now. They used to come home and they were weighted down with rats. That was 50, 60 years ago. The muskrat traps are about six inches in diameter and they have a trigger in the center. They look like the old bear traps without teeth. They set the traps below the waterline and the rats drown. If they set them in the shallow area, because tides go in and out, they'd still be alive. You come up and club them. That's the art of trapping. At one time it was a necessity. It was how you fed your family. You worked the land, as the ancients did. My grandfather told me, 'How do you think we learned many of these things that the watermen and the trappers know?' He said, 'That knowledge was passed down through the generations. It's oral history.' Oral teaching is how the Indians did it.

It was instilled in the older generations that to be Indian was something that one did not want others to know about. Indians were considered very low order, to say the least. Even animals were treated better. When people came here from Europe, they came with their thoughts and beliefs and they placed themselves on a pedestal. All other life forms were below them. So when they came here they felt they had the God-given right to assume ownership of the land. That was the difference between the cultures. Ownership of land was not something that was part of our language. You could not own the land. You could not own what Creator had made and placed us upon to be the caretakers of. It's even hard for me to imagine now, believing as I do, that one can own the land. I don't believe one can. We're here to share it and take care of it for the generations to come.

You'll notice I don't mind the word Indian. It's an identity that people gave us, and they understand it. You start talking Native Americans and First Nations People and aboriginals and people are thinking of Australia. It's semantics. What's in a name? My grandfather answered that very clearly. He said, 'We learn these things from the Indians. That knowledge was passed down. We just continued on with it.' He was right. He didn't know anything about Indians because he had been made to feel ashamed of being Indian. If you were black, you were better than Indians. So people chose on their birth records, going back as far as the late 1800's, to write in 'black' or 'free black' or 'white,' if they could get by with it. You didn't want people to know that your children were Indian. Indians were to be disposed of, to be moved to another place, so that you could then establish your culture.

It was from the time of first contact in the 1500's and in other places earlier, they just came and took what they figured was theirs and that they had discovered. They didn't discover a damn thing. They had discovered what had already been discovered tens of thousands of years earlier. They found people here and the people were numerous. In fact some archeologists believe that the villages were as close as half-mile to a mile apart along these waterways. They were dealing with other people in the region quite regularly through trade and exchange of partners. Traders would come here from as far away as the Dakotas, the Great Lakes, and the Gulf on a regular basis, across land and across water. From the Great Lakes we would get copper and good working stone from the mountains. We would get partners. Marriages were arranged and gatherings were held. Mica from the Carolinas, beautiful silvery mica schist, plates of mica that are like mirrors. Very ornate carvings. There were many villages and many people.

Over time I've learned different disciplines. Each art that you learn allows you to expand your ability to make other things. Each tool you create usually requires several arts or disciplines that are combined. I've made several bows. I plan on making several more. Out in the hallway there's a bow stave and some other raw materials that I bring in and set and work on, especially during the colder months. A bow stave is the raw wood that's split from the round or split from the tree you take. It has to be seasoned at least a year. I split out the staves and let them season, then sit down and make a bow. My preference would be hickory. Hickory is most forgiving. The bow that's hanging on the wall is made of pig-nut hickory. That's a replica bow patterned after one of three that they believe were taken from the Powhatan in 1654. I have the template for it. We call it an Ashmolean-style bow, and these bows are in the Ashmolean Museum in Oxford, England. It's a long, slender, very elegant bow, I think. It shoots well. It's about 55 to 60 pounds in draw weight. When you pull the string or pull the arrow back 28 inches, that's the full strength of the bow. Any bow you make is already half broken, as they say. The bow is stained with six-inch bands. They alternate natural color and a darker color, which is dyed from the green hull of black walnut. So it blends well with the forest. The pattern breaks up the shape of the bow.

The quiver is bobcat. It's uncut. They don't cut down the belly. They just pull the skin up over the head of the bobcat. The bobcat was trapped out in Minnesota. I came by him through trade. I still trade! The bobcat makes a nice quiver because it's very soft and supple and still has all the tail, the feet, and the head's still on. Makes a nice quiet case for the arrows. It's flexible and soft and the arrows don't rattle around in it while you're moving through the forest stalking.

I go out and harvest the arrows. They're primarily arrow-wood. Go figure, arrow-wood! It's a member of the viburnum family. Right along the river here is where I harvest it. They're quite common. I seek out the straightest ones. I cut them, bring them home, bundle them, let them season for a week or two.

Then I have an antler with a hole drilled through, the size of my shaft. I'll run the shafts through there and just scrape them down 'til they fit through the hole all the way down the length of the shaft. They're still bent because nothing grows straight in nature. Then you take the shaft after you've sized it and you heat it over the fire. You get it real, real hot, almost too hot to handle. Wherever the bends are, you press the bend out and hold it 'til it cools, and it will stay. So you can heat-straighten lance shafts, arrow shafts, fire drills. If you go through the complete making of a shaft, to make a long story short, you size, you heat treat, then you fletch it. You take feathers, split them, cut them to the right dimensions and shapes. Then you wrap the fletching, or the feathers, to the arrow. I do a spiral two-fletch or two-feather spiral on mine, in the ancient way. These are actually very characteristic of the eastern woodlands on the shore, and other places. I prefer waterbird feathers because they have oil in the feather, which is what makes the water run off of a duck's back, or goose or swan, or whatever. I will split the feathers, which is splitting them away from the quill so that they're long and flexible. Both feathers on each of the arrow shafts have to be from the same wing. They have to have the same curvature so that when you lay the fletching on the shaft it bends in the same manner. It allows the arrow to fly straight. I wrap them or tie them to the shaft of the arrow with either vegetable fiber, like that dogbane over there, or the tendon, or 'sinew,' of large hoofed animals like deer and elk. It's like thread, Indian thread. Then I'll cut a notch at each end. One is for the knock (where it fits into the string) and the tip of the wooden shaft you see there is slightly flared. Indians, when they pulled their bows they would pinch the arrow. And the flaring of the shaft at the end at the knock allows you to pinch and hold the arrow.

There were many ways to decorate your arrow shafts, various colors, paints, dyes. Each hunter had his own style, so you knew his arrows. Of course the kills were shared, always. The blade is Catoctin green stone, which is a course flinting material. You have to knap it, or flake it, first. Then peck it with a harder stone. I find these nodules of quartzite or jasper a little harder than the green stone. You don't want to chip it at that point. It's already been flaked. You've got the general shape of the tool you want. Then, to refine that shape, you will chip very tiny little bits by pecking with the harder stone. Tiny flecks will pop out of the surface of the green stone and you can slowly do the remainder of your shaping, 95 percent of it, through pecking. It's called peck and grind. The grind is the last part. You go to course quartzite or granite, followed by fine sandstone or siltstone. You grind the blade and smooth it and give it the final shape. I've done all these by hand, with authentic materials and techniques.

The stone blade or biface is glued into the slit at the end of the handle and then wrapped with the tendon of elk, in this case. Tendon has its own glue. If you boil it you can make 'hide glue.' Scraps of sinew are saved for making it; nothing is wasted. I try to waste very little in my life, as the ancients did. When you wet the tendon it expands lengthwise, not like raw-hide which swells in thickness, so you use it wet and as it dries it tightens. It never gets totally hard, it stays semi-flexible. You talk about tough stuff! Eighty pound bowstrings were made out of sinew. That's the strongest natural fiber we know. I'm doing nothing new here. This is not me. This has been done for thousands of years. I just do it in the traditional fashion. Good serviceable tools.

The animals and plants are our teachers. We believe that. Like the eagle. People see eagles, they don't feel eagles. They don't understand eagles. The eagle is a very sacred bird. It flies so high it disappears and the ancients thought that it was traveling to Creator and thereby they made it the messenger of the people. It would carry their prayers to Creator.

I remember a time when I was a child, standing on a beach. This beach that I went to is no longer accessible. I've tried to go back several times but it's private now, and they just don't want people down there anymore. I stood on this beach and I remember being overcome. This feeling was so strong. I felt it come in and I couldn't really place a direction on it. It just came in from all points. I mean it was so obvious,

I was so aware of it. I stood there and I wasn't able to under-stand what it was. And I've felt it many times throughout my life in different places, at different times. Then one day I read a passage that said, 'There were these people once who lived as one with the land and they knew of something they were inti-mate with, this all-encompassing spirit that moved through all things and bound all things together in a great web of life.' All of the sudden it became clear that this was what I've felt. Call it a life force, if you will. It's incredibly strong. And the ancients and I at times have sought out quiet places where we can open ourselves to this spirit. It speaks to us and teaches."

3

Historic Chesapeake

Captain Will Gates, *The Maryland Dove*

*My stepfather, actor/historian William Sommerfield, al-
ways likes to say, "American history is a rollicking good story,
one of survival and the struggle for freedom." American history offers all the drama and the humor of a great Hollywood
epic—and it's the story of us.*

*What do we know about the history of the Chesapeake
Bay region? To understand where we come from, we have to
get to know the people who came before us, both the native
people and the first European settlers. All of these cultures
contributed to the customs we live by today.*

One warm summer day in 2002, Voices *volunteer Paula
Phillips and I ventured out onto the City Dock in Annapolis
and happened upon an important piece of Maryland history.
We spotted a replica of the* Maryland Dove, *one of the original
ships to carry passengers to the New World, and to Maryland
in particular. The story of the* Ark *and the* Dove *provide us
with a glimpse of what early sailors and settlers had to withstand when making the long Atlantic crossing to reach the
new world.*

*In 1633 these two ships began their voyage across the
Atlantic. They almost immediately lost each other in a storm,
and reunited three months later in Barbados. After sailing to*

the new colony of Virginia and replenishing their supplies, the Ark *and the* Dove *went on to St. Clement's Island at the mouth of the Potomac River. They permanently settled in a shared Indian village nearby and called it St. Mary's. Not long after, the* Ark *sailed back to England. A year later the* Dove *set sail for England as well–but it never arrived, probably lost at sea.*

Captain Will Gates is Maritime Curator at the Historic St. Mary's City Museum and has served as the Master of the Maryland Dove *since 1989. He's a veteran of the Atlantic coast replica fleet, having previously worked on the* Mayflower *replica in Plymouth, Massachusetts, and in the educational windjammer trade. Captain Gates apprenticed as a rigger at Mystic Seaport, and was educated as an archaeologist. Captain Gates began our tour on the quarter deck, at the helm of the ship, peering forward over her solidly-planked decks.*

"The helmsman watches the sandglass as closely as he does the compass, because when the sand runs out that's the end of his turn at steering," Captain Gates said, while exhibiting the various navigational devices. "His responsibility is to turn the glass and call his forward shipmate, who is on lookout, to strike the bell then come back for a turn at the helm.

Included in the ship's navigation tools were a spool of rope and a spool of line marked off in 50 foot increments, with a little wooden chip or "drogue" on the end, which was used for determining the ships speed and was called a 'chip log.'

In addition to a chip log for speed, we keep track of direction with the compass and time with the sandglass. Not only does time factor in for taking turns at the helm, the distance that you travel is based on how fast you're going. This information is kept on a traverse board. It's a dummy compass face with peg holes in it. Illiterate sailors could place a peg for the direction that they'd been steering, at the end of their 'trick' at the helm. In addition, a row of pegs are placed for the speed that the ship is traveling, one for each of the eight half-hours on a four-hour watch."

Climbing down below, we approached the rear berth.

"Here in the master's cabin, a space roughly 12 feet by 10 feet, is the master's bunk, a small desk, a chest, some additional storage space for ship's weapons, gunpowder, and the only private space on board–the only space that can be closed off from the rest of the ship. It's ventilated from above with a small scuttle hatch which provides light and air, but also lets the master hear what's going on up on the quarter deck."

Moving forward through the ship we encountered a series of hanging cots, and he said:

"There's an element of speculation here. We know some details and we have to fill in some gaps. Rope beds in the fo'c'sle are a solution to the sleeping problem using period technology, but we don't know necessarily that rope beds were used on the ships."

We then entered a large open area about 30 feet long and 15 feet wide, the belly of the ship.

"Midships is the hold and would be exclusively for cargo. Cattle would probably not be carried in a small ship like the *Dove*. The hold has to be closed off entirely when you go to sea, so there is no way to get light and air in, or to get in and out to tend to livestock. The only livestock you might carry on a ship like this would be in cages on deck, probably only smaller animals, like fowl, poultry. The largest animal might be a sheep or goat.

The crew's quarters is in the forward end of the ship. The compartment is only 12 feet long by about 12 feet wide and narrows to nothing at the forward end. There's a hearth for cooking, a rack for storing rope, shelves for other gear, and a pair of rope beds that fill the space between the bow of the ship and the mast. This is where the common sailors slept, where they cooked, and where ship's gear is stored. They would have access to this space through a small hatch above and would be walled off from the hold, so they couldn't pilfer from the cargo.

Shipboard provisions usually consisted of a very monotonous diet of a staple grain such as corn, beans, rice or peas. Split peas was a characteristic English provision and would be served up in a pot with a generous portion of salt pork, mainly fat. The old rhyme about 'Peas potage hot, peas potage cold, peas potage in the pot nine days old' is very characteristic of a sailor's diet because you could only cook in fair weather. When peas potage gets cold it congeals to a semi-solid pasty mass, then you can cut it into little cakes and eat those cakes for several days after.

Sailors would certainly eat seafood before they would starve, but a large sailboat is usually a poor platform for fishing, since it's not very maneuverable. So there are only certain kinds of net fishing that are done from it. But, that said, they could trail a line with a hook, particularly if the ship was not moving very fast. So fishing might be a pastime for some of the sailors. If they did catch something it would yield a fresh meal that they wouldn't otherwise have.

If life aboard the *Dove* was rough for the average sailor, conditions were even worse for the passengers. On the voyage over, imagine yourself in a room with a low ceiling, perhaps 30 feet wide, 60 feet long. Exposed beams are everywhere, and creaking and groaning sounds are coming from both the ship and the passengers. The level below you has livestock and all their sounds and smells. Each family group is responsible for creating its own partition walls and also for their own provisions and cooking supplies. Sanitation is minimal. Chamber pots are emptied over the side during fair weather, but during foul weather are just as often emptied into the bilge. So you're adding that level of smell, odor, discomfort, and biological risk.

You can imagine that after a few weeks, only halfway through the voyage, the passengers were demanding a break. Happily enough, a break usually came in arriving in the Caribbean. The usual route to the New World involved a clockwise circle around the Atlantic Basin, taking advantage of prevailing trade winds and currents. So after a break in Barbados or perhaps in St. Marten or St. Christopher, the ship would again embark, most likely reaching Virginia in a matter of three or four weeks. If they were becalmed on route, they might not arrive in Maryland or Virginia, usually Virginia first at the entrance to the Chesapeake, for over two months.

The provisions usually didn't last the voyage across. They would be getting pretty spoiled by the end. After a few weeks water in casks would be rancid and full of algae. It would really only be used only for cooking and washing. The provisions of small beer, or harbor beer as it was called (today we would call it low-alcohol beer) was their main beverage. If the voyage ran long, the provisioning was not adequate, or the beer casks were damaged, they would be reduced to drinking that scummy water.

People would die on the ships. They were packed in close with the poor hygiene, and if there were diseases among some of the passengers they would run through everyone by the time the ship arrived. Many people did die. Even so, the hazard of mutiny was fairly small on an immigrant ship because the passengers are not experienced mariners, they don't know how to sail. They are completely at the mercy of the sailors.

For the most part, the mariners are not paid until they get back to England after a successful voyage, while the passengers have already paid. The mariners don't have a vested interest of keeping the passengers in good health, they just need to get them there or get them off the ship if they die. So there was typically an enmity between the common sailors and the passengers. The common sailors were a rough lot and would rather carry cargo that didn't talk back and get in the way. The Jesuit priest Father Andrew White did write a journal about the voyage of the *Ark*. Father White's comments about the crew are that they were a rough and unkempt and foul-mouthed lot."

Unlike other colonies, Maryland enjoyed a peaceful relationship with the Native Americans.

"It wasn't until crowding in the expansion of the English settlement, they encroached on the lands and territories and there was conflict," Captain Gates explained. "The initial relationship with the Indians benefited Marylanders in a terrific way. They were able to move into already-built shelters. They weren't what the English would like and what they considered proper shelters but they were more than adequate for survival. The Indians already had fields planted in corn that they turned over to the English, and they taught them how to till and harvest. So the Maryland colony in its first summer here actually had a surplus of corn that they were able to load onto the *Dove* and send to New England to trade for fur, thus furthering their commercial interests, and also livestock and lumber. Tobacco came within a few years; the Virginians had already pioneered tobacco cultivation and the Marylanders quickly followed suit.

In those first years of arrival the Marylanders used the services of Virginian Henry Fleet, who had been developing a fur trade in the Potomac, to communicate and negotiate with the Native Americans, to decide where they would settle. St. Mary's City was chosen. It's uncertain if that site was chosen by the English or by the Indians, but certainly it was by mutual consent. One version, I believe, is Father White's, who reported that Indians were already in the process of abandoning the village at St. Mary's City because the peninsula was being raided by another tribe, the Susquehannocks from the north. This placed an armed ally between the Indians of the Potomac tidewater region, the Wicomicos, and the Susquehannocks. The English were suddenly acting as a buffer."

Lucia St. Clair Robson, Author, *Mary's Land*

Like many other newcomers to Chesapeake country, I was drawn to the book Chesapeake *by James Michener. The book was written as a work of historical fiction, a style which allows the author to also create characters and events that might have existed had the historical record been complete. When this form of artistic license is employed effectively it's a compelling technique for historical storytelling.*

Like Michener, Lucia St. Clair Robson writes historical fiction. She is the author of Mary's Land, *a novel that recounts the exploits of early European settlers arriving and surviving in St. Mary's City, Maryland, during the 1600's.* "I've always liked historical fiction and I've always liked history," *she said.* "To me it's time tripping. I'm not saying that life is boring now, but, I'm pretty much used to it and this allows me to go to different times and places. I try to make it true to the times as best as I can, but the fact is you can explore motivations, you can speculate, you can go beyond the written historical record. You can assume some things. You can take some liberties that you can't do if you're a historian."

Like Captain Gates, Lucia Robson was fascinated by the story of migrating passengers on the small ships bound for the New World. "I had as hard a time getting off the ship as they did," *she said.* "That voyage seemed to go on forever because I read a lot of accounts. We don't know exactly what their voyage was like, that particular ship and that particular trip. But there are a lot of accounts of what life was like aboard ship at that time and it was really, really rough, especially for people in the 'tween decks (below the main deck). No standing room, no sanitation, no ventilation, very bad food. It was horrific. They would let them up sometimes, you know, to get a little air, but it was a hard trip. They really didn't have bathroom facilities, just a hole in the bow where the sailors would go. Someone wrote that when you walked across deck you could hear the lice crunching under your boot. Not pleasant."

Lucia knows what it is like to move around and see the world. She was born in Baltimore, raised in South Florida, and after college worked in Venezuela for the Peace Corps. She returned to Maryland to work as an Anne Arundel County librarian.

"I was interviewed at the old Reynolds Tavern, on Church Circle," *she said.* "That's where the library headquarters was at the time. I took one look at Annapolis and said, Wow! I'll take it!"

While working in the Eastport-Annapolis Neck Library, Lucia wrote the story of a young girl who was kidnapped by Comanche Indians and raised in their village, Ride the Wind. *It's now in its 17th printing, and made the New York Times and Washington Post best-seller lists.*

"I never even expected to write a book," *Lucia said,* "so making the New York Times list was just... I was flabbergasted by all of it because I just hadn't planned on that."

When I interviewed Lucia in the fall of 2003 from her living room overlooking the Severn River in nearby Arnold, Maryland, she told me that after completing her eighth book, Tokaido Road, *Lucia turned her sights on Maryland. She wrote about early St. Mary's City through the eyes of the Brent sisters.*

"The Brent sisters were two Catholics who came over with their two brothers in 1638. Things were pretty raw then. The colony had only been here four years. Margaret Brent distinguished herself as quite an entrepreneur and a very strong character. By 1650 she was in charge of 9,000 acres. Not only did she have her own estate, when Governor Leonard Calvert died, he named her as his executor. So she had his estates and his brother Lord Baltimore's estates. Those were the big guys and she was in charge.

When I started writing about the two Brent sisters, one thing that stood out about them was that they never married, as far as we know. That was odd because there were five men for every woman in the early colony and a lot of women came over here expressly to get married. The families would send them over here, looking for a husband. So I had to ask myself why the Brent sisters didn't marry. Now, I don't write romance novels, but I think romance is important. And so I wanted to show not only romance but also a side of life other than an aristocratic view, because the Brent sisters were aristocrats. I wanted to show what was going on below decks. I wanted to show the people who were transported, some of them against their will, and had it a lot harder than those who came over with money and privilege. We don't know much about them since they didn't leave records behind.

I made up a character, a little pickpocket who got taken up on the street, thrown into a ship, and carried off. Depending on your age, you'd usually sign a paper that you would work for someone for seven years. That would pay for your trip over and they would give you clothes and feed you. It was a way to get a foothold in the new world. And then when you were finished with your indenture, they gave you some land and clothes and a little bit of tobacco or corn or whatever and you were on your own."

Lucia's novel begins when the Maryland colony was four years old, after being established in 1634 by Leonard Calvert, Lord Baltimore's 24 year-old brother. Unlike his brother, who never came to Maryland, Leonard Calvert traveled to the New World and took charge.

"I am very impressed with Leonard Calvert," Lucia said. "He came over and kept this going in what they considered a howling wilderness. He was in charge of the whole shooting match. There was nothing here, so they had to start from scratch. The Indians, I believe the Piscataway, at that time, let them use their houses, gave them somshelter.

When Margaret and Mary showed up four years later, things were still pretty rough. They were probably expecting something different because, to tell you the truth, as with today in Florida real estate, there was some inflation of claims as to what you could expect. And there were pamphlets written to try to encourage people to travel to the new colony and settle it. They talked about the salubrious climate and all these wonderful things they could expect, which turned out to be not quite the case. I think she probably knew it was going to be a wilderness, but knowing it and actually being confronted with it are two very different things.

They came with their two brothers, but Margaret was the dynamo in the family. They came over because Lord Baltimore was Catholic and to be Catholic in England at that time was not healthy. They were persecuted and not allowed to worship as they wanted, so they were looking for religious freedom. To his credit, Lord Baltimore allowed religious freedom for others, too. He set up the Act of Toleration and any Christian could worship as they wanted. That was pretty unusual because you had the Puritans and Pilgrims up to the north, who weren't what you'd call tolerant. Virginia was Anglican, Church of England.

When Cromwell and his followers essentially started a civil war in England, it spilled over into the colonies. Maryland was reduced to maybe 100 people. And the Brent sisters, as far as I know, stuck it out through all of that turmoil. You had uprisings with the Protestants fighting the Catholics, and the Virginians had always been somewhat at odds with the Marylanders over fishing rights and things, which they're still arguing about today.

Maryland the colony very much depended on trade with England because they had very little here. They were growing tobacco. And you can't eat tobacco, you can't wear it, really it's not good for a lot. But it was profitable, so they were growing tobacco. And they didn't really have very many sheep or cattle, so they weren't making their own clothes. They were shipping out raw materials and shipping back manufactured goods, which can lead to an imbalance. But after a while they just really didn't use money much. Everything was done with the tobacco, so many hogshead of tobacco.

The Piscataway welcomed them because they were being attacked by Indians coming down from the north, from the Susquehanna, and they were ferocious. So here came these guys with guns. What a good idea that was! They were on quite friendly terms. Things went along pretty well, but it changed once the Calverts were no longer in charge. Plus, even with the best of will, the English brought all these diseases with them that the Indians had no immunity to, so eventually they were just about wiped out."

Lucia's research covered all aspects of daily life for the average person in colonial Maryland, including the most intimate.

"The whole subject of sex in the 1640's pretty much fascinated me," she said. "There's a book called *Wayward Women and Wanton Wives: Sex in Early Seventeenth-Century England.* I was like, yes! This book was written for me! There was a problem with sex because, number one, where are you going to do it? It was cold and there was no privacy. And number two, they really didn't encourage marriage among servants because if you have children, then you can't work. They were so short of labor that they didn't have people to spare to take care of kids, so you might be in your 20s before you could marry. The whole thing of getting together with someone was tricky, but goodness knows they were doing it a lot. Right there at the Hall of Records on Rowe Boulevard, in Annapolis, you can get the court records from 1634 to 1650. Go through the transcripts of these court cases, and you'll see–they were pretty active, with people they shouldn't have been. You know, other people's wives, other people's husbands. Put people together and they don't have cable, this is what's going to happen.

You know, we think that things are so wild and people carry on about the lack of morality. Oh, please! Give me a break! They would go to the court sessions every three months and get all the gossip. They had their own Court TV and Jerry Springer thing going, way before we did.

There's a book called *Crime and Punishment in Colonial Maryland*, by a guy named Semmes. And he gives some of the quotes of cases that came up. Of women pulling each other's noses and calling each other sluts and all kinds of names. Fascinating. The English are litigious and they wrote everything down, so we have this great record of who said what and did what to whom.

When you start researching daily life, it gets really, really fascinating. I'm not so interested in the dates and the huge battles, the coups, the kings and the queens. I want to know how people lived. It was fascinating to me to research the life in the public houses and the taverns and what went on there, and the songs they sang, and the activities that went on, and the fights that broke out. They would usually have a roast turning on the fire and to keep that spit turning, they had a little device with a cage and they put a little dog in there. Sort of like a mouse in a wheel, they'd make him run. And if he flagged they would drop hot coals in to keep him running. It's a sad, cruel thing, but the spit dog was actually quite valuable.

Margaret Brent is best known because she demanded her right to sit in the legislature, in the assembly, and vote. They turned her down because they said that it wasn't fitting for a woman to hear the kind of discussions that went on in the assembly. People definitely spoke their minds there then. That's something else I learned. They did not mince their words. I have a glossary that I put together of about 12 pages, single spaced, of terms for body parts, functions, and insults and things. I was amazed at how creative they were.

Margaret demanded not only a vote for herself, but as representative for Lord Baltimore and Leonard Calvert she wanted a vote for them too. She said that anything that went on there was not legitimate if her voice couldn't be heard. So they call her the first suffragette. But, I think the truth is Margaret wanted the vote for herself; she didn't care if other women got it or not."

John Wennersten, Author,
The Chesapeake: An Environmental History

*Another technique for writing about history entails tak-
ing a particular point of view and using it to explore a range
of time. The best book I've found for exploring Chesapeake
history in this way is one by John R. Wennersten called The
Chesapeake: An Environmental History. When we think of environmental crisis, we tend to think in the present tense. It
feels as if we have reached a point of no return, a crisis which
presents us with no alternative but to change course in the
face of impending disaster. A former history professor at the
University of Maryland Eastern Shore, Wennersten has written
other books about the Chesapeake Bay region and its history,
including The Oyster Wars of the Chesapeake Bay and Maryland's Eastern Shore: A Journey in Time and Place. But The
Chesapeake: An Environmental Biography should be one of the
books at the top of your reading list for understanding the
people and history of our region. Throughout this book, Jack
Wennersten provides not only a beautifully composed story,
but the opportunity to gain an invaluable perspective on how
we have related to the natural environment over our history.
He brings this same perspective to us, here.*

"I wanted the reader to know that environmental transformation is not something that is new," he told me back in
2002, at his home on Capitol Hill in Washington, D.C. "Nature
in the past was manipulated by slash and burn agriculture, by
setting the forests on fire, and by commodity agriculture like
planting tobacco in the 18th and 19th century. Today, with the
advent of the automobile and the technology of urban sprawl,
we have the opportunity to manipulate nature in ways that
previous generations would only dream of. What is new is that
the transformation that is taking place today may put an end
to what we know of as 'nature.'

You know, culture largely determines how people perceive a food base. Many of the people who first came to Virginia with John Smith perceived themselves as middle-class or aristocratic types who were not going to sully their hands with hard physical labor. And many people thought that everything would be handed to them, that the bounty would be just falling off the trees, that they could find things very easily. It wasn't like that, but it didn't have to be that difficult either. For example, the plentitude of sturgeon that John Rolf tried to encourage his fellow colonists to eat would have staved off scurvy. But they felt that this fish was foreign to their tastes and they didn't want it. To a great extent our attitudes about food and about life are determined by our culture. The culture got in the way of adaptation of the early colonists to the Chesapeake Bay. And indeed one of the things that is surprising to me is that early colonists in Maryland and Virginia starved when there was such incredible bounty all around them. All they had to do was look to the bay, forests, and the land, and they would have survived."

So just who were these European settlers coming all this way to build a new life? What convinced them to make the journey? And just how difficult was if for these people to survive in this new land?

"It's a misnomer to think of the early settlers as descended from some kind of aristocracy back in England. The people who rose to power in Maryland and Virginia came here and they got land grants. In the old days you used to get 60 acres a head for yourself and for every person that you would bring to the New World, and many ship captains forged lists of passengers to get large amounts of land. The people who got the large landholdings, if you go back in time you'll see that their beginnings were relatively modest.

The society that had evolved on the eastern shore of Maryland was pretty tough. The life spans were very short. If you lived to 40 you were considered an old man. People died of cholera, smallpox, they didn't have the nutrition they have today. They didn't have the medical care that they have today. If you look at the census of the United States, in the first census there were just a couple million people living in the entire country, which was then the 13 colonies, newly independent in 1790.

When the first colonists came to the new world land was plentiful, labor was expensive. And so land was quickly turned into a kind of commodity that was to be used up. These land use attitudes have remained in effect. For example, tobacco was a cash crop but it used up all the nitrogen in the soil. So the farmers were always planting new land and abandoning the old fields which had become less productive. This was a terrible way to do agriculture.

The genesis of American capitalism traces its roots to Maryland and Virginia. You can talk all you want and I'm sure I'll have some controversy from New England about the New England traders and the cod fishers populations and things of that sort. But it was really the tobacco revolution in Maryland and Virginia that set off the enormous boom in discretionary capital which could be used for investment in other things. The money that was gained from raising tobacco, the first major cash crop of the new world, was used for investments in other businesses. It was used for investing in status comforts and building the fancy homes that were on the James River and elsewhere on the Chesapeake Bay. It literally financed the social transformation of the middle Atlantic and the New England area from isolated dusty outposts into thriving, flourishing maritime and agricultural communities.

It also unleashed the slave trade. The first colonists resorted to using white indentured servants to pick the tobacco and harvest it and cure it and things of that sort. When economic conditions improved in England they still had a need for labor, and this was when they started importing massive amounts of slaves from Africa. I don't know if you've ever walked through a tobacco field and worked with tobacco but you get tar all over your hands and it is messy. It's also very labor intensive. Tobacco is a nasty crop."

Vince Leggett, Blacks of the Chesapeake Foundation

Another important contribution to the story of Maryland and the Chesapeake Bay which relates directly to the desperate need for laborers in the New World is that of African-Americans. From slavery to the Civil War, Maryland and Virginia abound in heroic stories, from that of Kunte Kinte (who came to Annapolis in 1767) as told by Alex Haley in his book Roots, *to the valiant work of Harriet Tubman of Cambridge, Maryland and her Underground Railroad. Vince Leggett is dedicated to researching and telling the stories of African-Americans in the Chesapeake region through his work as founder of the Blacks of the Chesapeake Foundation, based in Annapolis.*

Vince and his organization have recorded hundreds of interviews and collected as many artifacts in an effort to tell the story of African-Americans working on the bay as watermen, boat builders, sailmakers, and laborers in the maritime and seafood-processing industries. Vince is the author of The Chesapeake Bay through Ebony Eyes.

"It's so hard to capture the bay just through art, or music, or poetry," *he told me.* "We combined all of these things and stuffed the book with 24 wonderful recipes that we've collected throughout the bay, from Annapolis crab cakes to softshell, oyster and clam recipes. This is an eclectic approach to the bay and we try to make it multi-sensory, as the bay is. As we've traveled over the bay for the last 15 years, not only have we collected artifacts and oral histories, but some of our best times were around an old potbellied stove or wooden heater enjoying the catch of the day and hope for tomorrow."

Vince Leggett and I talked one afternoon in 2000 at the production studios of 103.1 WRNR, just steps away from a statue of Alex Haley at the Annapolis City Dock where slaves were once bought and sold from ships moored in the harbor.

"We have looked at the Chesapeake Bay as a waterway

of hope and a waterway of despair," Vince said. "Even when we look back to the slave trade, going back into the late 1700's and early 1800's, Maryland, Virginia, the ports of Annapolis, Baltimore, and Norfolk were major commerce centers, maritime commerce. And during that period, part of the commerce was slavery.

We have looked at the record and saw just how many of the slaves came up the bay and into Annapolis, even Alex Haley's Kunta Kinte landed right here. So we look at it from that standpoint. And also from a military standpoint. The record shows that blacks were involved in the American Revolution. Our major interest is the maritime work; blacks served as pilots, helping the British and the Americans navigate the bays and rivers in this area. We traced them to the War of 1812. Blacks were actively involved in that episode too, and on into the Civil War.

We've drawn a timeline through history to highlight the maritime aspect. For the last 15 years I've been going up and down the bay from Havre de Grace down to the Hampton Roads, collecting artifacts and so forth—oyster tongs, oyster canes, duck decoys, anchors, boat parts. Each one of those pieces has a story behind it.

I found that not only did they travel on the bay, but also coastwise up the Atlantic. They settled fishing villages on the Delaware River and the Cape May area, even up to Staten Island. So often we hear about the migrant farm worker that traveled from Florida to Maine, working in the trucking industry, but we know less about those that followed the fisheries in the Atlantic. So it was many of those stories that provided the links of the movement of people during that period. Free blacks and slaves that worked the bay enjoyed so much more freedom than if you were a field hand or a house hand. Somehow it was harder to police you on the water."

One of the legends which Vince depicts is of the vast network of safe houses, linked up along the Eastern United States to assist slaves escaping north to Canada. While there were no

trains or tracks, this is the famous system called the Under-
ground Railroad. It consisted of "stations" and "depots," and
a series of "conductors" who moved runaway slaves 10 or 20
miles from one station to the next. Financial supporters were
known as "stockholders." Some of the travel was conducted by
boat, on the Chesapeake Bay.

"I'm heading a research project called Chesapeake Underground," Leggett told us, "and we're documenting the ways
watermen used their boats and knowledge of the bay to help
Harriet Tubman and other slaves escape north. The period was
the 1830's to the 1860's. They dedicated a park to Mrs. Tubman in Cambridge and then a caravan followed the trail of the
Underground Railroad from Cambridge to Dover, Delaware, to
Wilmington, Delaware, to Albany, New York and it culminated
in St. Catherine's, Ontario in Canada. We headlined the initial
kickoff and traveled with the caravan up to Dover. I tell you, it
was a chilling experience traveling the very route Harriett Tubman had taken."

4

Chesapeake Bay Ecosystems

Pat Vojtech, Author, *Chesapeake Wildlife: Stories of Survival and Loss*

One sunny day in 2001, Paula Phillips and I had the great pleasure to visit with photographer and author Pat Vojtech in Centreville, on Maryland's eastern shore. In addition to her books about skipjacks and lighthouses, Pat has written Chesapeake Wildlife: Stories of Survival and Loss.

Through her own studies and from stories conveyed to her by parents and relatives, Pat has gained an understanding of what Maryland was like for the animals of the Chesapeake region before development and the population explosion forced many wild creatures out—or into extinction.

Pat Vojtech was born and raised outside of Centerville, along the Corsica River. She was the third of nine children from a large, multi-generational farm family. Pat's father sold John Deere tractors and farm implements, and she lives in the old 1800's brick house her father grew up in.

"My father used to tell me stories about what life was like on the Eastern Shore when he was a kid. He didn't see a lot of the animals that we see today, including the white-tailed deer and wild turkeys. He didn't even see geese.

When I moved out here we had honey bees in one wall. We had snakes in the attic and a raccoon underneath the floor-that's where the wealth was: animal hides, furs, and plumes from the birds that were harvested.

The first bounties were put on gray wolves. At about the same time the settlers realized that they were losing their white-tailed deer. They put into effect the first laws preventing foreigners, colonists from other colonies, from coming in and harvesting their deer. And the problem was that we were not just harvesting them to eat but, even in the early years, they were being harvested so that their hides could be sent back to Europe. If you think back and you've ever been to Europe you'll know there's not a whole lot of wildlife over there. They pretty much cleared out their wildlife early on. When all these areas were being settled in the 1600's and 1700's the king would ask, in fact he sent a letter to the Maryland General Assembly, asking that they send him wildlife including deer and birds and all sorts of things he wanted for his own collection.

The canvasback was one duck that my father used to talk about a lot. He used to see them by the thousands on the Chesapeake Bay. The animals that were really stressed were stressed because they were hunted for their beauty, their feathers, their furs, or they were good eating. In the case of the canvasback, it was evidently the best-tasting wild bird out there. And the reason was because it fed on the celery grasses that were in the Chesapeake Bay. You find a lot of the celery grasses and a lot of the aquatic grasses up in the Susquehanna Flats. As a sailor, I was interested to note that the Susquehanna Flats used to be about eight feet deep. Today it's only about one or two feet deep. That's because of the silting in, the cutting down of the forests uphill of the Susquehanna River, which of course goes all the way to New York. All this silt. It covers up the celery. It makes it impossible for these grasses to grow.

Canvasbacks and most of the ducks that were hunted for the market were hunted with huge artillery, huge guns that weren't even seen in war at that time. They were called punt guns or big guns. In some cases they would be battery guns where you would get 10 or 12 shotguns and set them up in a system where they all fired at the same time. Then they would go in with boats that were almost flat to the surface, so that the birds couldn't see them. The 'sink box' was actually like a coffin with wings on the side going out about four or five feet. You would probably get only one shot off, but the one shot might kill 20 to 60 birds. Gosh, if you look at them, some of them are 12 feet long. Like I said, they were worse than anything they carried into battle in those days. So the ducks were getting the brunt of the biggest artillery we could design at the time.

The canvasbacks were very much in demand in the finest restaurants in New York, Washington, and Philadelphia. You could get four to five dollars per bird, which was a lot of money in those days. It was more than an honest man could make working at a job. At its height in the 1880's there were an estimated 15,000 birds a day shot in one season on the Chesapeake Bay. Not only were they hunted with this huge artillery, but they were seeing their food destroyed by the silt and the chemicals. And the ducks, when they went home to their nesting sites, potholes in the Midwest, they were often drained and the edges were farmed. So the ducks experienced a severe nose dive in the early 1900's. And I remark in my book, that unfortunately things really didn't turn around until the hunters had nothing to hunt.

We often talk about how hunters were at the forefront of the conservation movement. Sport fishermen and sport hunters were noticing that the market hunters were killing off all the birds. And they were one of the first, Ducks Unlimited for example, was one of the first that drew the hunters together and went out and bought up land so that they could save the breeding grounds of a lot of ducks and geese and so forth. There are certainly some sport hunters that do a lot of hunting, but for the most part I think it was the market hunting that hurt; the market hunting combined with farming the land that was historically used for breeding purposes. But I think it's very important that people obey the laws because they're there for a reason. They're there because we need them. By 1918, market hunting with the heavy artillery became illegal.

We think of hunting as hunting deer and hunting geese, but back in the early 1700's, if not the 1600's, a lot of the egrets, with their beautiful feathery plumes, were hunted. Generally they killed them during the mating season because these birds develop many more feathers, which they display during the mating season. But it wasn't just the snowy egrets and the great egrets and the herons that were harvested. It was also the hummingbirds, with their beautiful iridescent feathers of green and red. Almost any bird that had any sort of beauty. Woodpeckers were being harvested for the red on their head and neck. It was up until the early 1900's that plume hunting continued. And it was plume hunting that really got the Audubon Society going.

The mountain lion, we always associate it with the mountains because most of us only know of them being in the mountains. But when Captain Smith came over here they were in the tidal regions as well. And the mountain lion–the names are interchangeable: cougar and mountain lion and bobcat–the mountain lion's main food was white-tailed deer. And so if the white-tailed deer disappears, the cougar is going to disappear. Plus they had bounties on their heads. Today it may be extinct. I say 'may.' Most officials say that you cannot find it in the wild, and supposedly the last ones in the wild were caught in the 70's. But there have been hundreds of sightings of mountain lions in the wild, particularly in the mountainous areas.

The mountain lion is a big animal. It's about 250 pounds. And it's probably one of the few animals that would have stalked people, and could pose a problem for people. The problem, of course, is that there are too many people in this region.

Animals can be a nuisance, but nuisances can be overcome. And some things we have to tolerate. It's important for us to have these animals because they create a balance in nature that we think we can do without. But, for example, back in the 1600's passenger pigeons would come in and eat every insect within miles and miles and miles. That was a natural way to control insects. Today farmers use a lot of pesticides.

Beavers do a lot of good. They create flooded areas and tidal ponds, and in their quest to create their perfect environment for themselves they're actually creating very good environment for other animals. They may hurt us because we want to farm our land and we want to build a house right on the creek and we don't want our backyard flooded. But I think we need to make an effort to work with these animals. For example, if you've got a raccoon that comes into your backyard and is going through your trash can, well, the thing to do is to get one of those lids that stays put. And the raccoon, he's so nimble with his fingers, he can pretty much get into anything.

Everybody loves the red fox. It's one of my best-selling pictures when I go to art shows. One person feeds the red fox, and the neighbor shoots it because it's grabbing his little kittens and is being a pest. You have to careful what you do with nature. The red fox is actually not a native of our area. We introduced it from Europe back in the early 1700's, late 1600's, for fox hunting. The red fox has done very, very well partly because it really didn't have any predators. But it does have a predator today, which is the coyote. And the coyote again is not a native of the Chesapeake region. A lot of people say that the coyote was another species that was introduced by man, but it wasn't. It actually just moved east as man has cleared the land and put lots of food out there in the form of little lambs and calves and so forth. Maryland and Delaware were the last states that the coyote entered in the U.S., back in the 80's. If we still had wolves and bobcats and cougars, we probably wouldn't have coyotes. But they will eat the fox. In fact, I was told that the red fox population will come under control by the coyote in a few years. That's happened in every other state."

Dr. Robert and A. J. Lippson, Authors, *Life in the Chesapeake Bay*

You haven't experienced the Chesapeake Bay until you've gotten your hands wet and your feet muddy. It didn't take our Voices *project long to arrive at the doorstep of Dr. Robert and A. J. Lippson. These two marine research scientists have written the handbook for anyone with a penchant for boating or just kicking around on the Chesapeake Bay. The book is called* Life in the Chesapeake Bay, *and it gives us an overview of most of the creatures and plants living in and around the bay. It's a fun book, geared toward students, boaters, and anyone who loves nature. The Lippsons' book is arranged into habitats, from wetlands to marshes and shallow waters to beaches.*

Life in the Chesapeake Bay is filled with beautiful illustrations by A.J. Lipson. A.J. is from Massachusetts where she studied medical illustration. She was once married to renowned ichthyologist-herpetologist-fisheries biologist Romeo Mansuetti.

"An ichthyologist is a person who studies fish," she said. "And a herpetologist is a person who studies snakes. In fact, we used to have bottles and jars of dead snakes all around the house. The kids got pretty used to eating dinner with a few reptile eyes looking at them. I worked with him on the bay. We would go out into the waters and haul for fish and take the right fish; in other words, the fish that were ready to spawn. We would take the males and the females and mix the eggs with the sperm, take the fertilized eggs back to the laboratory to a hatchery nursery, and we would do sort of a yeoman's work, up 24 hours a day, checking the eggs, making sure that they were in good condition. I would draw the developmental stages. Ultimately, I illustrated and described most of the major commercial and some of the recreational fish that we have in the bay. Dr. Mansuetti passed away at an early age."

There is a building named for Mansuetti at the Chesapeake Biological Laboratory in Solomons, Maryland. That's where Bob and A. J. met in the early 1970's. They spent countless hours working on the lab's research vessel.

"As a crab biologist, Bob went out on the Chesapeake Bay," A. J. said. "He would scrape a dredge along the bottom and go after small crabs, which were his main interest, but in the process he would gather up all sorts of other wonderful worms and shells and such strange creatures as mantis shrimp (that look like praying mantis) and even corals. At that time I was working on a book that would describe these creatures for the public. Bob got as interested as I was and we collaborated, spending many, many a day sorting through those samples, drawing and discussing, and looking things up in the reference books that he used. Ultimately, we got married and decided that we would put all of this knowledge together into the book that became *Life in the Chesapeake Bay.*"

These world-class scientists understood that they had a wonderful opportunity to pass on valuable knowledge to the lay person. The Lippsons felt that if the public were familiar with the myriad of animals and plants that live in the bay, they would help preserve them. Looking out their big bay window onto a creek near picturesque St. Michael's, Maryland, the landscape came to life as Bob began describing some of the waterfowl that inhabit their backyard.

"My favorite bird is the red-breasted merganser," he said. "If you go to Europe it's sometimes called a smew. That's a good word for a crossword puzzle. It mates and nests up in the north and comes down here during the wintertime. They are fish feeders. They're name is Mergus-serrator. Mergus means diving and serattor means that it has a serrated bill. It doesn't really have teeth because birds don't have teeth, but the bill has got serrations on it that are very, very sharp, and it helps to grasp the fish. They also have a wisp of feathers on the back of their head that looks like Woody Woodpecker. They're wonderful to watch. You'll see them all along the shorelines here and then around the middle of March they're gone.

We have two kinds of ducks, the diving ducks and the puddle ducks. Puddle ducks are like the mallards, which tip over. You'll see them with their little rear ends sticking up out of the water and their necks stretched out. They're feeding on whatever they can find in the shallows, whether it's vegetation or worms or small clams. They can dive to a certain extent but they're not great divers. They're very buoyant and their legs are placed in the center of their body.

Then you have the coots, loons, and the old squaws, and lots of the seabirds with their legs set way, way back towards the end of their body. When they get up on land they balance so badly they may fall down, but because their legs are in such a position they become very, very effective propellers and rudders. Some of the birds like the buffleheads and old squaws can dive 50 to 60, even 80 or 90 feet and stay under water. They'll go down in one place and come up an eighth of a mile away sometimes, or maybe just a few yards away. So there's diving ducks and puddle ducks.

Loons are particularly interesting birds. We have talked with loon specialists and there was one fellow studying loons who believes that from year to year there are somewhere in the neighborhood of 10,000 loons spending their winter here. Loons mate and nest in the north country, Minnesota, Canada, Nova Scotia, Maine, New Hampshire, up in the freshwater lakes. Canadians think so much of loons that their dollar coin is called a 'looney' and it has that wonderful engraving of a loon's head on it. They are beautiful, and when they're in their mating plumage they have this black and white striping with the elegant black head and some white on it and so on. When they arrive in Chesapeake Bay sometime in early September, and they come here by the hundreds, sometimes we'll see flocks of them out on the water. These are fish-eating birds, by the way, and they are great underwater swimmers. You'll see loons often swimming along with their bills immersed in the water up to their eyes. Birders call that peering. They're peering down into the water, they have the ability to see underwater. They're searching out fish. They're favorite fish in Chesapeake Bay is something called a menhaden. Some people call them pogies, some people call them bunkers. They're a bait fish. And they're here by the millions and millions in the Mid-Atlantic region, and there's a big commercial fishery for them. They end up as chicken food and other animal foods and fertilizers. Menhaden are very oily and human beings don't normally eat them, although they are edible. But they're a favorite bird food just packed with energy. So what they do is swim along peering underwater and all of a sudden there's a signal that goes through the flock. I don't know if it's a behavioral posture or some low-uttering yodel, but all a sudden they're under the water and herding these menhaden into the shallows where they glut themselves. You hardly ever see a loon coming up with a fish. They're feeding on them underwater and they just attack one after another.

They'll stay here around November maybe early December, and then they disappear. They turn up in North Carolina, along the Pamlico Sound and sometimes offshore, and all down through the Carolinas, maybe down as far as South Carolina. There they undergo a winter molt. And because they've molted they cannot fly for several days. When they molt they loose their feathers. Feathers wear out. So they go through these molts to renew their feathers. And they also molt to bring in their mating color feathers. So they'll molt maybe two or three times a year depending on the species.

As the winter turns the loons will show up here in the Chesapeake Bay in great numbers again. Now some of them have their breeding colors, that striking pattern that we recognize as a loon. They'll again stoke up on the menhaden, full of fat, full of energy, and they'll feed on those for the rest of the winter. And then, all of a sudden, they're gone.

One of the reasons that I think people don't realize that

loons are in the Chesapeake Bay is because they don't look like the classical loon that you see on T-shirts," A. J. added. "The beautiful coloration is always a favorite bird for photographers and so forth. But, the winter plumage that they're in when they come here is very dull and grey, and they don't have any of those wonderful black-and-white patterns. Most people would not even recognize them as loons.

Loons generally make that wild yodeling sound. It is so wild that there's nothing like it. It sounds like a crazy person's screaming. I think that's where the term 'crazy as a loon' came from. I've heard them yodeling in the upper Peninsula of Michigan in the summertime and it's just the eeriest and most wonderful sound. That's usually a mating call on their mating grounds, but every once in a while we will hear them yodel here as well."

The Lippson household was decorated with A. J.'s priceless illustrations, many of which are featured in Life in the Chesapeake Bay. *We asked A. J. to describe the process of drawing accurate illustrations of Chesapeake wildlife.*

"I went to Johns Hopkins Medical Illustration School where I graduated and learned how to draw livers and eyeballs and muscles and fingernails and things like that," she said. "But I married a marine scientist and soon I was on the bay. The beautiful bay. I had never really been associated with it.

I can remember the first time I came to Baltimore and had an encounter with a Chesapeake Bay critter. I went down to Lexington Market, a very vital place, and it was the first time that I saw the wonderful, delicious, savory blue crab, calinectus sapidus, which means 'beautiful swimmer.' I was walking down the aisle and I took sort of a short stop, a second look. 'My goodness, what a gorgeous animal,' I said. Because these were all alive, the beautiful azure blue of their claws just, as an artist, really took my eye.

If I am drawing a fish, I have to look at that fish so carefully that I have to count exactly how many spines are in the dorsal fin. The dorsal fins are the fins on the back of most fish. In many of the fish, such as white perch or striped bass, there are two dorsal fins and the first is very, very sharp. If you're a fisherman you know very, very well how sharp those spines can be. You have to make sure you get the exact count.

How about scales? I have to take the fish, and if anyone looks at a fish, most fish, you'll see a line going along the side. That's called the lateral line. It's important to the fish. It functions sort of as a sensory mechanism. They can sense currents and so forth through this lateral line. I have to count the number of scales exactly that are along that lateral line. And I have to draw that exact number. And then there are so many scales above the lateral line and so many scales below the lateral line.

Why do I go to so much bother? I mean, who cares? Well, the thing of it is that many fish look very much alike. And sometimes the only difference is in the number of spines or the number of rays or the number of scales. So, to make it a scientific drawing, rather than an artistic drawing, this is the kind of approach I take. But on the other hand we're writing a book that's for the public. I have to be satisfied as a scientist that I'm portraying the right species. But the public, the layperson that's reading this book, isn't necessarily interested in this scientific aspect. So what I've tried to do is integrate the correctness but also making beautiful pictures that give them a natural pose and put them in a natural habitat associated with a number of other animals they're usually found with. That's what makes it fun. It's not the usual straight scientific drawing.

And there's something very interesting. If you start looking at what we're talking about, scientific drawings, you'll almost always see the fish facing left. Somewhere along the line the scientific illustrators and ichthyologists wanted all of their fish to be standardized. But there is one fish that's very interesting. Go through a scientific fish book and all of the fish will be facing to the left. Ah ha! You come to one and, my goodness, why is this fish facing to the right? Well, that's one of the right-sided flatfish, like a flounder or fluke. Hopefully people know what they look like, rather than a filet on a restaurant plate. Very, very dark on one side with both eyes on that side of their body, and white on the other side. They're called flatfish because they're flat as a pancake, you might say, and they lie flat on the bottom with the dark side facing up, white side down below. There are left-handed and right-handed flounders. Left-handed flounder you would draw facing just like any of the other fish. But when you come to the right handed flounder you have to draw it facing to the right.

The purpose of having both eyes on one side in a flounder is pretty evident. If you look at their life habits, they're lying flat on the bottom. It wouldn't be very useful to have an eye looking down into the mud. Having both on the same side gives them both eyes ready to search for their prey. They sort of hunker down and their exposed side has the ability to change colors according to the color of the bottom. If it's a dark bottom they'll have very dark skin. If they move onto whiter sand they have the ability to change the color so that they camouflage themselves very well against the bottom. As they hunker down their two little eyes sort of flick around and as soon as they see perhaps a little shrimp come by they jump out of the mud and suck the shrimp into their mouth.

The interesting thing to portray is how they change their color. That's a mechanism of special cells in the skin called chromatophores. And these chromatophores–'chroma' for color–have cells that are like sacks with fingers that extend from the center. The chroamatophore has a pigment in it. It can be black, it can be yellow, it can be red, it can be brown. To change the color, the pigment retracts and becomes a tiny little dot in the center of the cell. If they want to be a darker color, the pigment spreads out into those fingers and creates more color on the skin. It's really fascinating."

Dr. Laura Murray, Scientist/Educator, Horn Point Laboratory

My first visit to the UMCES Horn Point Laboratory was in early 2004. In addition to Andy Lazur's sturgeon program, Horn Point Lab is home to a special program to study bay grasses in the Chesapeake.

These marine plants have drastically declined over the years. Due to a variety of issues beginning with runoff from the land, bay water becomes cloudy, blocking sunlight from reaching submerged aquatic vegetation (SAV). Plants can't grow without light. Another issue confronting bay grasses is algae blooms, which also block light. To make matters worse, when the algae dies it rains down, suffocating the plants and using up oxygen. In some areas this leaves no oxygen for aquatic life such as fish and crabs, to breathe. This phenomenon is referred to as a "dead zone." Without the requisite amount of dissolved oxygen in the water these areas won't sustain life. Marine animals will either die or be stressed to the point of exhaustion, like a person might feel hiking at high elevations in the mountains.

There was a time when bay grasses were so plentiful that they were considered an irritant to boaters. They would get caught up in the boats' propellers, making it difficult to get away from the docks. One solution back in the 1960's was to spray the water with chemical weed killer. That sounds unimaginable today, with what we know about water quality issues and toxic pollution, but that is what they did back then.

Scientists are taking a closer look at the habitat requirements of these grasses to see if we might be able to restore the SAV populations in the Chesapeake Bay. The SAV Restoration Ecology program at Horn Point Laboratory is run by Dr. Laura Murray. Dr. Murray was brought up in Mississippi near the Wolf River and attended school in Pass Christian on the Mississippi Gulf Coast. Her father was retired from the Marines and

her mother was a Russian whose family had fled to China after the Bolshevik Revolution. Dr. Murray's parents met in China when her father was stationed there after World War II. They married there and soon afterward moved to Washington, DC. After Laura was born, her father retired and moved his family to his home state of Mississippi and the Gulf Coast.

Laura attended college in Pensacola, then taught high school marine science and biology classes before moving to Virginia to attend the Virginia Institute of Marine Sciences (VIMS) in Gloucester Point on the Chesapeake. There she received her PhD while studying bay grasses.

"What we try to do with the education that goes on here at Horn Point Laboratory," Dr. Murray began, "is bring world-class science to teacher and student programs. We actually try to bring teachers and scientists together, all levels from K to 12, through various workshops and courses. We focus on science teachers more so than other areas, and we have had courses that cover first and second grade teachers all the way up through high school. Some teachers that have worked with me have actually published papers on their experience of bringing research to education."

Why are these grasses are so important to the Chesapeake Bay, and how they are doing in other bodies of water around the world? Do other places in the world have the same or similar problems to the Chesapeake Bay?

"Let me talk about the importance of submerged grasses to the global environment. If you look at a picture of the world, we've noted that grasses are disappearing from coastal waters where there are high population densities. Australia, Japan, Europe, all have reported declines in grasses because of water being cloudy. We know that human influence on these systems is detrimental to it, mainly from the things that come off the land and end up clouding the water. These are very, very important habitats globally because they act as nursery areas for small critters. Crabs that shed go into these grasses for protection from predators. Small fish use that grass to hide.

Historically, bay grasses covered predominantly the shallow areas throughout the bay. In the late 60's and early 70's they began disappearing, and you could see it in areas that were more susceptible to runoff from the land. Up in creeks and rivers they disappeared first, and where the water was cleaner they hung on for a while. The disappearance continued through the 80's. We started to implement some policies to protect the grasses, try to curb nutrient and sediment inputs into the waters, and in the late 80's and 90's the grasses started making comebacks. Probably, in part due to our efforts of trying to curb what runs off of the land, increasing water quality, and also in part maybe because we've had some dry times when not as much rain fell.

Sediments come from development, agricultural fields, and erosion. When it rains the sediment washes into the water. Once sediments come into the water they remain suspended in it and cloud it so that light cannot reach the bottom, where the grasses grow. So if the water is cloudy from sediments the SAV doesn't get enough light for photosynthesis and they die.

Nutrients are a little more convoluted story. Nutrient inputs have various sources. We call them point and non-point sources. The point sources are sewage treatment plants, and industrial waste that can have nutrients in it where the effluent comes out of a pipe. Non-point sources are off of lawns, agricultural fields, parking lots, development, anywhere there's not a pipe you can point to.

When the nutrients come into the water, nitrogen and phosphorus primarily, they cause micro-algae (phytoplankton) to bloom. The water then turns cloudy from too much algae and the light can't penetrate to the bottom where the grasses are growing. Phytoplankton is good because it's the basis for one of the food chains in the bay. Phytoplankton is eaten by zooplankton, small little animals, and then zooplankton in turn are eaten by larger animals. There's a balance. But if you have too many nutrients, the phytoplankton grow to the point where the little animals, the zooplankton, can't keep up with grazing on them. Not only are they shading the water column, but when they die they start to decompose and they use up oxygen in the water.

The algae can grow in the water and also on the surface of the leaves. We call those epiphytes. If you add nutrients to the water not only are you causing algae to bloom in the water column, but your also causing these algae to grow on the surface of the leaves of the plants, which further blocks light to the plant. We found out from our early studies that the light required for SAV to grow is somewhere between 10 to 20 percent of light that hits the ground out of the water. We also found out that this light was being blocked heavily by suspended material in the water and by the epiphytes growing on the plants themselves.

We lost probably between 90 to 95 percent of grasses back in the 80's. Some of that has come back, maybe 5 to 10 percent of the grasses we had before the die-off started. The problem with trying to restore grasses as opposed to restoring marshes is that first you have to have good water quality. If the water is too cloudy for the grasses, they won't grow. So one of the things that we need to look at in selecting a site for restoration is, is that site suitable? Is the water clear enough? Are the sediments right? If the sediments have too much organic material or decaying material from other sources they won't grow. If it's too exposed to turbulence they won't grow. So a site has to be carefully selected before you even go in and plant or restore submerged grasses.

The Severn River has one of the nicest grass beds in Maryland waters that I've ever seen. It's beautiful. It stretches about a mile and it has a predominantly redhead grass bed that was there even through all of the rain that we had last year, it persisted throughout the whole year. After Hurricane Isabel it was still there. So in certain areas of the Severn you have the right conditions, obviously, for grasses to grow.

One of the things that we've looked at and are still looking at is the fact that grass beds, when they're large enough and dense enough, can actually modify the water quality. They can clean the water by trapping sediments and phytoplankton and depositing it to the bottom. As the water comes into the grass bed it slows and particles that are suspended then fall down to the bottom. One of the things we're looking at in terms of restoration is how big and how dense must a grass bed be, in order to modify its own environment. If you go out to try to restore a grass bed, larger, very dense plots might be able to survive because they can modify their own environment.

Why do we want to restore the grasses? Why not just clean up the water and let the grasses return on their own? Well, I can't argue with that point of view. Our efforts to continue to clean up the water of the bay are very, very important to restoration of submerged grasses. However, we can help that process along in areas that we find suitable for grasses to grow. If you couple restoration projects with education you're increasing your knowledge by the citizens, and, hopefully, the citizens will understand the importance of clear water, the importance of submerged grass habitats to the bay, and maybe even act to help protect and help clean up the waters of the bay."

Dr. Tom Miller, Fisheries Ecologist, Chesapeake Biological Laboratory

Within the bay grasses we find many fish and crabs living in their natural habitat. Though the decline in bay grasses has affected the blue crabs, they have not always been under such intense pressure. John Flood, a former pile-driver and longtime environmental activist in the upper bay, remembers eating crabs as a kid growing up on the Chesapeake:

"We had seaweed beds so thick that they were a problem for navigation, and we had loads of crabs. We didn't bother with hard crabs. If you went crabbing it was assumed you were soft crabbing. If you caught some hard crabs, which was unavoidable, and you wanted some hard crabs later, you'd have them before you'd have a soft-crab supper. Now hard crabs are $120 a bushel at Memorial Day! Your neighbor would have given them back to you then."

Monitoring reports from the Chesapeake Bay Program spanning from 1968 thru 2004 suggest that the overall commercial harvest for blue crabs is down about 26 percent. The population of blue crabs does fluctuate, making some years better than others for the overall catch. It is thought that harvest pressure, loss of habitat, and poor water quality all contribute to the decline in numbers of Chesapeake Bay blue crabs.

In late 2006 I met with Chris Conner, Public Relations Specialist for UMCES, and he was kind enough to arrange interviews with some of the CBL's top scientists. One of the people I spoke with was Fisheries Ecologist Tom Miller. Tom was working on a series of projects to determine how abundant the crab population is at any given time. He also was trying to discern how fishing pressure and natural changes affect the crab population from year to year.

Tom Miller is British, and as a kid growing up near London, had visions of becoming a veterinarian. "My mother tells me that ambition stopped dead in its tracks when I watched James Harriott's All Creatures Great and Small and witnessed a cow giving birth," Tom said. "That turned the ambition off cold. But I suppose that reflects an interest in the world around me in general. I've always had an interest in coastal and river systems. I've been fishing since I was a boy and always had that interest in the aquatic realm."

Tom Miller moved to the States in the mid 90's to attend North Carolina State University, before further schooling in Canada. He arrived at Solomons shortly afterward and has been here almost 12 years, studying our superstar, the famed and symbolic Chesapeake Bay crustacean callinectes sapidus. He began his research knowing nothing about his subject and expecting the project to be short term.

"The more I got to work on crabs the more I realized that they really are a remarkable organism," Tom said. "They have this complex lifecycle where they have to go down to the mouth of the bay to spawn. They have this complex growth pattern, and shed their carapace (shell) every time they grow. There are different commercial sectors exploiting crabs at different times of the year, in different parts of the bay. It makes them a very challenging species to work with, and interesting from a scientific point of view because they offer new challenges in how we represent growth, how we represent their behavior, and how we represent their reproductive biology. All those things have led me to continue working on crabs now because I find them an interesting organism. They offer very unique challenges.

When you come to work on a new project you try the tools you already have in your toolbox. I started developing models of crab populations that had been used for quite dissimilar organisms. I'd used them before for turtles and stream insects. It was in understanding why those original models weren't working that it began to clarify in my mind what had to be understood. It pointed toward growth dynamics and this special variability in crabs, that what's going on in the upper bay can be somewhat uncoupled from what's going on in Tangier Sound in the southern part of the bay. Up until I began my work, that variability had been largely overlooked.

Because female crabs are tied to having to go to the lower bay to release their offspring, the upper bay tends to be more male-dominated. From many points of view, if you've got a male-dominated stock in the upper portion of the bay, once they've inseminated all the females they've done their job evolutionarily speaking, and you can harvest more of them. In the lower bay, those crabs have not yet produced the next generation so they have a higher value, if you like. So perhaps we should be more cautious about how we exploit crabs in the lower bay. In a nutshell, that sexual difference in the distribution really has profound implications for how we could manage the fishery.

I started making sure that we were representing how crabs grow as accurately as possible. How we estimate growth in any model is really vital to understand the dynamics of a species. It tells you how fast they go from the new offspring to the mature. If you get that growth estimate wrong the population grows too slowly or too quickly. If you think a population is growing faster than it really is you risk fishing too hard on it. If you underestimate the growth you're foregoing opportunities to fish them. Growth turns out to be a very fundamental parameter and so that's where our initial work started.

We looked at bringing crabs into the lab and monitoring the growth of individuals. We estimated how much they grew at each molt. They increase in size about 25 percent each time they shed their skin. Then we estimated the amount of time between molts. That period is very dependent upon the water temperature. The warmer the water temperature the shorter that period is. As water temperatures get down around 50 degrees they stop molting. They can't get enough energy to molt and so they go into this over-winter period. This torpor characterizes the crabs in the Chesapeake Bay, but not where water temperature stays high all year, for instance, in the Gulf of Mexico.

That study, representing how crabs grow, led eventually to what's called a stock assessment. We go out and we use as much information as we can about the biology of crabs and the fishery to try and estimate the abundance and the exploitation rate, and compare that to what we call thresholds. Thresholds are limits that you don't want to exceed. If crabs become lower in abundance than this threshold you would recommend drastic action to stop the fishery. We also recommended an exploitation rate threshold, and that's a rate of removal. Once we set those two thresholds up we estimate where crabs are relative to that. The results of the assessment indicated that between 1998 and 2004 we had been fishing crabs at too high a rate. That had driven their abundance down below the long-term average abundance. But the good news is that in 2005 we were below that exploitation rate threshold. We were down at an exploitation rate that is likely to be sustainable. If we continue to maintain that level of exploitation, crab stock should increase again.

The natural mortality of crabs is a very, very hard parameter to estimate. The first assessment conducted estimated natural mortality rates based upon how old they thought crabs could get. That was very controversial because the assessment estimated that crabs could live to eight years of age. Most of the watermen and, in fact, many in the scientific community, found that to be too high, an almost incredibly long lifespan. They felt that crabs perhaps could only live two or three years on average. Certainly with the fisheries exploiting as heavy as they do, two to three years is probably the reality for crabs in the bay at the moment. What we need to know to estimate their natural mortality rate is how long they would live in the absence of the fishery. But there isn't any information out there for how old they might have been before we started exploiting them. So this maximum age proved to be an almost impossible number to estimate. Rather than try and convince people of a number that we could prove neither right nor wrong, we took a different approach this time and used direct estimates from a tagging study, where individual crabs are marked and released. By knowing how many of those marked crabs you released and how many of them you recaptured over a period of time you can estimate what their survival rate would have been. That study produced a higher estimate of natural mortality rate than we had used before. It actually translates to an estimated lifespan of about four or five years.

In most fish stocks the individual organisms are so fecund, they can produce so many individuals each time they breed, that if you can protect the spawning stock they have the potential to recover fairly rapidly. Certainly in crabs, if you're thinking about an individual female giving birth to five million offspring each time she spawns, spawning four or five times, there's a tremendous potential fecundity if we give it the right conditions. Most of the other research I've been doing has been focusing on trying to determine what those conditions are.

The moratorium on the rockfish was imposed because that species was ecologically threatened–it was at tremendously low levels of abundance–not because the fishery was threatened. The blue crab, I think, is somewhat different. Here abundance is still relatively good. It's below the long-term average but I don't think the ecological function that the blue crab plays in the Chesapeake Bay ecosystem is threatened. What's threatened is the sustainability of the fishery. So I'm not sure a moratorium on the fishery is necessary at this point.

The crab fishery certainly has an advantage in that you can set a size limit. In a trawl fishery, once you've caught the fish in a net the mortality of them, even if you discard them, is very high. So in a sense the crab fishery is a very green fishery, or it has the potential to be a green, environmentally friendly fishery, because we can be very careful about setting limits that are enforceable. We can say 'don't have any sponged females with black sponges,' and they can be picked from the harvest. We can say 'make certain crabs are always over a certain size' and fishermen can throw back those that are too small. Those crabs have a very high survival probability. There's probably no impact of them being in a crab pot for a day or two only to be released again. So there is the potential to manage this fishery very wisely. There just has to be the will.

What we need to think clearly about is: What do we want the fishery to look like? Who do we want to be able to participate? How do we want the balance of hard shell and soft shell to be struck? Do we want it to be a sort of organic soft-shell fishery? Do we want it to be the hard-shell fishery that provides crabs for the July Fourth and the Labor Day weekend market? So there are a lot of questions that are not particularly scientific questions. They're sort of socio-economic questions about the role this fishery to plays in society. Do we want it to be a fishery that employs the most people possible? Generates the maximum profit for the few people that are in the fishery? Or some balance between those two? It becomes a question of the political will between the stakeholders and the agencies that regulate the fishery themselves. Scientifically we can tell them what they can't have. We can tell them what limits there are to the abundance, or what limits there are to exploitation rate. But above those limits there isn't a scientifically correct answer to what the fishery should look like. We can provide guidance on the consequences of choices, but we can't tell them which one of those choices is correct. That really is a political question. That's the hardest question! We can tell them how big the pie is, but we can't tell them how to divide the pie. Who gets a slice and how big is that slice? It's a hard question because there are no right answers."

Photo courtesy of Joe Evans

Bill Goldsborough, Senior Scientist,
Chesapeake Bay Foundation

Bill Goldsborough, a Senior Scientist with the Chesa-peake Bay Foundation, has been a friend and source of infor-mation for the Voices *project since it began. He's a great guy and someone I always look forward to talking to about various bay issues.*

Bill's family settled in Talbot County on the Eastern Shore of Maryland in the 1600's, and has lived there for many generations. He grew up there, fishing and crabbing as a kid. He has always been passionate about bay issues. As an under-graduate he studied the decline of the striped bass population, and as a graduate student at the University of Maryland he studied underwater grasses. When I met with Bill in 2006, he was working on the hotbed issue of menhaden in the Chesa-peake Bay.

Like the oysters, menhaden are filter feeders. While the menhaden eat, they also filter impurities from the bay's wa-ter. According to the group Environmental Defense, menhaden have the ability to filter a volume of water equal to the entire bay in less than one day.

Menhaden are valued as a fishery, but not because they are good to eat. We use menhaden for other purposes, such as making cat food, plant fertilizer, and fish oil supplements, trademarked Omega 3 oils by the Texas-based company that fishes menhaden in the Virginia waters of the Chesapeake Bay (Omega Protine).

Menhaden are known by other names depending on where you live, such as bunker, alewives, fatback, bugfish, or bait fish. Every fisherman knows that other fish, including rockfish, sea trout, bluefish, tuna, and shark, crave menhaden as food. Menhaden travel in very large schools making them easy prey for these larger fish. This also makes the menha-den easy prey for industrial fishermen using spotter airplanes and huge purse seine nets to surround the fish, and vacuum them into the ships' hold by the millions. According to the National Oceanic and Atomspheric Administration (NOAA), more pounds of menhaden are landed each year than of any other fish in the United States.

"One issue that I'm directly involved in now that's proving to be a challenge," Goldsborough said, "is trying to put some simple conservation measures in place for one of the most ecologically important fish in the bay, and that's the Atlantic menhaden. In this part of the bay we typically call them alewives. But it's not the same as an alewife herring. It's a similar fish but its real name is Atlantic menhaden. Some people call them bunkers. They're schooling fish that you'll see out in the bay in summer time at the surface of the water. Boaters should be familiar with the menhaden. People that boat and fish are probably also familiar with the sad observation that we don't have as many as we did at one time. Numbers of menhaden in the Atlantic coastal population have been going down steadily now for over a decade and their reproductive success in the Chesapeake Bay has been at a very low level for just as long, yet we continue to maintain an industrial-scale fishery for them in Virginia, removing over 200 million pounds annually.

We do catch menhaden in Maryland as well and in Virginia, with other gear like pound nets and gill nets. They're sold as bait for crab potters or fishermen. That level of harvest is entirely sustainable in this system, that's really not a problem we're concerned about. We're more concerned about the industrial fishery which catches them by the millions of pounds to process them into oil and meal. The gear that they use is a large net called a purse seine that's deployed with two boats encircling a school of fish found with a spotter airplane. They encircle the school with a net and then they use a pursing mechanism to enclose the net into a sort of bowl that actually takes up the whole school. They'll cinch that up and then throw a huge hose into the mix and pump the mass of fish onto the hold of the boat.

We're not so used to that scale of industrial fishery in Maryland. That gear was banned in Maryland in 1931. I'm not saying that we were so conservation-minded at the time. I'm not sure why that happened. It was probably a result of gear conflicts between different users of the bay, as typically is the case. And I'll not say that gear is something we should not be using, period, either. I think our problem, as with many of the fishery issues we deal with, is it's a matter of scale and extent, and just keeping the concentration of those activities down to a sustainable level. The problem that we've had in that fishery in recent decades is that other states along the coast have, one by one, closed their waters to that gear and concentrated this fishery in the lower Chesapeake Bay. In 2003, 75 percent of the coast-wide catch of menhaden with that gear came out of the bay–and yet the population of this fish is evaluated on a coast-wide basis and doesn't take into account this aspect of the fishery.

That's the problem we're dealing with now. We're trying to get the interstate body that manages fisheries across states boundaries, the Atlantic States Marine Fisheries Commission (ASMFC), a very important forum for interstate fisheries management, to move a little faster dealing with the issue of multi-species management with an eye toward the menhaden. The ASMFC was mainly responsible for bringing back the striped bass.

Multi-species management looks at not only individual species, the way we've done it historically–how much can we take of this population and allow it to continue to persist–but it also looks at the interactions between different populations, trying to account for them. For menhaden that's a huge issue because so many species depend on it. Striped bass, for example, prefer menhaden above all other prey. It's highly nutritious for the same reasons we want to take them out and process them. The problem is that the very complex models and tools that they're developing to understand these dynamics a little better is taking a lot of time. We and our partner organizations, in a coalition called Menhaden Matter, are promoting some interim stewardship so that we buy the time to do those more detailed studies."

I tried to interview representatives from Omega Protein but my calls and e-mails went unanswered. Since my original discussion with Bill Goldsborough in 2006, the ASMFC did put a cap on the fishery, limiting the allowable catch to 105,800 metric tons (the average catch from 2000-04) for each of the next five years. This cap is considered a stopgap measure that will buy time to allow more research on the Atlantic menhaden fishery management issues.

Dr. Carole Baldwin, Marine Biologist/Author, Smithsonian National Museum of Natural History

Understanding the Chesapeake Bay inevitably leads us to a better sense of planetary issues, especially those related to plant and animal populations worldwide. Why should we care about the health of animals and plants in other parts of the globe? Dwindling populations, ill health, and even extinction are sometimes rationalized as nature's way of creating balance in a changing world. A closer look reveals that all of us are affected by events near and far away. You've all heard of the canary-in-a-coal-mine theory. If the canary dies from poor air quality, then the miners can be sure they're next. Worldwide fish populations are feeling intense pressure from overpopulation, over-development, and unsustainable industrial fishing techniques. You do not need to be environmental scientists to know that as plants and animals disappear, as air quality gets worse, and water becomes undrinkable, we have immediate work to do to protect our bountiful and healthful living standards. Lucky for us, we have plenty of folks who are focusing on better understanding these health, management and sustainability issues.

On one extraordinary day in early 2004, I trekked into Washington, DC, to the Smithsonian Institution's National Museum of Natural History, to meet with marine biologist Dr. Carole Baldwin. I was escorted through a maze of long hallways, away from all the museum galleries and visitors, into a large, no-frills room highlighted by a desk and various tables. It seemed as if every surface was covered with numerous jars of preserved fish surrounding a high-tech microscope. Dr. Baldwin began to explain both her life's work and her surroundings.

"My specialty is the study of fish, particularly the diversity of fish. So, I'm an ichthyologist," Carole said with a laugh.

"Not the most attractive title. It's even a little more technical than that. I'm actually known as a systematic ichthyologist. Systematics is the study of the diversity of organisms and how they're interrelated genealogically. So I study diversity of fish. My research specialty is the study of diversity of coral reef and deep sea fishes worldwide, but primarily Western Atlantic and Eastern Pacific.

My dad likes to tell people he threw me in the ocean at three and I never came back out, which is partly true, I think. I grew up in Beaufort, North Carolina, right on the coast. I spent a lot of time on the various barrier islands along there–Hunting Island, Fripp Island, Hilton Head. That was way before it became so overpopulated and busy, as it is now.

Why do I work here in Washington, DC if I'm a marine biologist? The reason I'm here, and what the public doesn't actually see in this building, are the enormous collections of organisms that we have. We have the largest reserve fish collection in the world. Estimates vary, but we have about five million or so fish specimens from around the globe, freshwater and saltwater. That collection is what makes my job a lot easier."

Carole Baldwin's work has resulted in a couple of extraordinary and perhaps unexpected career opportunities. As part of a research expedition to the famed Galapagos Islands, she became the featured star of the IMAX 3D film Galapagos. *More recently, Carole became the author of the charming, timely, and informative cookbook,* One Fish, Two Fish, Red Fish, Blue Fish: The Smithsonian Sustainable Seafood Cookbook.

"My work in the Galapagos Island was part of the history of this *Sustainable Seafood Cookbook,* in that the water surrounding the Galapagos Islands is supposed to be protected as a marine reserve," Carole said. "Yet every time I've visited the islands I've seen examples of illegal fishing activities. And I'm not talking here about some local Ecuadorian fishermen, some of whom have permission to fish in certain areas. I'm talking about huge foreign industrial-type fishing boats that are in the area illegally. When you come to care about a place like, it's really disheartening to see the marine life being abused by foreign vessels. I think that was one of the things in the back of my mind that sort of prompted my interest in marine conservation issues.

Years ago I visited the Tokyo fish market in Japan. That is the most enormous, mind-boggling seafood market you can ever imagine. I mean it's just city block after city block of fresh seafood. Looking at that I had to wonder how there could be anything left in the ocean.

In 2001, I was part of a Smithsonian research expedition to El Salvador. One day we had the chance to work aboard a commercial shrimp trawler. We were sampling the fish that they caught in the nets along with the shrimp. Every four hours these nets are brought in, the contents dumped on the deck of the ship, and the shrimp are sorted out. I'm not exaggerating when I say that less than 10 percent is shrimp. The rest of it, after the shrimp is sorted out, is shoveled overboard several hours later, almost all of it dead. This is called 'bycatch' and it's an enormous problem worldwide. I think the most recent estimate is that more than 60 billion pounds a year of bycatch is discarded worldwide.

Stocks and populations of commercially important species have declined across the board. I don't think there's any arguing with that. Clearly what you see if you start looking at individual species is that some have suffered more than others. Things change, so in the past we might have had more emphasis on, say, Atlantic salmon or Atlantic halibut. But now if you look at the population sizes of those fish they're so small that they can no longer support any commercial fishery. It's what we call 'commercially extinct.' So fishermen have gone on to other species.

The red drum is a classic example of how human impact and individual choices can affect fish populations. In the 1980's the commercial catch of red drum increased by 10 million pounds in three years, when blackened redfish hit the American seafood scene. It was such a popular dish that everybody wanted it. The fishery collapsed as the population disappeared. Now, on the bright side, there is a fishery management plan in effect for the Gulf of Mexico red drum, and the population size is increasing. It's not back to pre-decline levels yet, but I think it's one of those examples of how fishery management plans can work, given time.

Without a doubt, fisheries management takes on another whole level when you talk about international fishery management plans. There are some excellent examples of problems, such as the Atlantic swordfish. The severe declines are believed to have been caused when several countries undermined the international management plan that was put into effect. More stringent measures to monitor fishing were put into place and the most recent estimate that I read was that the Atlantic swordfish populations are back to about 94 to 95 percent pre-decline levels. These are still small fish not yet at an age where they can reproduce, but still that's on the way to being a success story.

Another example of a problem with international management plans is the fishery for Chilean sea bass. Chilean sea bass is actually a common name for two species, lumping the Antarctic and the Patagonian Toothfish together. They occur in cold waters throughout the Southern Hemisphere. There is a management plan in effect through the Antarctic Living Marine Resources Group. But there's so much demand for that fish that illegal poaching is common, and the ability to monitor commercial catches throughout the world is difficult. It's just such a broad range species. You can consume Chilean sea bass that has been caught in accordance with these regulations. At some stores, even locally, I've seen it advertised that it was caught in accordance with the regulations. However, both of these species are overfished, so we encourage people to look for something else.

You really do need to be diligent while you're shopping, to do so responsibly. One thing that makes that a bit difficult, even if you're familiar with all the issues, is how poorly seafood is labeled in this country. It's quite tough sometimes to know whether you're buying a product that is imported or domestic, or farmed or not. A farm bill has been passed that is supposed to put labeling procedures into effect. With that information, plus information you can find in our book, every single person can make good seafood choices."

5

Watermen of the Chesapeake Bay

Earl White, First Mate, Skipjack *Stanley Norman*

In the Chesapeake Bay region we call our fishermen watermen. Watermen work year-round catching more than just fish. Different kinds of seafood are caught in different seasons–male crabs are plentiful in the summer, for example, while oysters are harvested in the winter. What watermen catch is not just based on what they are good at catching, but on which species is plentiful in the bay at any given time. When the fish aren't biting many watermen reluctantly turn to other pursuits, such as building houses and boats. All the watermen I've met and talked with are multi-talented. Each seems to have various specialties but they're all adept at catching fish, crabs, oysters, eels, muskrats, waterfowl–you name it, using whatever gear is necessary.

When it comes to gear and technique, there are more ways than one to catch a Chesapeake Bay blue crab. Recreational crabbers might use a string hung from a dock or boat with a piece of chicken attached. They get the derogatory title "chicken neckers."

Crabs also can be cornered with a crab scap, a long pole with a hoop and wire net on the end of it used to scoop up crabs in open shallow water or off a dock. This technique is often used for catching molting crabs. Another method is trot-lining, which entails a long rope with baits tied onto the main line or on dropper lines called "snoods." The trot lines of professional watermen stretch out up to three-quarters of a mile, but most are perhaps a couple hundred yards for recreational crabbers. The crabber's boat plies the water from one end of the trot line to the other, pulling up the line from the bottom. As the line appears just below the surface of the water the crabber nets the crabs off the bait and tosses them into a basket, before the next bait appears seconds later.

Some recreational crabbers use pull-traps, small cages with collapsible sides, which are set open on the bottom about 50 to 60 feet apart. They are marked at the surface by floating buoys made from Styrofoam or old plastic bottles, and the sides swing closed when the trap is pulled up. Larger crab traps called "pots" have a wire mesh, with a one-way door that lets the crabs in but not out. These are commonly used by watermen to catch multiple crabs. Boaters on the Chesapeake Bay know when they are dodging crab pot buoys that they're in a waterman's territory.

Some watermen use a crab scrape, which is a three-foot-wide chain basket with an edge of metal teeth that combs through the grasses and across the bottom, scooping up crabs and other bycatch. These are just some of the best-known methods for catching crabs. We could mention crab fykes or pounds, bank traps and crab seines—there are dozens of ways to harvest blue crabs—but you will have to ask a waterman what those are all about.

Watermen also use several different methods to harvest oysters. One, requiring extreme arm and back strength, uses a scissor-like wire trap attached to long poles called oyster tongs. The tongs are lowered into the water hand over hand. When they hit bottom, the waterman rakes in the oysters before pinching the tongs shut. The tongs are lifted out of the water, the cage is opened, and the oysters are dropped onto a culling board where they're sorted by size. Undersized oysters are swept into the water to settle back onto the oyster reefs below. As you can imagine, this is very labor-intensive work.

Modern technology involves a motorized winch and a larger version of the hand tongs, a three-foot-wide pair of claws called patent tongs, which grab the oysters in a scissor-like fashion and hydraulically raise them out of the water. Skipjacks like the Stanley Norman *tow large, heavy dredges, which scrape the oysters off the bottom. The watermen commonly call this method of harvesting dredging, or in slang, "drudging."*

Some of my favorite interviews have been with the watermen of the Chesapeake. Some say that watermen are a little hard to get to know. It is true that they keep to their own and they live a somewhat solitary life out on the water. But my experience with watermen has always been friendly. The watermen usually are happy for an opportunity to explain their lifestyle and the techniques they use to catch the bounty of the bay. When it comes to talking about the government regulating their harvest, there is an understandable hesitancy. Nevertheless, in talking to the watermen we begin to get a picture of their daily lives and the challenges they face.

In 2000 we interviewed Earl White, who has since passed away. Our friend Vince Leggett, of the Blacks of the Chesapeake Bay Foundation, summed up Earl's life: "Born November 17, 1918 in Dames Quarter near Deale Island, Earl White was practically baptized in the Chesapeake Bay. During 60 years as a waterman, Earl experienced its beauty, tremendous bounty, and sometimes, its wrath."

Earl had a long history with the Stanley Norman. "I've done it all on this boat," *he said.* "I even remember the guy that had her built in Salisbury. He named the skipjack after his two sons, Stanley and Norman." *Earl worked on the boat with Captain Ed Farley, of St. Michaels, when it was used for oyster dredging. After the Chesapeake Bay Foundation acquired the* Stanley Norman, *Earl was its First Mate. Working with several captains over the years, Earl took thousands of school children out on the* Stanley Norman *to teach them about the bay's history and aquatic life.* Voices *interviewed Earl White aboard the* Stanley Norman, *as interviewers Dr. Robin Jung and Claudia Donegan listened, along with the Chesapeake Bay Foundation's*

John Rodenhausen.

"My father was a waterman. In water season, he worked on the water. And when that was over with, we'd go working in fields, canning factories, all that. So when I got big enough to hit the water, that's where I been. And the first me hitting the water with my father was a'tonging, and he was taking me out when I was about 13 or 14 years old."

What's that mean, a'tonging?

"Tonging for oysters. And so, I went out with him that one time. The next day I got ready to go again. He said, 'Boy, you ain't going nowhere. It's too cold out there for you.' And I didn't go on the water no more until I got about 19 years old. And I've been going ever since.

I really helped raise all my brothers and sisters, 'cause I was the oldest of 16. I love my family and all my family act like they love me right today. And if something was to happen to me here today, they'd be here.

Well, I tell you what, people around my home would do a season. Season's work. And when tomato time come, they would all get together in big trucks and would come pick them up from Hebron, Maryland. And we'd stay over the whole to-mato season, sweet potato season, and then we'd come back home for the winter. And doing that, my mother and father would buy stuff and store it away for the winter. Father used to raise hogs and chickens for the winter. When it got cold, we didn't have to do nothing, only had to get wood.

Mother was a worker. She was a hard woman. All my brothers were watermen. The way I got on the water was a friend of mine, during the time I was young, I was going with his daughter. The boat he was working on got so he didn't have enough crew and he asked me did I want to go. So, I went with him and I've been going on the water ever since. A guy from Smith Island, a boat named *Ralph T. Webster*. That's the name of the skipjack I was on. Skipjacks, schooners, and bugeyes. I worked on them all. Well, it was a lot of fun. 'Cause when I first started there were a lot of oysters. We had plenty of oysters. We'd put 3,000, 4,000 a day on a boat. That's a lot of oysters.

That schooner was big. Oh boy, she was something else. I tell ya what I used to do when I got of age to go for myself. I used to work on the Chesapeake Bay from November to the 15th of March. Maybe spend two weeks home, then I'd go to Jersey. See, they'd drudge in New Jersey first of May. Then I worked there until the last of October. Sometimes I'd go crabbing in Jersey up until the first of November, then I'd come right straight back on the Chesapeake Bay. That's the way I worked."

How long were your days, doing that?

"On Chesapeake Bay was from sun up to sundown. In the winter, in New Jersey, we used to work sun up until three or four o'clock. Generally go in. See, in Jersey they'd plant oysters on their own grounds, so they could catch them anytime they want.

That's been my life. Yep, been my life. Now, my wife wants me to quit. My sisters want me to quit. But I want two more years, then I'm willing to quit.

I've been on boats two months before hitting the shore. I just didn't go. Most in generally, on a lot of these boats, I was the headman on them. Nobody didn't go nowhere on the days and weekends. We sat up and sing and play the guitars. I got a whole lot of people in my family that can play guitars. In fact, most of the people around my hometown, mostly all the guys play guitar. I had an uncle who could play, he helped teach me. If I'd do something wrong he'd crack me across my fingers. 'Play it over!' Once upon a time I used to play guitar, but I can't play no guitar now."

What kind of stories can you tell us about Annapolis back in the 40's?

"Oh, Annapolis was a drudger's home. Yeah, a good time. Annapolis was a good time. One time when we used to leave Deale's Island and come up there to Annapolis, the women in Annapolis used to put the men out and take the drudgers. Yes, indeed that's the truth.

When I was young, sometimes, God know this true. I would go out in Annapolis and when I get back into the boat it'd be time to go to work. I stayed out on the street all night long with the women and drinking and going on.

I'll tell you the truth, a lot of people will tell you the same thing that I'm gonna tell you now. I've seen the time going into Annapolis harbor you could walk to the other side on boats. You could see like them little yachts and things they got out there now, there'd be skipjacks and bugeyes and schooners anchored out, just like that. Annapolis used to be a little, rough town. I tell you one thing, many oyster come through there. That's for sure.

Well, this captain, I'll tell you, his name. Willie Anderson was the captain. This was a few years back. Who the guys was, or when, I can't remember...this captain and this cook named Harvey, we'd been out drudging and we were on our way in. And see, during that time they had woodstoves. They didn't have gas stoves like now. And he was cooking. He'd been working. He was cooking our supper and the stove started smoking. Oh, she was smoking... Captain said, 'Harvey, what they hell is you doing there?' And he said back 'Captain, this old stove, I can't do nothing with her.' Me and the boys were up forward and I was mate. He said, 'Earl, goddam it, come here.' He cussed all the time. Cussed the wind and rain. Everything, he'd cuss it. I went back there and couldn't even see the wheel 'cause of the smoke. He said, 'Throw that son of bitch overboard.'

I said, 'Hadder,' the boy's name was Hadder, he's dead now, 'Come here. The captain said let's throw it overboard.' We grabbed that stove. We throwed it overboard right into the harbor in Annapolis. That's the truth. I guess it's still down there. And tell you what, I think it was 11 or 12 o'clock that night before we went over on West Street and found another stove.

When I had just started sailing this captain told me, 'Earl I'm gonna learn you how to sail a boat.' He was a good sailor. And he would give me the wheel, tell me where to steer and how to steer. And we was working that day with some boys that had been older than me, had been drudging. And one of the boys told me, 'Earl, if you cut cross right by here you'll get in there a half hour earlier.' Here I go, put her across there, where this guy told me. The captain didn't tell me that. It was on a Friday, I never will forget it. And everybody was figuring on getting in and going to the bar, or going uptown, somewhere or so on. Here I go across here, struck that bar, high and dry she went!

The captain was shaving. Never will forget that. 'Goddam it, what the hell you doing out there?' He cussed me and he cussed me. And I didn't get mad with him. I knew he was right. He said, 'Did I ever tell you to go across there?' I said, 'No, you didn't.' And I couldn't say nothing 'cause he was right. And this other boy looked like a fool. I remember he told me, 'Who told you to do it? Crawford? Hell. Goddam it, Crawford ain't the captain aboard this boat.'

Always take the word of the captain, if the captain's wrong, that's his fault. If he tells you to do something, you do it. Even if it's the dumbest thing in the world. Do it. That's his fault. If it's wrong, if it goes wrong, it's his fault. Ain't but one thing the captain can tell me to do that I ain't gonna do. If he tells me to jump overboard, I ain't gonna do it. He'll have to throw me overboard!

Look, let me tell you something. When you're on the water, you're not the boss of nothing. You just go along with it, 'cause you can't change it. You better believe it. You can't change that. The wind start blowing, you can't change it. Tide starts running wild, you can't change that. You just have to wait it. You gotta have patience. That's all you have to do. And realize that you can't conquer it. Man conquer a lot of things, but he can't conquer the water, the sun, and the wind. You can't do it. You get that in your mind you'll be all right."

Captain Dallas and Kaki Bradshaw, Smith and Tangier Islanders

During an outing to the triangle of Crisfield, Smith Island, and Tangier Island during the midsummer of 2000, we had the chance to gather at the home of Captain Dallas Bradshaw and his wife Kaki. Dallas is from Smith Island and Kaki from Tangier Island. They met at an inter-island baseball game more than 50 years earlier.

Captain Bradshaw is retired now after a long career as a Chesapeake watermen and a subsequent career as a captain and educator at CBF's learning center in Port Isabel, on Tangier Island. Claudia Donegan and I talked to the Bradshaws about music, social life, and the culture shared by the people of these tiny Chesapeake Bay islands.

In the 2000 census Smith Island registered 364 inhabitants. Tangier Island, in Virginia waters, has a population of about 600 people. Like the island shores that are eroding at a fast clip each year, the number of Smith and Tangier Island inhabitants is declining. The sustaining force of the islands has always been the bounty of the bay. As the catch of fish, crabs, and oysters decreases, the number of watermen also shrinks. Even with the mainland culture drawing kids away, the island way of life, symbolized by a dialect said to be similar to Elizabethan English, is still largely left intact. The stories told to us by the Bradshaws illuminate simpler times in Chesapeake country.

"I played baseball for Smith's Island," Dallas said. "She couldn't keep her eyes off me.

Her aunt was always nice to young people. She had a little party for her. I wasn't even invited! But I went down there. I knowed her aunt and her husband. And I danced with her. First time I seen her, I knew her in high school, I said, 'Who is this girl?' My sister knew her and she said, 'She goes with

somebody.' I said, 'He's got competition!' She never did go with him no more."

How'd you feel about being from Tangier and meeting somebody from the other island? Was that a normal thing, for people to intermarry between the two islands?

"Yeah," the Bradshaws said in unison. Then Kaki said, "Two of my good friends married. The young man was from Tylerton (on Smith Island.) One of them's his cousin." "And her sister married a man from Tylerton," Dallas noted.

How'd you decide where you were going to live?

"My business was Tylerton," Dallas said. "I was a waterman."

Your father a waterman, too?

"Yeah," Dallas said. And his father, same thing. My great-grandfather had a big schooner. My grandmother was born on Shank's Island. That's the lower part of Smith's Island, in Virginia. She told me that her father and his two brothers, they had a farm on this island, Shank's. It's all gone now, washed away. And they dealt with pirates. They really did. It was either deal with them or they'd take what they wanted. And they got twice as much money for their produce, salted fish, and everything, and the pirates could come in there and not be bothered and get their stuff, you know. And they paid them in gold. And when they left there and come to Tylerton they bought all of Tylerton. My great grandfather's house was the Noland's house and the other one was that great big house right in front of the church. That was one of his brothers, and another one was right down the road.

We been married for 50 years. And I've said, and this is the truth, if I've been to Fox's Island three or four days, then when I come back here and I see her, I feel different in my heart. And we've been married 50 years. I'm serious! She says that she does the same thing on me."

"He was in the service from '45 until '48," Kaki said. "Weren't you, Dal? We were married in '49. The worst that happened in our life was our son getting killed. He had just graduated from high school two weeks to the day of his funeral. That broke our heart. He was on the island in a boating accident."

"He played basketball at Crisfield High School," Dallas said. "He was good too. He had just graduated and on June the eighth, '91, that happened."

Tell us about how you got started with music, singing, and playing the guitar.

"Growing up on Tangier," Kaki said, "I was real small and my father, he was a good singer. He used to set me on his knees and teach me choruses. And then I took piano lessons. A lady and her family moved to Tangier from New York, and I took music lessons from her. And I always love to sing, sing in the choir. And then with our quartet we traveled. Leave Smith Island every Sunday morning, cross the water, and go up and down along the Shore. We sang to the Naval Academy once. We had good years doing it. I've sung at I don't know how many funerals. And we got our paper and pencil out and just tried to remember all of them. The first funeral I sang to on Tangier Island I was 12 years old. And from then I tried to think of them all, and until last year I have sung in right around 400 funerals. Weddings, funerals, you know different affairs, Lions' Club and watermen's. I sang the National Anthem at a Shorebirds baseball game last year.

It was a honor to do it. Yeah, I was nervous. I love to do it. I'm getting older now and you wonder how much longer you'll be asked to do it. And I thank the Lord for giving me the talent I have. I give God the praise for it 'cause He's the one that gives us our gifts."

Kaki then played and sang the Meredith Willson hymn May the Good Lord Bless and Keep You *beautifully.*

David "Bunkie" Miller and Marybelle Miller

Ed Klein is a songwriter from picturesque St. Michaels, Maryland. A semi-retired dentist, Ed had written a musical play called The Last Waterman. *I invited Ed and his group, the Royal Oak Musicians, to open the second* Voices *concert with a medley of their songs. The trilogy* "Don't Marry a Waterman," "Life of the Wife of a Chesapeake Waterman," *and* "Born the Son of a Waterman," *beautifully reflect the life and times of watermen and their families. The tunes were performed masterfully that night, on short notice, by Lynn Henderson, Jay Brown, and Ed himself on guitar. I later learned that Ed's musical was being produced with a family gospel singing group, which featured three generations of watermen: grandfather, father, and son, augmented by another brilliant Tilghman Island gospel singer, Larry Gowe. The group performing in the play was a variation of a touring gospel group from Tilghman called the Fathers & Sons Quartet. It also happened that the three related family members in the singing group were all named David Miller.*

Tilghman Island is a watermen's community, accessible by drawbridge, located a few miles from Easton and St. Michaels on Maryland's Eastern Shore. In the spring of 2004, I met up with (grandfather) David Miller and his wife, Marybelle, at Ed Klein's dentist office in St. Michaels for a chat about the life of the Tilghman Island watermen. David began by explaining his island nickname.

"Everybody on Tilghman's got a nickname, so mine is Bunkie. When I used to swing through the trees they used to call me monkey and they just changed it to Bunkie. Ha! That's what they told me, that's how they got the name. Some of the older guys named me that. They just pick a nickname and that's what you're stuck with for the rest of your life. In fact, half the people on Tilghman Island didn't even know my name was David. They always thought it was Bunkie. I was growed up with that name.

I've built houses and I've worked on the water for 50 years. I built boats for 20 years and it's been a wonderful life and I wouldn't change a thing I've done. All my kids were raised. I have three children, 10 grandchildren, and four great-grandchildren. I have a son, David, a grandson, David. Well, they call him Jordan but his name's David."

Marybelle added, "Aaron, he's our grandson. He's in Italy. He's a civilian engineer working for the Navy in the building of the Anitra's Blockades, and so forth. He worked on the water in the summers along with his brother. He graduated from Bucknell and went for two years in the service and then became a civilian engineer."

"My dad was a waterman," Bunkie said, "and also farmed some in the summer. He'd put in the crops and then they'd go crabbing, my uncles and him they'd go crabbing 'til the crops come on. So, as long as I can remember, you know, we been watermen. My uncle farmed all the lower part of Tilghman, which was about five farms, which is all being built now with homes. Everything is great big homes now. The farmland is pretty much gone down there.

Both sides of my family were watermen, so, I mean, I've growed up as a waterman. Never knew anything else. I started tonging with my dad when I was about nine or 10. That was my way of life and I loved every minute of it. I was on that boat and the same thing with my son. I started my son when he was five years old. Wrapped him in a blanket, carried him up, put him in the cabin. He slept, but then he'd come out and sit there with me when I was crabbing. But when he got seven, he came out with a big pair of rubber gloves on and he said to me, he says, 'Dad, it's time for me to work.' Seven years old! And he started picking up a crab here, and picking a crab there. But when he was about nine he could pick as many crabs as any grownup. He loved it.

I built his first boat at 13, and he loved it. I let him crab alongside of me. I would lay his line out because I was always afraid of laying a line out in the dark. Afraid he'd get his leg wrapped around it. That's a very dangerous job, when you're laying out a trot line in the dark. You've got maybe three quarters of a mile of line coming out of a barrel. So I would lay his line out first and then lay mine out. And then I would make sure when he picked his line up I always had a spotlight where I could keep my eye on him. It was real early, like four o'clock in the morning. Now you have to wait 'til about a half hour before sunup, but then you could crab to 12 o'clock at night. One year we crabbed all summer from 12 o'clock until nine o'clock in the morning because you couldn't catch the crabs during the day. The water was so clear, crabs would drop off, so we crabbed at nighttime. Water's so clear that they can see eight, nine feet down and they'll see the bottom of your boat and drop off. You could actually see the bottom. You could see the crabs coming off the bottom. They're very smart, very smart. I only had to do that one summer, two summers.

And of course I've haul seined and I've pound netted. Haul seining was probably one of the worst jobs I ever done on the water. It was all night time. You never left until just about an hour before dark and you fished all night. Fish come ashore to feed at night time. Along all the edges real early in the morning you catch your fish most of the time. But at night, just about the edge of dark, they would come ashore on your tides. They would come ashore and we would start dragging our haul seines ashore. That's when you catch your fish. They would cover probably a mile, and then you would pull them around, like, Bloody Point Light. You know where Bloody Point Light's at? We would start right inside the Bloody Point Light and we would haul that whole Kent Point with a haul seine. You haul around the edges. You go off the deep edges and haul around and you pull them into shallow water. Once you get them into shallow water we say we 'bunt 'em up.' We tie them together and then you wind them in shallow water so you can dip your fish out. But that was probably the worst two summers I ever had because I was crabbing and building a shop and haul seining. My wife was working in the bank and the only time I saw her was Saturday. And we had nine in a crew and there was five different crews on Tilghman and each one of them worked in a different area. One time we had like 70 some ton of hard heads (Atlantic croaker). We had 27 ton and the crew on the other side of us had 55 ton, I think. That was a lot of fish. I mean we hauled all day the next day in boats to get them up, get them down to Tilghman. That was '57 and '58."

"I was working at Tilghman Packing Company in the office," Marybelle said, "and that's where they brought the fish in. Mr. George Harrison, who was President, he took the herring and would send a lot of them up to Vida Foods in Chestertown. And we did some down at Tilghman Packing Company. But most of them we did for Vita Foods too. So it was something to see all those tons of fish come in. We had ice coming from everywhere for those trucks. We had Tilghman Ice and Fuel then. Russell Harrison ran it. It was right across the causeway, so it was close. But it wasn't enough ice for as many tons as we had that time. So they had to get ice from other places too. Cambridge and Easton, I think."

"We all haul seined that whole summer and never made a dollar," Bunkie said. "And we were all $1,250 in the hole, each person in the rig. So we had to pay that off when we went tonging. It's all we could see, was that bill. It takes money to run your boats, and then you have your food and everything. And it all counts up. And they were ticking our gas bills and stuff like that. Finally we looked at what we owed. This was all summer work, plus I was crabbing. I would come in from haul seining, which you get in about four o'clock in the morning. I'd come in at four o'clock in the morning, pack my sandwiches, and go aboard my boat and I'd have my crab line in pickle brine, and go out and crab. And I would crab until about 10 or 11 o'clock and then I would come home and I would work four hours building a garage for a guy. And then I went on home and packed my lunch for haul seining. And then at six o'clock we went aboard the boats and went haul seining. So I never seen my wife because my wife never got home until five. By four I was gone. We slept on the boat whatever hours we got, you know, like running down. One guy would steer and all the other guys would take a nap.

We had some storms 70, 75 mile an hour winds while we were in the back of that net. The job that I had in the back of the net was one that nobody else...me and one other guy were the only ones that would do that job. And it was diving down 12 foot in the middle of the night. Now, this was pitch dark, no lights, and the nets would hang on the bottom. There was a lot of pound net poles where they'd have old pound nets and stuff. The net would hang in these broken off pilings, so we would have to dive down and pull the net over the top of the poles. I really wasn't never scared of the water, only when we started catching these big sharks. Then I kind of got a little bit scary. Because that was a bad job being at the back of the net and we, me and George Harrison, and George was too heavy to dive. So I would dive, or Orin Hadaway would dive, one or the other, we would take a chance on going down. Now that was one job nobody wanted.

I had other jobs in there too. I mean, when you pulled her ashore I had to go all the way around and take the brail, on which is called brail line. And then we walked out in the middle of the net and ties it together. That's when I found out we had sharks in the net. There was one big old grey shark. They figured he probably weighed around 1,500 pounds or something like that. One that we brought in weighed 900 pounds. That was a white shark. We figured it was female and a male shark. We got the female. But when I walked out it was a moonlit night. This was a gorgeous night. I mean it was just gorgeous, not a ripple on the water. And I walked out and I seen these big things laying there. They weren't moving. I mean they were just laying there. I thought we had picked up a couple cedar trees that had come off the shore or something, because you do catch trees every once in a while in your net. So I walked right out through the middle of them and tied my brail lines together, you know, and then they started moving on out as I got closer. They just kept moving and I kept looking, you know, and I kept thinking, these things are moving just like

I'm moving. It never dawned on me that it was sharks in there until I got out. Then when we bunted out the net, kept pulling the net in 'til we got it in the back, all of the sudden we saw a tail come out of that water that was unbelievable! And then we saw fish coming to the top of the water half eat up. He was mad and he was just chompin' them. Course we had a lot of fish in the net at that time. Then all of a sudden—this was a brand new nylon net—this shark went out of it and left a hole in there. It looked like about seven foot. We mended on that thing all the next morning so we could haul seine that night.

One night we were out into the bay, and they had said it was going to be a bad storm. We saw lightning off to the westward and I kept telling the captain, I said, 'I think we better wait and not set this net because I don't think we're going to beat that storm.' He said, 'Well, if we get around far enough, you know, then the wind'll take us in. But we didn't get around far enough and me and George Harrison, the guy I'm telling you about, he weighed about 240, we were in a 16 foot rowboat and it blowed 70 mile an hour. And we held onto this net, and I said, 'Whatever you do, don't let go of the net!' because the water was running into the boat and running out. So, I mean, she was literally sunk, but she wouldn't sink. She had enough wood into her she wouldn't sink. So we were holding onto the net, and we rode that thing out. We didn't have any idea where we were at, because the work boats left us. They figured they were going to sink in the shallow water so they went on around the point. Me and him was out there in this boat. Oh, they thought we were gone. I mean there wasn't any doubt. What happened is about a 50 foot yacht came across in this storm, and they come right over the top of the net and they caught the net in the prop. Well, that choked both motors out. She started dragging us, this big boat with the wind on her, and we knew we were moving but we had no idea we were moving that fast. So when the guys came out to find the net, there was no net and there was no us. And they panicked. They had spotlights and they were going all around and there weren't no way they're going to find us. They were more panicked, I think, than we were. You know, we were just holding on."

Marybelle said, "I was home praying that as a seasoned waterman he had better sense than to be out in the midst of that storm. I kept telling myself he's up in a cove somewhere, you know, waiting it out. And so when he did come home and tell me what he'd been through it sort of panicked me. You know, the women stay behind and worry. But the Lord always takes care of them it seems."

"'Course I'm a Christian," Bunkie said, "and I think that you pray about it and put it in the Lord's hands and it gives you the peace. But they take a lot of chances on the water. Even though they're seasoned watermen a lot of times I think sometimes that goes against them. 'Cause they get too confident sometimes and take chances that they shouldn't. And we've lost a lot of lives on Tilghman from that. It's a good life, but it's not a life that you take for granted. You've got to love the water to be on it full time, I think."

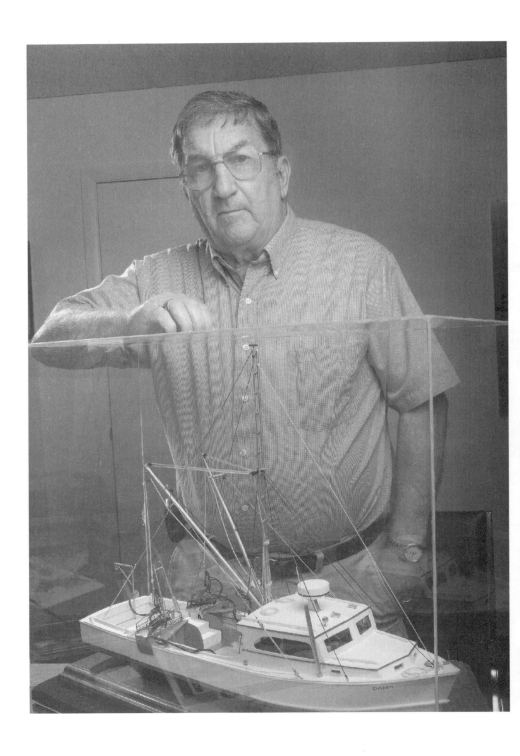

Larry Simns, President, Maryland Waterman's Association

There is nobody more respected in terms of their civ-ic and personal commitment to standing up for Chesapeake Bay watermen than Captain Larry Simns. Larry, a commer-cial fisherman and charter boat operator, is the President of the Maryland Watermen's Association (MWA), headquartered in Annapolis, Maryland. MWA is the advocacy group for Mary-land watermen. The organization gives input to legislators on formulating regulations, works to create an atmosphere of ca-maraderie among watermen, and provides an outlet for shar-ing the tips of the trade. Much of MWA's efforts are directed at simply keeping watermen working and somewhat prosperous. While the watermen have always been rugged and intelligent businessmen, the MWA, under Larry's leadership, has become a savvy and engaged political association, adept at looking out for watermen's business interests and for the bay itself.

I had many questions for Captain Simns as we sat aboard his 28 passenger, 46 foot charter fishing boat Dawn II, *which was moored at his homeport in Rock Hall during the winter of 2001. Located on the Eastern Shore, Rock Hall is a pictur-esque, quiet fishing village facing the Chesapeake Bay. Once an important tobacco port, it celebrated its 300th birthday in August of 2007.*

"I was born in a house right here in Rock Hall. Worked on the water from a little kid with my great-grandfather. Used to row the boat down the trotline for me. Back in those days you only went to school enough to pass. Anytime something's go-ing on fishing, fishermen needed help getting fish out of the nets and we'd take off from school to do that. In the evenings we'd wait for the watermen to come in, pick the fish out. Then on weekends we'd go fishing with them. Sometimes we'd take off from school to go fishing with them. My father started out on the water, then he hurt his back and he become a barber.

But he built his own boat, a wooden boat about this size, in the side yard while he was waiting for customers. He'd also run fishing parties.

On my mother's side and on my father's side, we worked on the water. My great-grandfathers, they all worked on the water, so you can get it back a long ways. But, you know, you grew up in Rock Hall there wasn't anything else to do but to work on the water or to work on a farm or be a carpenter or something like that. You didn't have many opportunities. The most prestigious job around when I was coming up was to be captain of your own boat. That was as high as you could get in this town. So when I got out of high school I got my captain's license and I had my own boat. I'd run fishing parties, then oystered and commercial fished in wintertime.

I wouldn't have this job if I wasn't an optimistic person. I always think that mankind is going to win out in the end and do what's right for the bay. We have low times and good times but we're kind of used to working with nature and nature is up and down. You never gonna control nature. Every time man thinks he's gonna control nature he winds up messing it up. When you think you can regulate a species so that you have an even flow all the time of that species coming in, you're doomed for disaster. That's not going to happen, because nature it flows from plenty and it flows into almost nothing. So we're used to that but the general public is not used to it. They want to see an even flow of fish, an even flow of crabs, and that's just not going to happen no matter how many laws and restrictions you pass. And it seems like the more laws and restrictions we pass, the more man upsets the balance and flow of things. It makes it so an abrupt season ends and an abrupt season starts. You got a big glut on the first of the season. Shut it off and everybody rushes off into something else. That's wrong because it doesn't work that way. You need overlapping seasons 'til you have a tapering off for some people and a tapering in for others. It makes it all work better.

But as far as the health of the bay, you know back in the early 70's we were seeing the bay deteriorating pretty bad;

worse than it is now even. And Senator Mathias was in this slip right here where we're talking, on my other boat. He was doing a photo thing for a campaign. And he was talking about the health of the bay, and I was telling him a lot of things that I've seen going wrong. How you'd see a plume from a sewage treatment plant that nothing grows in, all these things. And he asked me, he said, 'Well, why don't they do something about it.' I said 'Well, I guess we're not scientific enough about it and they don't believe us.' He said, 'What do we need?' I said, 'We need scientific evidence that what we're saying is true.'

Well, he went back and appropriated 27 million dollars for an EPA study of the Chesapeake Bay. And in two or three years, after that study was done, he called me up one time and he said, 'I can't believe what I'm looking at. I'm reading this study and outside all the scientific stuff, all that jargon, it's the same conversation I had with you on that boat. They've proved everything you said. Now we've got to get to work and change it.' Then everybody got on the bandwagon. Governor Harry Hughes, he jumped into the bay cleanup. They started cleaning the bay back up. And I saw a lot of improvement.

It's peaked out now. In fact, I think it's on a downward trend again. But, what really happens here is, if the population had stayed the same and they did all the things that they did then the bay would be pristine. But the population is increasing faster than the cleanup is taking place. So we've over-enriched in the bay with plankton and all the other things that's over-enriched from nitrogen and phosphorous. It makes all these algae blooms and they're smothering out the grasses, and they're changing the whole ecology of the bay. And if we don't do something about that the bay's gonna go downhill, and all these regulations they're passing are not going to save anything.

The other thing is, we look at the surface of the water. When I look out over this bay, I don't see the surface, I see the bottom. Just like a farmer looks out over his field, I see every hill, every nook, every cranny, every oyster bar, every stone on the bottom. Because I've picked that bottom up and looked at it. Everything we do, we're picking the bottom up and looking at it whether we're oystering or clamming or whatever. Even if it's fishing, we know if its mud or sand or whatever it is because it comes up on our nets. So we know what's on the bottom. When that changes we know something's wrong. I've got faith in mankind that we won't let it go to the point of wiping us completely out. And I don't think that the watermen's going to disappear, because I think seafood is going to be a major player in the food production. And if we can hang on and don't get too many regulations passed to keep us from working, I think we'll always have watermen and they'll always prosper. And I think the public is better served by having watermen out there watching the bay and feeling its pulse, letting people know when something's happening there. We're right there, we see it, we put people on it. We let CBF know, we let the government know. If the watermen aren't there, it'll be 10 years before the general population knows that something bad is happening. By that time, it's too late to change it. They won't pick up on these little things that we see because we're in tune with the bay."

Mick Blackistone, Executive Director, Crab Restoration Around the Bay (CRAB)

As disease and inconsistent fisheries limit the watermen's trade, they have created their own contributions to the restoration effort. Programs such as the Oyster Recovery Partnership (ORP) and Crab Restoration Around the Bay (CRAB) are both run through the Maryland Watermen's Association. These organizations, which provide watermen with work in the off-season, use watermen's unique talents and perspectives. Their programs include rebuilding and reseeding oyster beds and participating in joint efforts to study the lifecycle of the blue crab.

Mick Blackistone is a watermen, and is Executive Director of CRAB. I spoke with Mick, a longtime Voices *friend and supporter, about CRAB and the important contribution made by watermen to managing and sustaining Chesapeake Bay fisheries.*

"I had previously worked with the Marine Trades Association of Maryland for a number of years, and then I went to Washington to work with the National Marine Manufacturers Association (NMMA) for 11 years. The Marine Trades Association of Maryland represents all marine businesses in the state, from marinas to brokers to dealers, suppliers, fabricators, and so forth. The NMMA represents manufacturers of boats, engines and accessories all across the country. They also have, I think, over 20 boat shows a year including the Baltimore Boat Show, which is owned by NMMA. When I left NMMA five years ago, a year or so after that, Larry Simns, the President of the Maryland Watermen's Association, asked me if I would run this upstart CRAB Program. The watermen were doing it in conjunction with the University of Maryland Center of Marine Biotechnology (COMB) and a consortium of other interested parties: Virginia Institute of Marine Science, North Carolina

State University, University of Southern Mississippi, NOAA, the Smithsonian Environmental Research Center, and the Maryland Department of Natural Resources. That's the consortium. The Maryland Department of Economic and Business Development helped to get the blue crab program off the ground. There was also a significant amount of money from Phillips Foods, and the help of Senator Barbara Mikulski.

What CRAB and the Watermen's Association are responsible for is for the operation, maintenance, education and public relations for the new Piney Point, Maryland, crab hatchery. We have a 10 year agreement with the Maryland Department of Natural Resources to use it at no charge. Piney Point is located near the southern tip of St. Mary's County, on a creek out of the Potomac. It's a beautiful piece of ground. There was an aquaculture facility there for oysters and, at one point, for rockfish.

The impetus of this whole project is to increase the brood stock, the breeding stock of the blue crab, and do research on the species. We've seen the population of the blue crab decline, then remain stable but low for the last five or 10 years. If we can increase the breeding stock by growing crabs in the laboratory environment and then releasing them into the wild, we'll learn about the crab's lifecycle—predation, migration, spawning—and, hopefully, we can sustain or increase the population of crabs.

For over 20 years Dr. Tuck Hines, at the Smithsonian Environmental Research Center, has been studying and researching blue crabs. And then Dr. Yonathan Zohar and Odys Mora up at the COMB lab in Baltimore, they're world renowned for their work with the blue crab. And when you look at the contributions from the scientists at VIMS, NC State, Southern Mississippi, and watermen, and you put it all together, you have quite a team to research, study, and follow the blue crab, the lifecycle and what we can do to sustain the population. The scientific community asked the watermen to be participants and in 2006 voted for them to be a formal member of the blue crab advanced research consortium, which was quite a compliment to the watermen and what we can bring to the table.

More often than not people don't understand what traditional watermen do for fisheries aside from catching them. We're trying to change that, putting our hands-on experience together with the scientific research.

The university scientists at COMB take the embryos and grow them out. There are seven different scientific stages of crab larvae. When they are just before a cannibalistic stage, which is somewhere between a quarter of an inch and a half an inch, shell point to shell point in size, they have to keep them separated using screens inside very large tanks. Everything is done by hand. Hopefully we'll be able to automate that a little bit somehow in the near future. But right now everything is done by hand.

We call it a grow-out nursery because these crabs are ready to grow out to maybe an inch or so before they're at the release stage. They go from the hatchery at COMB in Baltimore over to SERC, where graduate students and volunteers tag each crab. Since we started in 2002 we've released 300,000 juveniles, and each one has to be tagged individually. When they're released the watermen and recreational crabbers will turn in the tag information, and they're paid for calling it in. We need specifics so there's a reward from five to 50 dollars, depending on the tag. One of the things the scientists have made great strides in, and which will happen in the very near future, is that we'll begin to tag and identify these crabs through DNA. That will give a lot more information when they're recovered.

We have found that hatchery-raised crabs adapt extremely well in the wild environment. Right now we're seeing about a 15 percent survival rate, which is quite high. The scientists are very happy about that. We've also always thought that crabs spawn once a year. Now they have crabs in the COMB lab that have spawned five or six times in a year.

Our hope is that we'll expand the hatchery release to a million crabs. We will continue to learn about the lifecycle process and educate everyone from school children to adults about how important this knowledge is; then we may be able to not just sustain the blue crab population, but increase it. That was never the intent of the program, but we do hope that may be an end result.

Watermen are very supportive of the hatchery program, but one thing we all have to realize is that watermen are like everybody else. If things are going well and they have a really good crab year, like last year compared to the two or three years before, then they don't worry about doing something like this. It's when things get rough that they ask, 'What are you doing to restore the crabs,' and, 'what are you doing to restore the oysters?' These programs, oyster, rockfish, yellow perch, blue crab recovery, whatever it is, are long-term, big-picture issues that the watermen have been obligated to and are heavily involved with. But I wouldn't say that the typical waterman stays up at night thinking about it. They are very supportive, they want it to work. Watermen worked on the rockfish moratorium. They helped start the Oyster Recovery Partnership and still work tirelessly on planting seed oysters. Watermen are the ones that put spat out, the baby oysters, creating disease-free oyster beds where scientists think they should be put.

In the last 10 or 20 years we've seen an annihilation of the oyster population. MSX and Dermo are two parasites that invaded the oyster population in the bay and killed off at least 90 percent of all the oysters. That was a significant income for the watermen, but also a significant income for restaurants and the tourism industry and everything else related to the bay and the oyster fishery. Then we had the moratorium on the rockfish, another huge impact on the watermen's income source. Next we saw the decline and now relative stability of the blue crab which is, I think, by far the largest income-producing fishery for watermen on the bay today. If they don't make their money during crab season—peeler crabs, selling soft crabs, and so forth—it's a very big hit for them. Frankly, there are very few full-time watermen compared to 20 years ago because you can't make a living doing it anymore. It's a barometer to look at in terms of the health of the bay and what the fisheries are producing. In my mind you can't blame the watermen for the decline of the bay or the fisheries.

You know, you go into that 20 year, 30 year time period where you see people could catch bluefish until they were pouring out of the boat, and now you can catch two. They're not there. The same thing happened with rockfish. I think for too many years everybody thought that everything was cyclic and that Mother Nature would reinvent itself, recreate itself after a certain amount of time, and that when one fishery went down another one would come up. I think that was true for a long time. However, for some fisheries you'll never see them bounce back to historical highs, and it takes them longer to bounce back.

I always considered watermen to be the barometer of the bay. If they're making a living and catching enough of the fishery to make a living, then we're relatively healthy. Watermen know what's happening out on the water. They know what's happening with the fisheries. It's how they make their living, how they support their families. One of the things that frustrates them is the amount of time it takes for changes to be made that would help the bay or the environment at large, and the politics that have to be played. Watermen realize that they don't have the money to play in some of these arenas, and it's disappointing to them and frustrating, but its life. They understand it. They feel that people should listen to them and I think that people are now, at least a percentage of them are, with Oyster Recovery Partnership, with the Blue Crab Advanced Research Consortium, and so forth. But there are too many things that are against them, whether they're criticized for over-fishing, or whatever. Those things, true or not—mostly not true, because their fisheries are highly regulated by the Department of Natural Resources—are all about perception."

Captain Ed Farley, Skipjack *H.M. Krentz*

Captain Ed Farley sailed south from Massachusetts, landing on Maryland's Eastern Shore in 1971. Like other watermen, Ed has made his living with a variety of skills and occupations, all tied to the water. He spent a good portion of his life restoring and repairing traditional Chesapeake skipjacks and other wooden boats. In the late 70's he worked with author James Michener, doing research for Michener's book Chesapeake.

Ed has owned and restored two skipjacks since moving to the Chesapeake Bay region. His first skipjack, purchased in 1975, was the same Stanley Norman *we visited earlier. Built in 1902, this boat is currently owned and sailed by CBF as part of it's skipjack environmental education project—a program that Ed helped start. Ed purchased and restored his second skipjack, the* H.M. Krentz, *in 1990, and has recently converted it to carry charters out of the Chesapeake Bay Maritime Museum in St. Michaels, Maryland.*

I met up with Ed in 2002 for an interview at a boatyard in Rock Hall where he was restoring a traditional oyster schooner. Along with Ed's lifelong dedication to outdoor, environmental, and experiential education through ecotourism and oystering, he is committed to keeping the heritage of the working watermen's fleet alive.

"Oysters are an interesting animal. They start off as larvae that swim for about three weeks, and then settle to the bottom. The larvae glues itself onto shell or other substrate and metamorphoses into an adult, a biologically mature oyster. In the first year they start spawning. As they grow bigger, they spawn more. The majority of those spat will be males, and when they reach around three inches in their third year, a large percentage of them will change sex and become female. I used to read that the average lifespan could be 15 to 25 years if left unharvested. I have harvested oysters that were eight and nine inches in diameter, even a year ago. In the Choptank River we were catching oysters that were eight to nine inches long.

When an oyster is, say, three inches long, and you pick 50 to 60 oysters out of the dredge, it's not enough to be worthwhile catching. The volume isn't enough and we don't sell them by the piece, we sell them by volume. But when those same 50 oysters in a dredge go to being eight to nine inches long, then it's going to fill the tub pretty well. We were catching oysters that had survived and had been living there probably six or eight additional years, and, hopefully, did some spawning during that time. A lot of them were dying as we were harvesting them. Some of the oysters would be gaped open and you could still see meat attached to the inside of the shell. The ones that we were harvesting that were not dying were fat and healthy.

I have a piece of a shell that I dredged up one time that I saved because it's an inch and a quarter thick. If you look at the layers and layers and layers of shell there, and basically the oyster will produce like a tree, one layer of shell every year, there's probably about 35 to 40 layers there. So that oyster was a lot older than the average. And whether any oysters that old are still alive in the Chesapeake is hard to say. There are little pockets of places.

Some people have the idea that when a waterman comes in to harvest oysters that he takes all of the wealth. We're not allowed to sell anything under three inches. At the same time, if you get to the point where you're not catching enough to make a living, than you leave and what you've left behind, because of our inefficiency with hand-tonging, patent tonging, scuba diving, or dredging, will be there for spawning for the future.

The big change I'm seeing in the whole bay system, the articles that are coming out about the oyster industry are no longer focusing on over-harvesting. People are realizing that the harvest has been there for a long time. Because it's a stationary resource and it's not like fish that swim away from you and migrate, and so forth, it's a resource that you can do calculations on more easily. And for a long time we've had the rules that have worked to maintain a very stable, efficient industry. And because the Chesapeake Bay is this incredible ecosystem, with incredible amounts of nutrients that grow the algae to feed the oysters, all the conditions are just right. Maryland's portion of the Chesapeake Bay historically has produced more oysters than any other body of water in the world. And the regulations simply help protect that biomass and that resource so that the oysters can continue on forever.

One of the reasons I got into the oyster industry, or stayed in it, was because I felt like I was a part of this natural system and didn't have to feel guilty about just raping a resource. I felt that here's a resource that's been harvested at different levels for a long, long time. If the rules are followed and enforced and if nature doesn't fail us as the oysters regenerate and reproduce and if we're careful with the Clean Water Act, my feeling was, gosh, it can only get better. The problem is that a lot of our legislation has in the past focused on single issues and tries to solve one problem at a time. These days we're looking at legislation and concepts where we take a look at the whole system, work towards a larger goal.

I dredged oysters this year (2002) from November first until the end of November, and I could have continued. There are friends of mine that are dredging up through the New Year here and are still making a living. There are not as many oysters as there have been in the past, and not a very bright future since we're seeing high mortalities again even in areas like the Chester River and the Eastern Bay. Even in the Upper Bay just below Hackett's Point, below the Bay Bridge, we're seeing high mortality. So, there's a real potential for the oyster population, or the harvest population, dropping very low again. We bottomed out in 1994 at about 80,000 bushels for the whole state. That's down from an historic average of two to three million bushels. But with the present regulations, within five years it rebounded to 400,000 bushels, and that looks like a recovery. But we could drop right back down again. Or it could double to a million. Right now it doesn't look very good for the immediate future. But that doesn't mean there are no oysters out there; it just means that the harvest-sized oysters are scarce."

I keep hearing people say that it's just the cyclical quality of nature and that you're going to have your down years.

"That's true to a certain degree, but we've never seen cycles that were so baywide before, where there weren't some oysters in high volume somewhere. If you look at the harvest yields historically there was never this kind of a collapse before. They fluctuated up and down and when they were down in one area they might be up in another area, so that averaged out. Right now, the watermen in Deal Island tell me that the whole Tangier Sound is just loaded again, that every shell and every oyster is just peppered with spat. That could well be. Will they survive the three years to reach market size? We don't know that until three years from now. But no matter how successful the spawn is, if they don't survive the MSX and Dermo then it's a moot point. Whether the oyster goes through a cycle of becoming resistant or not, scientifically we still don't know.

When the oysters died the basic structure on my lifestyle was radically altered, because then I was making 90 percent of my income dredging for oysters in the winter, moving seed oysters in the spring, and then living out of my garden all summer. I was also doing some boat carpentry in the summer months. But I mostly worked on the *Stanley Norman*, rebuilding one section at a time for five years. And just about when I had it rebuilt, the oysters died. So, I had to come up with an idea of how to make a living. I could have gone crabbing like other watermen. I did do that some. But I decided to make a skipjack work year round. I developed the idea of taking people sailing on the skipjack and talking about the bay, the environment and history. I got a permit to drag a small dredge to show people how we dredge oysters. That worked out very nicely over time and led into working with CBF and taking school children. At the end of that time I sold my boat to the Foundation, thinking I would stop being self-employed and continue working for them. In the meantime I bought another skipjack to work on part-time. It just worked out better for me to continue to be self-employed, so I upgraded that boat. I would say I make more money today from talking about catching oysters than I do from actually oystering. But I do love the oystering, and I feel that it's a very valid part of our lifestyle here on the bay."

What's the balance now between the watermen who own working skipjacks that have licenses and the people in that group that are actually turning toward taking people out on eco-tourism trips?

"One other captain has started carrying some charters. Maybe two others are talking about doing it. Tourism is a growing market worldwide, so in spite of September 11 we're going to still see tourism. In my mind it stabilizes the ability to take care of a skipjack. If you relied only on the oyster industry you just can't do it. You can't even make enough money to properly maintain the boat, from the amount of oysters you catch. To a certain degree we don't harvest on the sailing days anymore. We're allowed two days with our push boat (a small motorboat which is tied to the stern of the skipjack, and pushes it through the water under power.) We've gotten to the point where we are dependent on those two days and if the weather isn't pretty near perfect the rest of the week we go home and do something different."

Since this interview was conducted back in 2002 the business of dredging oysters with skipjacks has pretty much dried up. Oysters are still being harvested from powered workboats with mixed results. Captain Ed is successfully running eco-tourism trips on the H.M. Krentz *out of the Chesapeake Bay Maritime Museum.*

6

Boats

William Fox, Editor, *Chesapeake Sailing Craft: Recollections of Robert Burgess*

Wooden boats have always been synonymous with the Chesapeake Bay. Throughout his life, the late Robert Burgess traveled the region taking pictures and informally interviewing crew members of various Chesapeake sailing craft. From 1940 through the mid 70's, Burgess was a curator at the Mariner's Museum in Norfolk, Virginia. His maritime collections were purchased recently by the Chesapeake Bay Maritime Museum and are the subject of an exhibition there. Boats photographed by Mr. Burgess included bugeyes, pungies, sloops, schooners, skipjacks and log canoes, among others.

In late 2006, I had the opportunity to talk with Naval architect William Fox, who recently edited and re-released a book called Chesapeake Sailing Craft: Recollections of Robert Burgess. *Fox was a lifelong friend and neighbor of Robert Burgess and grew up with his son. During our interview, he talked about Burgess and outlined the progression of these traditional boats, many of which are gone from the Chesapeake Bay.*

"*Chesapeake Sailing Craft: Recollections of Robert Burgess* is broken up into sailing craft that developed, and generally they developed exclusively from one kind to the other, starting with log canoes," Mr. Fox began. "Bugeyes, the next type of Chesapeake sailing craft, were really glorified and larger log canoes. Then there were pungies, sloops, two-masted schooners and rams, which were very particular to the bay, and skipjacks.

Mr. Burgess made some kind of humorous remarks in the beginning about log canoes. They've obviously got to be about the oldest vessels because at one point someone just climbed up onto a log and that was a boat. Then they started being hollowed out. The colonial people here learned from the native people how to make dugouts, but the colonials enhanced them because they had good tools. They were able to graft two and three logs together and they could get a smooth enough joint between the logs to make a much larger and stronger three-log canoe.

The log canoes from colonial times were made from three to five logs. They had center boards and they were made from big, three-foot-diameter pine trees. There was lots of pine around this area, almost unlimited building materials. The log canoes had very fine, very fast hulls. They were really sleek and beautiful boats. Very narrow beam and no straight lines at all. Usually they had two unstayed masts and bowsprit and huge sails and jibs. Sometimes they had a little triangular sail, called a kite, way up on top, just as high up as you could possibly get. That gives the canoes a really distinctive look, a very unusual sail plan. Since there was high sail, excessive sail, they'd have to use springboards, boards that the crew gets out on. When the boats heeled, the crew would go on the windward side springboards to keep from capsizing.

All of the principles of naval architecture are the same. You are basically trying to get the most speed you can with the least power. In the case of the sailing vessels you're trying to get the best speed you can with the least sail. That's why, I guess, if you go back to the log canoes, they were almost perfect. One of the stories that Robert Burgess tells in his book is about Sid Vincent, who was a naval architect at Newport News Shipyard in the 30's. He measured the hull and took the lines off of a log canoe in 1925 and compared them with the latest destroyer designs of that time and they were really close, as far as the basic hull form and lines. So the log canoes were hundreds of years old but they were very efficient.

Maybe I should add at this point that I'm interested in sail. My primary interest has always been powered vessels, in particular tugboats. But I'm learning and Mr. Burgess is my teacher. I'm not trying to pass as an expert on Chesapeake Bay sailing craft but I've certainly learned a lot doing this project and will continue to do that.

Log canoes were replaced by the bigger bugeyes. The bugeyes were generally bigger than 40 feet long. They also had center boards. Just about all the boats in the Chesapeake have center boards because the Chesapeake Bay is so shallow you can't really build a boat with a keel and sail it practically on the bay. Typical size for a bugeye was 60 feet long, 20 feet wide and eight feet deep. They had very beautiful lines, again barely a straight line on them. They were gaff-rigged with two raking masts. The masts were stayed with a very long bowsprit and a jib. They had cabins forward and aft with beautiful carvings on them.

The log canoes, as I understand it, were basically replaced by the bugeyes because there were so many oysters to be caught in the bay then, unlike it is now, that the log canoes were just not big enough to handle it. So the bugeyes were mainly oyster boats. A lot of these sailing craft were built for oystering, and out of season they would carry cargo. They carried produce and lumber, wheat and tomatoes, watermelons, that sort of thing. Some of the best pictures I've seen are taken in Baltimore Harbor of bugeyes loaded down to the gunwales with watermelons in the summertime. Bugeyes were built from the 1860's to the 1920's. That was their heyday, 'til about 1920. There aren't many left. The *Edna E. Lockwood* is at the Chesapeake Bay Maritime Museum. The *Dorothy Parsons* is at Piney Point, Maryland.

Pungies are another type of really beautiful boat, with basically a schooner rig but a very distinctive shape and type.

Burgess says that they 'have a full flowering bow, long lean run, deep drag aft, sharp floor, flushed deck, log rail and raking stem post and stern post.' The pungy had a main top mast that was bowed forward with a little mast on the forward mast that was canted forward.

It was also an oystering boat, used a little bit for freight. Some of them went about 60 feet long. Once in a while some of them would go to the Indies and pick up a cargo of pineapples. They were built from the 1840's to the 1880's and they were around in the bay until the 1940's. Pungies were basically built in the Accomack region of Virginia on the Eastern Shore, in the Pungoteague area. That's where we think the name came from. The only survivor that I know of is the *Lady Maryland*, originally built in 1904. One thing that's really interesting about these vessels is that they were painted pink with green topsides. We're not sure where the pink came from. Either the paint was white and it had oxides in it or one theory was that the red-bottom paint and the white paint mixed together and they liked the effect.

Mr. Burgess points out that sloops were not indigenous to the Chesapeake Bay. You hear about Long Island sloops. Sloops were built here but some of them came from other places. They have a round bottom and kind of a full, chunky hull with a center board. They were 30 to 60 feet long, again with a long bowsprit. They have a gaff mainsail and topsail and one or more jibs. They are sloop-rigged. Most of the sailboats you see are sloops with a main and a jib. They have a huge boom. The booms were as tall as the masts were in a lot of cases. They were really impressive boats. Burgess called them 'handy, handsome little craft.'

These sloops were all professionally built. They had a crew of five or so and were primarily used for oystering. Sloops were built from colonial times until sometime in the 1890's and they tended to replace the bugeyes. They were very expensive to build because of all the shape. They also needed a larger crew to sail, so the skipjack took over from them. Many sloops were built in Dorchester County and Taylors Island, Maryland.

The sloop *Charles M. Kelly* was built in Gloucester, Virginia in 1892. At 74 feet long it was one of the largest. And there are a few survivors. The *J. T. Leonard*, built in 1882, was the last sloop on the bay and it's at the Chesapeake Bay Maritime Museum. The *Rebecca T. Ruark* is now rigged as a skipjack. It's got a sloop hull and was built in 1886. The *Rebecca T. Ruark* still cruises out of Tilghman Island as an ecotourism vessel."

Mike Vlahovich, Chesapeake Maritime Museum Skipjack Restoration Program

In 1865, Maryland passed a law forbidding the taking of oysters by boats under engine power. By 1884, a whopping 15,000,000 bushels of oysters were harvested from the Chesapeake Bay. The number of licensed dredge boats also peaked that year at 955 vessels. Five years later 860 vessels harvested 6,500,000 bushels of oysters from the bay. Two years later the harvest was 4,400,000 bushels. Skipjacks took over the oyster business around the turn of the century as larger oystering vessels became unwieldy and the harvests grew smaller and smaller. The skipjacks were designed to operate at less cost with less crew, they were easier to maneuver in tight and shallow places, and they could be built at half the price by the watermen themselves. Even as motorized boats took over other methods of harvesting the Chesapeake, the oyster dredging industry thrived under sail, albeit on a smaller scale than during the previous century of schooners and pungies.

In 2005 the harvest for Maryland's oyster industry was just 100,000 bushels. The devastation of the oyster population in more recent times is attributed to disease and parasites rather than overfishing in a highly regulated fishery. During the past decade, the skipjack has gone from being a very small working fleet of about 20 boats, to a fleet of purely educational and eco-tourism vessels. According to a number of watermen that I've spoken with, there are currently no skipjacks captains making a living from dredging oysters.

Work to save the last of the skipjacks from sinking into oblivion has being ongoing for a number of years. Skipjacks are an important part of our heritage and worth preserving, whether they are actively harvesting oysters or being used for ecotourism and educational field trips.

Captain Ed Farley said, "Some of the skipjacks have been

in really bad shape for a long time because the oyster industry has been so down. With the strain on the crabbing industry it's really affected people's abilities to take care of them, which is why when the millennium came around the State of Maryland had this program of choosing treasures to be preserved to make sure that they don't disappear. They decided that the skipjacks are a Maryland treasure. We're nationally unique. Skipjacks represent the last fleet of vessels in the country that work under sail, harvesting a fishery product."

For a number of years the Skipjack Restoration Project at the Chesapeake Bay Maritime Museum was in high gear, thanks to support from the National Trust for Historic Preservation and leadership from people like fisherman, master builder, and restorer of wooden boats Mike Vlahovich. The museum instituted an apprenticeship program led by Mr. Vlahovich, to teach traditional wooden boat building skills to a new generation while restoring or repairing some of the skipjacks.

Mike has left the museum since I interviewed him in 2002, and now heads an organization called Coastal Heritage Alliance, a non-profit educational organization that is dedicated to preserving the commercial fishing family cultural heritage of North America, including its vessels, skills, and stories.

"My appreciation of my own heritage, which had a lot to do with working on and near the water, probably has keyed me in to working for a museum that cares and preserves heritage," Mike began. "The bay heritage is not mine in particular, I was raised on the West Coast, first generation in this country actually. My father came from the island of Brach in the Adriatic, off the Dalmatian Coast of what was then Yugoslavia. He came to America with knowledge of fishing, and some knowledge of boat building. They immigrated from 1900 to about 1930 and established themselves out in a little place called Gig Harbor in a larger community called Takoma, on Puget Sound in the State of Washington. There were plenty of fish there and there was plenty of timber, so the talents and the skills that they brought from the old country were put to good use in America. I actually learned my trade from the old-timers that brought these skills with them. My family was into commercial salmon fishing. They used purse seines, similar to what they call a snapper rig here in the bay, used to catch menhaden. It's a big net. We fished Washington State and southeast Alaska and then also fished for anchovies, mackerel and tuna in California and in Mexico.

I started in the maritime trades when I was 15. That's when I first went to sea. I was the youngest crew member by maybe 45 years. They were all old guys that took me in. So it wasn't 'til I was about 21 that I got any interest in actually building boats, but I remember, I can pinpoint the trip that I was taking to Alaska. I was in my bunk. I was off watch. And I'm lying in my bunk just about a foot below the wooden deck beams down in the forecastle of this boat. Because of the rough seas and the age of the boat you could actually see the timbers working. The diesel engine was pounding in my head so hard you couldn't hear the timbers creak but you could actually see some movement. Paint would chip off. And it got my attention. I wasn't concerned about the boat going down, but it got my attention, and I thought, 'Gee, how'd they ever fit these pieces together? Because you saw every hanging knee and every deck beam was notched into the sheer clamp or what's called the shelf timber. And so in the off-season I started to pick up some skills. And it was a natural for me to work with the owners of these purse seine vessels. Many of them also worked in the shipyards in the wintertime.

I picked up a little here and there and was eventually encouraged to go to a trade school. And that's where I went so I learned some drafting, some boat design. I went to a place called Bates Vocational School which is now a community college in Washington State. I eventually became an instructor there. So I kind of went full circle. This is my 31st year in the trade. I was probably in the trade about 25 years before I thought about teaching it. And that interest in teaching was truly a response to an appreciation that I was starting to develop for the old timers that taught me. As trades people became more and more scarce I felt a responsibility to give something back. So that's what I did.

I first came here in the 80's after reading Michener's book *Chesapeake,* and just felt like I had to live it. I think Michener had an office here at the museum and did quite a bit of research here. I waited until I located a job opening at the little boat yard down in Reedville, Virginia, on the Western Shore. The yard used to be owned by the Rice family. It's since been bought out by a fellow named John Jennings. I stayed there two years. It took a year to really be incorporated in the yard with the old timers. There were only five or six of us that worked there but the two head carpenters had been there 30 years at that same facility. That yard, at one time, had a very healthy new boat building reputation and business, but as boat designs changed and of course materials changed, this yard was slow to change. So they eventually lost their market share and then most people went down to Deltaville and had boats built there. Our repair work was on everything: charter boats out of the Inner Harbor in Baltimore, which would come down to Virginia because our rates were so low and we also had a marine railway big enough to haul up to 90 footers. We worked on many boats from Smith Island and Tangier Island, which was just a real bonus for me, getting to know the islanders.

After I'd been there for a year and the owner had some confidence in me he asked me if I would design and build a prototype of a deadrise hull for Atlantic blue crab fishing. He wanted to get back into the new boat market. I was a young guy, so I was a little bit more open minded to different designs. So I went about to Deltaville and I went and talked to watermen who recently had wood boats built, and just found out about what they liked about 'em, you know... what do watermen want? And I went back and designed a 46-foot deadrise boat using some West Coast construction."

Mike laughed, then said "That's the way I had learned. And I made some changes. It still looked like a bay boat. But the way I fit the timbers together and made a one-piece bow stem...but before the boat was even halfway done, a gentle-man from Tangier Island, Lonnie Moore, who was a hotshot crab fisherman, came over. He didn't say anything to me, he just watched, standing in the boat shop, looking. And then the next day he came back and he had about eight of his friends and they were gabbing away, talking in Tangierese, and I didn't have a clue what they were saying. But it was obvious that they were talking about the boat or talking about me, so I was flat-tered but uncomfortable. Finally he approached me—of course Lonnie could speak in a way that I could understand when he wanted me to understand him—and he committed to the boat. Because of Lonnie's reputation as a tough fisherman that, no matter what the weather is he doesn't go back in, he took that boat and he gave it one heck of a reputation. He bought the boat and he dredged crabs in the winter down at Cape Charles and did some of the toughest fisheries in the bay. He still owns it. It's called the *Lonnie Carol.*

Lonnie was eventually approached by Chesapeake Bay Foundation to become one of their captains and an educator and eventually a manager and they also leased the *Lonnie Car-ol.* I had gone back to the West Coast by then, but I came out to help Lonnie get it certified to carry passengers. We never built it to carry passengers, so we had to make some changes. And as Lonnie moved up in the ranks of Chesapeake Bay Foun-dation, occasionally there were opportunities for me to come out and work for them, repairing some of their boats. On two instances I worked on their skipjack the *Stanley Norman.* Once with Captain Ed Farley, who owned it before the Bay Founda-tion. Ed and I worked together on the *Stanley Norman* down at Severn Marine Services on Tilghman Island, and that was in '93 or '94. At that time we saw that the *Stanley Norman* needed a whole new bottom, new keel, new skeg, a massive job.

I had done some skipjack work in Reedville. We put a new side in the *Sigsbee* before it sank. I'm sure it was the side that didn't give way. And I think I worked on another skipjack, but I really can't recall the name. Skipjacks were not our main-stay at Reedville. The very first skipjack I worked on here at the museum was the *City of Crisfield* and it had been built at the Rice Yard in Reedville. So I thought that was an interesting set of events. On the day Captain Art Daniels launched here, he got up on our little podium and said, 'I thank God and this here museum!'

In any commercial fisheries it's all about making a buck. That's what business is about. It's also about loving what you do. But the skipjacks, like any commercial fishing vessels, were built to have a certain lifespan—20, 30, 40 years. I know the salmon boats that I'm most familiar with, although many have lasted 70 and 80 years, most of the highliners that had these boats built would pay for them the first year or two. Five or six years later, they'd build another one. There was a time on the bay when it was the same situation, when the oystering was a lucrative business. So the longevity of these vessels was never really a great concern. I think that what we're faced with now is about half the vessels were built quickly and cheaply, and of course that's what a skipjack's about. That's why there are no more round bilge boats built to harvest these oysters. They were the precursors, the schooners, the Chesapeake pungies, all fairly sophisticated in design but boats that needed time, a higher degree of craftsmanship, and exquisite lumber when you started to plank the boat fore and aft. Skipjacks were a way to beat the system; another way to skin a cat. But skipjacks performed as well or better, so it wasn't just cutting corners to save money. It was saving money and still getting the performance. But they didn't get the longevity.

In the building of boats, there's no building inspector, there are no codes, unless it's Coast Guard inspected to carry passengers. Other than that there's a real freedom in boat-building that just doesn't exist elsewhere anymore. People moan about the difficulty in getting building permits if they build their own house, and it all makes good sense. But in a boat the only test is if it works. No one's looking over your shoulder. You can make your own decision on how the boat goes together and maybe that's why boat building may be viewed more as an art than as an actual trade.

An owner of a traditional wood boat becomes tightly connected with that boat. I refer to it as a real intimate connection. The hours and care that need to go into that. If you're building it new you handle every piece of wood hundreds of times. Quite honestly your fingerprints are on it from sweat or blood. I remember when we launched the skipjack *Lady Katie* and we had a bit of a celebration here with the National Historic Trust, and there were six captains on stage. I was speaking about the *Lady Katie*, saying that she looked beautiful, freshly painted. But I didn't want people to forget that underneath that paint were all the fingerprints of a lot of people. Real human toil, which I think is a wonderful thing."

An update from the National Trust for Historic Preservation dated May 7, 2007 reads almost as an obituary to skipjacks oystering on the Chesapeake. "Only one or two skipjacks dredged for oysters under sail in 2006. A taskforce appointed by Maryland Comptroller William Donald Schaefer is no longer active. The once-impressive Chesapeake Bay Maritime Museum's skipjack restoration project is stalled. The National Trust, Preservation Maryland, Maryland Historical Trust, Save America's Treasures, and others are working to bring financial and technical resources to the support the rehabilitation and continued use of these endangered, nationally significant symbols of the maritime past."

Pete Lesher, Curator of Collections, Chesapeake Bay Maritime Museum

From the early 1800's until the mid 1960's the "Grand White Fleet" of Chesapeake Bay steamboats was the preferred method of transportation up and down the estuary. These magnificent vessels transported people and connected goods and produce to merchants and markets. At one time 50 steamboats connected Baltimore City to major hubs at Norfolk and Washington, DC, linked by steamboat wharves along 2,000 miles of navigable coastline.

The advent of better roads, railroads, and the Great Depression spelled the end for the steamboat. But there are still many folks around who remember when steamboats were a common sight on the Chesapeake Bay.

I visited with Pete Lesher, Curator of Collections at the Chesapeake Bay Maritime Museum, in 2007 to learn more about the steamboat era. Pete had recently overseen an exhibition on the collections of Robert H. Burgess, who was enchanted by the Chesapeake steamboats and chronicled them in his writings and photographs. Even from an early age, Burgess sensed that someday, like other Chesapeake watercraft, the steamboats would disappear from the landscape.

"Steamboats started on the Chesapeake in 1813," said Lesher. "If you remember that Robert Fulton had his steamboat on the Hudson River in 1807, you realize it didn't take very long for steamboats to get to the Chesapeake. The Chesapeake was really an ideal body of water for running steamboats. All the tributaries of the Chesapeake form fingers up into the land that allows you to get to the Tidewater towns.

It was a great network that ran out of Baltimore. Steamboats proliferated particularly after the Civil War. For many towns around the bay this was really the connection to urban markets. This was the way of getting out of the locality before the train arrived. When a steamboat stopped at a rural wharf that was where everything happened, even if it was at two o'clock in the morning. The steamboat's arrival was the lifeline of the community.

By the 1930's we were building road networks around the state, around the bay. Truck transportation began taking a lot of cargo away from the steamboats. The Depression further took freight away from the steamboats, and that was the nail in the coffin for most of these lines. Most of them went out of business in the 30's but some steam packets survived until early 1962. Those overnight express steamers you would board in Baltimore, and get a fine dinner as you were going down the Patapsco River. You turned in to a stateroom, to wake up in Old Point Comfort or Norfolk, Virginia, or vise versa. In those last few years that they were running I think everybody realized these things were complete anachronisms, and that they couldn't last much longer. People really savored those last opportunities to ride them. The steamboats were a thing of the past. They were entirely outdated. The comparable thing is like a skipjack today, dredging under sail. It seems totally out of place in 21st century America for a sailing vessel to be involved in the fisheries. And really we're seeing the end of that, I think. That's an example of the old ways surviving beyond their natural time on the Chesapeake Bay.

The early steamboats were wood-fired. They later became coal-fired. The last ones in the 20th century would have been oil-fired. So they took away the labor of feeding the wood into the boiler, of feeding the coal into the boiler. Of course, in the early days of steam transportation steam technology was a feat of engineering that was done by trial and error, and there were errors. Until these things blew up they didn't necessarily know what kind of pressures they could take. In fact, there was a lot of fear of high-pressure boilers. Most steamboats on the bay had low-pressure boilers just because of that fear. If they got too much pressure in the boiler or something stopped up, steam could make a very forceful explosion. Some people were injured and some people were killed, scalded to death in these boiler explosions. It would be like an airplane crash today. It made the headlines. It aroused public fears.

There were a variety of steamboats in the Chesapeake. There were the overnight packets, which could be up to 300 feet or so long. They would have had two and even three decks, lots of staterooms, a sumptuous dining room usually on the stern, where you could get really a good meal rather cheaply. There were the steamers that stopped at all the rural wharves. One might have run out of Baltimore up the Choptank River all the way to Denton. Another one might have made this run to all the wharves along the Potomac River and up to Washington. Their purposes were for passengers and freight, picking up the produce of all these rural communities and getting them to urban markets, and bringing the products of the cities out to these places. From the plantations certainly farm goods were traveling this way. If you look at some of the packing slips from these steamboats that would have called at these rural wharves you'll see absolutely everything from clothing to furniture, maybe the occasional piano, livestock. This is how you got your cow to market. Everything traveled by steamboat, everything but bulk cargos. If you were shipping fertilizer or grain or something like that you loaded it on a schooner.

Some were day ferries that would have connected, say, Baltimore to Love Point, or Baltimore to Claiborne, where you met a train that then connected you to Ocean City. This was the way you got to the Shore before the Bay Bridge and Route 50. Another type of steamboat on the bay was the excursion steamer. Some of the were owned by the Tolchester Line, which owned Tolchester Beach on the Eastern Shore, almost straight across the bay from the mouth of the Patapsco River. It was about a two-hour ride from Baltimore on the broad, open decks of the steamboat, taking in the summer breezes. You'd get to what was just a picnic beach at first, later a swimming beach, and ultimately a full amusement park with all kinds of rides—a roller coaster, bumper cars, dance pavilions—all the things that you would associate with an early amusement park. Its remarkable how little survives from Tolchester Beach. We do have the bandstand, that's been relocated to the grounds of the Chesapeake Bay Maritime Museum. Live music was an important part of these parks as well. If you can picture Baltimore in the days before air conditioning, in the days before paved streets, in the days before public sewers, there were a lot of really good reasons to get out of the city and to get to a place like Tolchester Beach.

The steamboats really used the Chesapeake for what it was best suited for. Although the bay is rather shallow, the land is beautifully intertwined with the water. You've got this incredible length of shoreline, this incredible access to the land from the water in any place that's deep enough to float a boat. Most of these steamboats were relatively shallow depth craft and could get up these rivers and creeks, in some cases even before they were dredged.

An aspect of steamboating that we have utterly no appreciation for is how a big steamer would get up into a creek and manage to maneuver. It really is hard to imagine if you think of the typical smaller river steamboats, which were side wheelers. Your rudder is nowhere near the wheels that are pushing the water forward or back. They used side-wheelers in the Chesapeake because they could operate in very shallow depths. You can get into those shallow places with the wharves on the creeks, where there's barely enough water to float that steamboat. Steamboats did occasionally run aground. My grandfather was fond of telling me about a time when, he could never remember which it was, the *Talbot* or the *Dorchester* (sister steamboats that ran to Easton Point at the head of the Tred Avon River,) ran aground just across from Easton Point and couldn't get herself off. She spent the night, and my grandfather, a young teenager at the time, and other boys in the community had run of the steamboat that evening. They made their way out there and explored the whole thing. There was hardly anything better than for a 12 or 14 year-old boy.

The decline of freight during the Depression, that was really a nail in the coffin. But the immediate cause for the demise of a lot of the steamboats was a spectacular fire aboard a steamboat named the *Morrow Castle* off of Asbury Park, New Jersey. Congress got to work on new safety legislation for steamboats. And in 1937, as Congress was considering that, there was another spectacular fire aboard a steamboat named the *City of Baltimore* right off the mouth of the Patapsco River. I think there were three fatalities in that fire, and Congress rushed through legislation. All of the sudden these steamboats, many of which had steel hulls but wooden super-structures, now they were required to put in sprinkler systems to arrest fires. The expense of installing sprinklers meant that some of these steamboats had to immediately tie up and ultimately got sent to the breakers yard. Because of that in the 1930's really most of the steamboats disappeared. The express liners between Baltimore and Norfolk continued for a while and some of the excursion steamboats like the Tolchester Line steamboat ran for another couple of decades.

It is remarkable that none of the steamboats from the Chesapeake survive. There is not a single one left that operated on the Chesapeake Bay. Steam tugs, yes, but none of the steamboats. There's one interesting wreck that I love to see, right on the Baltimore waterfront by the Baltimore Museum of Industry, along Key Highway. It's the wreck of the steam flagship of the Maryland Oyster Navy, the *Governor Robert M. McClain.* Just the remnants of her iron hull in the waterfront."

7

Chesapeake Bay Families

Mary Parks Harding

Over the course of the Voices *project we've had many opportunities to sit and listen to stories about Chesapeake families. It is always a pleasure and honor to be invited into another person's house. In that personal space are echoes of the past, clues about generations of Chesapeake people, and insights into our own lives.*

Lower Dorchester is a once far-removed region filled with people who have a history of living off the land. Dorchester County is home to the Blackwater Wildlife Refuge, a marshland considered one of the world's most beautiful natural wonders. It's also the site of the National Outdoor Show—a bizarre yet fun event which combines an annual muskrat-skinning contest with a beauty pageant (as documented in Amy Nicholson's recent film, Muskrat Lovely). *Beyond the hoopla of the festival is an area filled with ordinary people living extraordinary lives, including Mary Parks Harding. Ms. Harding grew up in Dorchester County, the daughter of a well-known boat builder. In 2003, Paula Phillips and I visited with Mary Parks at her current home near Cambridge. We were greeted with smiles before feasting on homemade Chesapeake Bay crabcakes and watermelon.*

"I went to a one-room schoolhouse, seven grades in the one room, right next door to the little Wingate church. When I was at Wingate growing up, my mother taught us so many things. She'd take us out in the yard at night to look at the stars, and point out the different constellations. I knew every leaf on every tree. You couldn't show me a leaf in South Dorchester that I didn't know what kind of tree it came from. I knew every bird, I knew every kind of duck; there were so many things that we learned about the outdoors. That's what our life was all about.

My father had five daughters, no boys. He used to say I was the only boy he had. My sisters were all very feminine and dressed up, but I didn't care if my socks matched or not. I didn't even care if I had shoes on. I used to go into the woods with my father. He used to go into Mr. Spicer's woods to measure trees. My father would send me home and he'd say, 'Mary, go tell your mother to put a little bow ribbon in your hair.' I think he didn't like for people to say, 'Is that your little boy out in the forest?' My hair was straight and cut short.

The roads when I was little, they were called corduroy roads. They were built by laying pine trees crossways and filling them in with oyster shells from seafood processing plants. They had little pull off places where if you met another car, one would pull off. If you wanted to drive from Wingate to Cambridge, which was about 30 miles, then you had to change a tire about three times because those oyster shells cut into them.

Not many people had cars. Most of them came on a bus. And lots of people liked to come to town on Saturday night. As a small child, I got a quarter every Saturday night and I could go to the movies for a dime. Mostly westerns on Saturday night, I think. It was a big deal, to get to go to the movies. There was a restaurant I could spend a dime for a hot dog and five cents for a Coke.

My sisters were in college at Salisbury State Teachers College. It's now Salisbury University. We would go on a boat to see them. That was about 15 miles by water, but to drive around from Wingate you had to come into Cambridge, which was 30 miles, and then go another 30 miles south. So it was much faster to go by water.

We had a car, but really and truly there were only eight or nine cars in the South Dorchester area, and it had to be a business person who had it. My father and my uncle at one time owned a crab house, a picking house, but that was well before my day. That was all within two miles and the pickers walked to work every day. In later years they had transportation, but early on the pickers walked to work every day, sometimes very early in the morning before daylight. And they picked crabs until lunchtime or two o'clock so they could get home and cook for their husbands when they came in off the water.

It was always a pleasure to pick. All the crab pickers were happy. They were singing and laughing and joking. They sang lots of hymns, church songs. They sang other songs, but you know I don't remember what they were. I remember they sang 'She'll Be Coming Around the Mountain' lots of times. The crabs were big and they were fat. There were not many nine inches! They were a lot bigger than that. It was almost unreal. They had some that I'm sure measured 11 inches tip to tip. And they didn't pick over them to ship the big ones away. You picked them as they came.

As a kid I was slow, but I could pick five pounds an hour and that was a quarter an hour I made. And I think it's like $2.50 now. I cracked claws at one time for two and half cents a pound, but that soon changed. That changed almost as soon as I started cracking claws and we got five cents a pound.

At first, my mother taught me to pick crabs. You took it by the point, held on near the back fin, and pulled the shell off. Then you cut the eyes off, and the fins, and then raked away all the membrane. And there is a neat little way you know exactly where to put your knife to cut across that hard membrane, and we just made a straight cut across that so that you didn't mess up the big piece of lump meat, 'cause that was kind of special. That went into the can all by itself. We picked right into the cans, then we carried it up to the window to get it weighed. And we always made sure our cans were full. The supervisor would take a little bit of meat off and put it back in your pan. You had a couple of, two or three cans sitting in a big basin. You picked your crabmeat right into the appropriate can because they were different. And when you went to the window to get it weighed, he'd put on a chalkboard how many pounds you had brought up that day. Everybody knew who the fastest pickers were.

I finished high school in '44, and even before I finished high school I was cracking claws and picking crabs. That was my summer job. Well, it doesn't sound like much when you say you made a quarter an hour, but way back then you could buy a yard of fabric for 39 cents. I had many skirts out of a yard fabric. My mother made lots of clothes. She made everything. There were three picking houses in Wingate. There might be two there now. But they don't handle the volume of crabs that they did at that time. That was big business way back.

My folks were primarily European. I guess they came mostly from England, Ireland, Scotland, Wales, that area. And they were all watermen or boat builders. My father's father, well, he had a boat at one time, a dredge boat. He also worked for a furniture company here in Cambridge, Nathan's Furniture Store. He was a salesman on the road, and then he'd come around every month and collect the money that you owed to pay for your furniture or whatever you bought.

My father and my uncle owned a packing house and that was around 1918 to 1922, somewhere in there, to the best of my recollection. But they only stayed in business a couple of years. It was hard for them to run it and make a profit. That's when my father started building boats.

My father was Bronza Parks. He is most famous for his skipjacks, commercial fishing boats, and fast motorboats. There were three boat builders that I recall in the Toddville and Wingate area. My father was one of them and then there was a man named Lane Todd and one named Harvey Hurley.

They were in competition, and all evidently were pretty

good at what they did. They had lots of customers. Yet if Mr. Hurley had boats that needed painting and he needed brushes, he'd come over to my father's shop. If dad wasn't home, he went into the shop and got paintbrushes or whatever he needed. Dad could do the same thing with him, and Mr. Hurley would do the same thing about dad. So I just always thought that was a wonderful way for those people to work.

Counting the little ones and all, he built over 400 boats in his lifetime. The ones that are most famous, I suppose, are the skipjacks. The first one he built was the *Wilma Lee,* and then the *Rosie Parks, Martha Lewis,* and *Lady Katie.* The *Martha Lewis* was named after my mother's mother. The *Rosie Parks* was named after my father's mother. And the *Lady Katie* was my mother. And those boats happened to be named after my grandmothers because the boats were built for my father's brother and also his brother-in-law.

My father first started building boats probably around 1932 or '33. They were built in the side yard of our home right along the county road, right at Wingate. My father had a fairly large piece of property attached to our yard and he built a long shed-like boathouse. It was 50 feet long. Then he wanted to be able to build two boats at one time, so he added another 50 feet, and then another 50 behind that. By then he had some mechanical tools. He had a big band saw, but when he started everything was done by hand. He added the last two 50 foot sections so he could now build five boats inside. Others were built outside, but he still had a lot of space. If the weather was bad he could go inside and work on other boats. And do you know my father never ever had a blueprint. He never ever sketched out blueprints. I think he probably just figured it out. He never ever worked with anybody else. He was kind of an artist in his own right. He'd work all day long, and they had to work very hard on the heavy lumber. At night he'd go down to the boathouse and feel the sides of the boats to make sure they were nice and smooth.

My father was killed when he wasn't quite 60. He was killed by a man he was building a skipjack for. The man was from Wheaton, Maryland, over near Washington. And he came, and I didn't know this at the time, but we learned later through the court trial that this man had bought another boat and he couldn't afford to pay for both of them. His mind must've been just warped enough that he thought it would be a good way to take care of it, by killing my father. My father was a big, burly man. He didn't pay dad and dad took a lien out on the boat. I was with my father that day when he went to the States Attorney's office, and he said, 'Hold up on that lien. Mr. Rose is coming and I'm sure we can work something out.' Rose told dad that he thought he had overcharged him. Dad said, 'Stop and bring any boatbuilder you want to. We'll charge whatever that other boat builder says it's worth. If he says I'm charging you too much, I'm willing to go by... You and I can make the decision.' Rose said, 'That's all well and good, but I don't know anyone.' Dad said, 'Ask them about Captain Jimmy Richardson, a boatbuilder here in Cambridge.' He said, 'You'll be satisfied with all the references you get. Don't even tell him that you're coming. Just walk in there and ask him.' He evidently was satisfied with all he got. He went down to Richardson's and Captain Richardson said, 'Look, you know, I can't leave, I'm too busy.' And Rose said, 'Bronza Parks said all I had to do was ask you and you'd come.'

Captain Richardson put a man in charge of his shop and he went. Rose told him it's such-and-such an amount due. Should I offer him...? And Captain Richardson gave him a figure that was a little bit less. Richardson said to Rose, 'Look, both you and Mr. Parks told me this wouldn't be embarrassing to me. I told you what I think. It would cost you a lot more if I were doing it because the decking was all hand done and all.' So when they got there Rose said, 'Okay I'll go in and settle up.'

When Richardson heard the first shot he thought there were two boards, one falling on top of the other. When he heard the second one, he thought, 'Oh my gosh, that's a shot.' He jumped out of the car and ran into the boathouse as Rose shot my father the third time.

What had happened was my father had a little office in the front end of the shop. When Rose walked in daddy said, 'I'm in here, in the office.' And dad walked out and walked ahead of Rose and sat on a board. When he did, when he turned around to talk to him, that's when Rose shot him.

I remember one time when someone died in the community and the poor widow was wondering if she could afford a tombstone for him. Dad came in and said, 'I hope no one wastes money on a tombstone for me. You know, I hope they'll remember me for what I did in life.' And they sure have. That has come to pass."

Captain Buddy Harrison

Just about everyone knows Buddy Harrison of Harrison's Chesapeake House on Tilghman Island. Captain Buddy is known for running one of the foremost charter boat fishing operations on the Chesapeake Bay. His family restaurant and inn has provided comfort and delicious meals to faithful customers for more than 100 years.

Harrison's Chesapeake House continues a proud family tradition. When people arrive the expectations are the same as they were during the age of steam: "Relaxed atmosphere, great sport fishing, and no-apologies-lots-of-butter country cooking."

Their web site offers the following disclaimer: "If you like chrome and glass high-rise hotels, hot tubs, and sushi bars, we're not the place for you. On the other hand, if your taste tilts toward waterfront decks with picnic tables that groan under the weight of huge platters of hot steamed crabs and sweating pitchers of icy beer and brewed tea, we're for you." Robin Jung and John Rodenhausen visited Buddy Harrison one evening back in 2000. As they sat at the bar sipping drinks and sampling Chesapeake Bay delights with Captain Buddy, a much-treasured family story emerged.

"I grew up right here in this house. I was born here in 1934, right upstairs. Been here, except for four years at the University of Maryland, left there and came right back, been here ever since. My grandparents started this business in the 1890's. I'm the third generation. My grandparents started it, my mother and father before me, and now my wife and I. I have two sons and five grandsons, so it should continue on.

When I was a child it was mostly watermen here, crabbing, and oystering. Only part of the tourism in those days was fishermen that came to visit our establishment. It was kind of a primitive way of life in those days. The guys used to use pushcarts to take their crab lines and their baskets of crabs down to the pier, and their culling boards and their shaves, rakes, and tongs back to their house.

My grandfather and grandmother built this place in the early 1890's. He was a successful waterman, had a nice house, and in the summer there was nothing for those watermen to do. Believe it or not, in the 1890's there was no crabbing here. My grandmother was a schoolteacher, and she got him a job as the captain of a steamboat. That was the only mode of transportation in those days. Back and forth to Baltimore, or if you wanted to go to St. Michaels, you went by steamboat. If you wanted to go to Easton you'd go by steamboat, or Oxford. You know there was no other mode of transportation. There was hardly any roads. If there was it was a primitive oystershell road. When my grandmother sent his résumé in, they hired my grandfather very quickly because there was hundreds of steamboats plying the bay.

In his occupation my grandfather got to know the people in Baltimore, where they loaded and unloaded. Some guy said, 'Do you have a place down on the Eastern Shore where you can send my wife and family down for a week?' So he asked my grandmother and she said, 'Yep, bring the family down, no problem. We got this big house!' So they brought a family and they had a wonderful time. This was like in 1898. They enjoyed the sun, the crabbing, the swimming, the eating, and the Eastern Shore fresh air.

My grandfather told me the story. He said in those days in the harbor of Baltimore the stench was terrible, because they used animals to load and unload everything. They used all the old oxen, and horses and everything. The people that ran the loading and unloading of the steamboats lived upstairs. And he said he could understand why they wanted to get their family out of there.

When he went back to Baltimore the following week, there was 11 children and two ladies, 13 people standing there, waiting to come down the gangplank. He's up in the pilot house and the purser said, 'Captain Harrison, these people want to come onboard.' Well, from the Eastern Shore they took livestock, they took bulls, they took pigs, they took all kinds of produce, they took everything. But they had to let the livestock off first. So he said, 'Tell those people to get away from the gangplank.' Because the bulls, he said, they would get really, really ornery on the trip, especially when it was rough going up. The purser said, 'No, the people want to get on the boat.' So he came down and talked to people. In the meantime they let all the livestock off.

He said, 'Who are you people?' And they said, 'Well, you let Will's family go down with you, so we're Jim's and Bob's, and we're going too.' He said, 'I can't make arrangements all of a sudden.' They said, 'Well we're going.' He said, 'No, you're not!'

So then here come two guys in charge of loading and unloading and they said, 'Okay Captain, you've got one of the best times loading and unloading on the bay. If you want the worst unloading time, then you leave our families standing here. 'Cause you're going to be in big trouble. We're never gonna unload you.'

'Oh,' he said. 'All right, get on the boat, get on.' So they got on the boat. But he said he agonized all the way down the bay because he had no way of letting anybody know anything. He got to Tilghman and my father and uncle were down there with the horse and buggy. He said, 'I got 13 people.' They said, 'My God, we can't even carry 13 on the horse and buggy.' They had to make two trips. But they brought them up.

Our family always had a sense of hospitality and it's a damn good thing they have. So anyway, they get here and he's afraid to come home. My grandfather was only 28 years old, and that was the only night of the week he could spend with my grandmother. He was a young man. You know he wanted to come home. But he said he stayed on the boat that night right down here on the pier. The next morning he took off and went on his trip. When he got back, he picked up all the passengers and they went on back to Baltimore.

That following week when he got back he came home and he said, 'Well I guess I got to throw my hat in first.' My grandmother said, 'No, no, you know, my being mad's over. But if I'm going to work like that, then I'm going to make money. I've had two little signs painted up and I want you to nail them to the pier where you dock up there. It says, Harrison's boarding house, five dollars per week, all you can eat.' And so that's how the place got started. By accident, you know.

My father said at first the ladies and children were content to swing in the swings and catch soft crabs. Wade out here and do a little swimming. For 10 years it was just ladies and children. Then the men started coming and they were anxious to go fishing. By that time my father and his brothers were old enough to have boats. That's how the fishing fleet got started. They took them fishing, brought them in and cleaned their fish. They made something for the men to do.

Our food was so great that once the Bay Bridge was built all the customers that used to come here fishing started bringing their wives over for Sunday dinner. That's how our restaurant got to be really popular. A lot of people would argue the eating is the best part. Maybe I'm biased, but fishing, I think fishing is the most fun. I have a fleet of fishing boats and everyone says to me, 'Why do you go? Why do you fish?' I'm in the office in the winter and spring and all, and I enjoy it. I fish almost every day in the summer.

When I got home from the University of Maryland, we only had three boats. At University of Maryland I took business and public administration. And I'd say, if you don't advertise it's like winking at a girl in the dark—nobody knows you're doing it but you. So, I started to advertise a lot, and our name got out. Now ours is the largest privately owned charter fishing fleet in the United States. We average about 1,500 trips a year and they average about eight people a trip. Right now, we're catching a lot of striped bass. Later on that'll evolve into croakers and sea trout and drum fish and bluefish.

I take people out five days a week and I enjoy it. I take people that request me. I only fish if somebody requests me, or if it's a celebrity or a sport figure, or what have you. Brooks Robinson fishes here, and he always requests me. Ed Hale, who owns the Mariners Bank, Governor Schaffer and Barbara Mikulski all fish here. And Bob Pascal, who was the governor's appointment secretary, he won't fish with anybody but me. He brings a lot of ex-Colt football players. He was an ex-Colt himself. The pictures are right here on the wall: Brooks Robinson, Willie Mays, Joe DiMaggio, and Stan Musial. All Hall of Famers. So I've had some notable people."

As people grow increasingly aware of the health of the bay and become more concerned, what do you see as the future of the Chesapeake Bay?

"I see a great future for the Chesapeake Bay. The Chesapeake Bay is cleaning up. A lot of people have made everyone aware of what we were all doing detrimental to the bay. Everyone was being detrimental to the bay and we didn't know it. The Chesapeake Bay Foundation had a lot to do with letting people know. They let people in Baltimore City know what they were doing to the rest of the bay. They let the watermen that were working every day know what that they were doing. There was a lot of people that were doing a lot of different things that now have a better understanding of the bay, and the bay is cleaning up. I see a great future for the Chesapeake.

The lowest point was right after Agnes in the 70's. Oh man, that was bad, and we lost our oyster business. We had tremendous oyster harvests every year before that. And we lost the rockfish. I'm very optimistic, very optimistic. Now everyone knows what they were doing wrong and anybody who thinks anything at all of the Chesapeake Bay is gonna try to keep improving it."

You said that crabs weren't a big fishery back in the 1890's, but now it's the most important fishery on the bay. What happened?

"Refrigeration. There was no refrigeration in the 1890's. Also what made the crabs very important was after people started eating hard crabs in restaurants. They didn't start eating them until the late 50's. Before that it was all crabmeat, picked and served as crab cakes. Then people started eating them in crab houses and restaurants. That never happened before that. That made the crab industry. That gave a lot more income to the crabbers because the restaurants could pay more for them.

In the summer months I think they were just eating fish. There were a lot of croakers and a lot sea trout. There were a lot of all kinds of fish in those days. Our family made a living for years catching herring and shad in the spring. My father and my uncles had big rigs of pound nets, from here to the head of the Bay. And they caught millions and millions of herrings. We packed them for Vitafood Company. Put them in little jars. Pickled them. Vitafood. It was a big industry in those days. And all of a sudden the herring vanished. And that was the end of our pound net career.

Shad are coming back. We used to catch the big ole roe shad. Great big roe. Wonderful roe. A lot of technical things are bringing them back. They figured out what was happening, what was making them depleted. I think they even eliminated another dam up there so they could get them further upriver to spawn.

The Chesapeake Bay has been good to me. I don't know how I can ever repay the Bay. I mean, without it none of this would be possible. And I'd just like to say whatever I can do in the future–I don't know how many years I've got left, I hope a lot of them—but I gotta try to do all I can for the bay. I've lived on this island for a long time and I've had a great life. I go fishing every day and I come in here, and it's like the Fourth of July every night, cocktail hour. I told them on my tombstone I want to put, 'All men die, but few men live. I've lived.'"

Dr. Harry C. Rhodes, Author,
Queenstown, The Social History of a Small American Town

In the spring of 2007 I visited with Dr. Harry C. Rhodes of Queenstown to learn more about rural family life on Maryland's Eastern Shore. Dr. Rhodes has written a book called Queenstown, The Social History of a Small American Town. *From Dr. Rhodes's sitting room we looked out on the Chester River, where steamboats and schooners once arrived to load passengers and produce for shipping back to Baltimore. There had been grand hotels and entertainment here then. All that is gone now, but through the scholarship and personal recollections of Dr. Rhodes I was able to relive a slice of Maryland history.* "I've done research on about 11 generations of Rhodes going back over a period of about 400 years," *he told me. Two weeks after the interview, Queenstown celebrated its 300th anniversary. Dr. Rhodes had recently celebrated his 90th birthday.*

"I was born and raised on a farm about two miles out of Queenstown. Our home farm's been in the family for over 175 years. My mother and father both went to Washington College. Never graduated, they dropped out after their sophomore and junior year. He came home and went farming with his father. My mother went to millinery school and learned to make women's hats and so forth in the trade. Her father was a mortician and a furniture dealer, a one-term delegate to the legislature, and second president of Queenstown Bank. He was a pretty well-known person here in the village. My father, grandfather, and my great-grandfather William Washington Rhodes, were farmers. When my great-grandfather died, around 1890 I believe, he owned about 10 farms. He had a large family of 11 children. My family ancestors prior to my great-grandfather basically were farming people. They moved up here from St. Mary's County and settled in Talbot County and Caroline County, after Caroline became a county, around Revolutionary War time.

In my immediate family there were four boys and two girls. The oldest girl I never knew. She died in infancy. And then I had an older brother, who is now deceased. I was the second boy. The third boy died at the end of his freshman year at Western Maryland College, which now I think they call McDaniel. The fourth boy never did attend college. He spent most of his years farming and as a rural mail carrier, and was in the mercantile store business in Queenstown for a few years. The youngest member of my family was my sister.

My wife's family is from Dickerson, in Montgomery County, where I first started to work. She was one of five girls. Her mother died at around 40 years of age. Her father raised these five girls and I'm sure he and St. Peter got along alright when he arrived at the gate—hah—because he did his hell on earth raising those girls, I guess!

I graduated from Queenstown Elementary School and then from Centreville High School. Of course in those days there were only 11 grades in public schools. I went to Washington College in 1931, the year I graduated my high school. I graduated in 1935 and took a teaching position at Poolesville, Maryland, up in Montgomery County, and I taught until the Second World War broke out. At that time I had been granted a leave of absence by the school officials in Montgomery County to develop a program for low-income farm workers, a housing program. Just about the time we were organized and ready to go, war broke out and that ended that endeavor at that time. So I went in the Navy as an ensign in 1942. I kept telling the navy people what a great mathematics teacher I was, thinking they'd send me to one of the schools to teach math, but I ended up spending four years on minesweepers in the South Atlantic and then in the Pacific. Our last big sweeping operation was in the North China Sea at the time the Armistice was being signed in Japan.

When I came out of the service in '46, I went back to

teaching in Gaithersburg, for one year in science and math, and I coached baseball, basketball and the soccer team. After that year, '46 to '47, I was sent back to Poolesville as principal. I worked there as principal until 1952 when I was offered the Superintendent of Schools position in Queen Anne's County, my home county on the Eastern Shore. I returned to my present home in Queenstown and served as Superintendent of Schools from 1952 to 1967. After building the Queen Anne's County High School I resigned and I accepted a position with Anne Arundel Community College. That was in the summer of 1967. It was the year they moved from Severna Park High School, where we were having temporary classes, up to their present location in Arnold. At the end of my first year I was appointed Faculty Representative. I was Dean of Faculty until about '72, I think it was, where I retired again, and been in so-called retirement ever since."

Dr. Rhodes, talk about your childhood days, on the creek and on the river just outside your window.

"As a young kid growing up there's a lot of things I remember of Queenstown, such as when the freighters (schooners) used to come in here. This used to be a great tomato-growing country. You had hundreds of baskets of tomatoes piled up on the wharf waiting for a sailing vessel to come in to take 'em to Baltimore. The early boating was all sailboats. This house right next door was a granary up until the 1930's. The man who owned it, Mr. Mitchell, would charge them so much a bushel to store their grain there. The ships came in on high tide and during the low tide the ships would be aground, on their side almost. They didn't have to prop them up or anything. They would haul that grain out by mule and cart, dump it into the ship, come back and get another load until they got it loaded. When the high tide came again the ship got afloat, they'd take off and take it to the city.

Queenstown was an important hub back near the turn of the century for vacationers traveling by steamboat and train from the Western Shore of the Chesapeake to Ocean City beaches. One of the great highlights as a kid was when the railroad used to run a midnight excursion, they called it. We'd get on the train about eight o'clock in the morning in Queenstown, go to Ocean City and take our big fried chicken and country ham lunch with us, and go up to the hall where they had a lot of tables. The kids would run ahead and reserve a table for the family. We'd have a big lunch and spend the rest of the day swimming or on rides, or whatever you wanted to do in Ocean City. The train would leave that evening and get back to Queenstown about 10:00 or 10:30. We kids would all be dead tired, but we had a big time. We'd spent all the dimes and nickels that we saved to make the trip, but it was a great affair.

Later in the 1920's there was another dock here that carried the people and automobiles to Bay Shore, over near Baltimore. If you went to Bay Shore and you wanted to go into Baltimore City you'd go in on a streetcar and spend the day, spend your money, and come out and get on the boat and come back to Queenstown again.

All those days are gone because the railroad terminal was shifted from Queenstown to Love Point in the early part of 1900's. Then, of course, old *Smokey Joe* and other boats they used started the run from Love Point to the Western Shore. *Smokey Joe* was an old-time steamer and it hauled everything—automobiles, cattle, freight, people. It had a dining room on it and snack bar. It was just a good ole general boat. People used to look forward to it coming in and going out. The *B.S. Ford* was one of the most famous steamboats that used to run in here. They would carry passengers and freight. Now, when I say freight, that would be any kind of freight, including livestock. I can remember as a kid we'd sit over here where we had a bench between two trees, over there in front of my grandfather and grandmother's house. While we were visiting them we kids would sit out there on the bench and yell and yell that they were losing cattle, trying to scare them, hoping that they would jump overboard. One time I think we saw some calves jump overboard, which they were able to fish out. They hauled livestock and baskets of tomatoes. Peaches were a big thing here in the county at that time also. The local merchants would be down there meeting to get their shipment or whatever they'd ordered. Linens or sugar, whiskey, products that stores were selling that you couldn't get local. They used to come right in here and turn around at Love Point and go 'cross the bay to Baltimore.

We lived two miles from here out on Route 50. We would come to Queenstown every Saturday night. That was a great outing. We'd get in the old Model Ford with the isinglass windows you'd take off and put on. We had a Ford and then had an Essex after that. We'd come to Queenstown, do our shopping, bring eggs and barter eggs for whatever basic things that we needed at the store, things we couldn't raise or get on the farm. After we did our shopping then mother would take us kids and start at one end of the town at Grandmother and Grandfather McConner's. Usually we'd try to be there for the Amos & Andy Show, because they had a radio at that time that we could listen to. We'd visit there for a while and have cookies and lemonade or something and then go on up the street and visit the aunt and stop there and end up at Grandfather and Grandmother Rhodes, who used to live on the corner right across from here. In the meantime, my father would be making the rounds of the stores, picking up all the local gossip in the town.

In that time we had a drugstore, a hardware store, and beer tavern. We had, I guess, about four grocery stores back in those days. We had a shoemaker, newspaper office, barbershop, and things of that type. My father would come along 9:00, 9:30 or so and pick us up and go home with our groceries. It was always a big time for us to come to Queenstown."

You'd think that the kids would be spending their idle time fishing and swimming along the shores of the creeks and the bay. Not necessarily so. Family life on the farm required everyone's participation. Plus, there were classes to attend.

"We boys used to fish or crab a little with a chicken neck or something sitting on the end of a dock up here or at Love Point, but we didn't do much fishing. We didn't have time. We were busy on the farm. We worked on the farm as kids. We didn't have to worry about what you were going to do for recreation like they do today. We were up at four o'clock in the morning and four thirty we had to milk cows, feed hogs, feed chickens, feed sheep. I can remember many a morning I got up and my father had mules hooked to a cultivator or a disc or a roller. I was out in the field working until about 15 minutes before I was to catch the school bus. This was when I was in high school. I'd run in to change my clothes, run to the road gate and get on the school bus. Oh sure! Then we'd come home in the evening we had the same kind of thing to go through. You had the cows to milk and wood to gather and things of that type. You feed the chickens. You never ran short of jobs, and you did them. Now Saturdays, we pretty much had our work cut out for us. We had to clean kerosene lamp chimneys from the soot. We had one of these carriages it looks like an Amish buggy. It had a windshield on the front. You could pull it up and tie it up inside, sliding doors with glass in it. On Saturday—it was my job mainly—I had to take those wheels off, grease them, wash the windows, clean it out inside. That was a Saturday job, and nobody had to tell us to do it. We knew when we got up that's what we had to do.

We didn't have running water back in those days. We had a pump at the barn and you had to pump water in the water trough for the livestock, and we had a pump at the house and you had to tote the water from that pump into the house for your use, and so forth. And you had to be sure you had enough kindling and wood for the fire and we got into burning coal, and had to clean the ashes out. We had stoves at every chimney. The stove in the dining room was a small stove but boy, it could throw the heat out. Don't back too close to it 'cause it'd burn your rear end every time! And then the stove in the living room became a coal stove. We kept it going all night; we had a pipe going through ceiling into mom and pop's bedroom, and they got a little heat. Rest of the house upstairs had no heat in it. Cold as the devil! You got under those old comforters that they made back in those days. They were pretty snug and feather ticking was in the bed. Wasn't hard; you'd sink right down into it. 'Course you'd take that off after winter when it didn't matter, then sleep through summer that way. We lived a different kind of life then. A good bit of the time we had to beat biscuits, Maryland beaten biscuits. You put this dough on top of a block and you beat it with an axe to get air in it. That was part of our job.

I can remember as a young kid coming with my father and men and wagons and mules. In the wintertime they came out here, and with axes and saws they cut great big hunks of ice out of the creek over there, and put it in the wagons and hauled it out to the farm and put in what we called the ice house. The ice house was a big hole dug in the ground with an A-type roof over it. It was a fair-size building and they would fill that ice house up, then they'd cover it with sawdust to help delay the melting. If you wanted a piece of ice in the summer you'd go out there and get a piece out of the icehouse, put it on the pump and wash the sawdust off, and take it in and put it in your icebox.

That's how it was 80 years ago, growing up a farm boy in little Queenstown, on Maryland's Eastern Shore. The ships are all gone now, as is the railroad. And a simpler way of life."

Lawrence Hartge

The Hartge Family Yacht Yard in Galesville, Maryland, is beloved by all as a focal point for recreational boating and quality maritime services. The yard was started back in 1865 during the Civil War years by Henry Hartge, an imaginative and resourceful German immigrant. Five generations later I sat with 90 year old Lawrence Hartge at his home in Annapolis, Maryland, to talk about his life, family and the famous maritime business they created.

"My great-great-grandfather arrived by sailing ship in 1832 from Germany." Mr. Hartge began. "He evidently had some training in pianos in Germany because the first thing he did was to form the Hartge Piano Company. We have one of the three surviving pianos in our family museum and I always thought how remarkable it was that this man came here and within a few months had a piano company of his own. He had to learn to speak English. He had a job with somebody else working about 14 hours a day. And within less than a year he sent to Germany for his wife and children. His name was Henry Hartge and he lived in Baltimore.

Henry Hartge loved getting on the steamboat and coming down from Baltimore to different parts of the bay. He fell in love with Shadyside and bought 400 and some acres, all of which was the west side of West River."

There is a great tradition of boatbuilding in the Hartge family; Lawrence points out a rendering of a sailboat he himself had designed, called the Quatrant class. So I asked how the boatbuilding tradition of the Hartge family began.

"Because of the Civil War and his piano business dying out, he built a home and then another and then another, in which he got people to come down from Baltimore and stay

primarily a weekend or a week, in some cases all summer. Henry also had the ingenuity to build a pavilion out over the water with a roof over it, where visitors could dance and his own family could play the music. Then it occurred to Henry that they could also be enjoying the river. So he got his son or somebody and learned how to build rowboats, and got the rowboats going on the river too. People could swim or go sightseeing or sail or whatever it was. He did real well in that respect.

Henry's grandson was a professional boat builder, and he not only built boats for his forefathers but for other people. Emile Alexander Hartge, at 18, could build any kind of boat they wanted. Emile got sick and tired of so many Hartges living in Shadyside, so he went across the river to what is now Galesville. It was called Galloways then and that's where he started up building up his own boats.

So my father was a born seaman. At a very young age my grandfather was a very smart man. He had three sailing boats that he traded with on the bay. My father was the oldest of the sons. At 17 he was made the captain of a bugeye. A bugeye's a pretty good-sized boat. In those days people traded all over the bay with each other. For instance, in some parts like Galesville and that area they would load up a bugeye, let's say, with tomatoes, sail it primarily to Baltimore, and sell them. But from Baltimore they would try to buy something to take, let's say, to St. Michaels. Sometimes they wouldn't get home for months and months.

When I learned from my father about the boats that my grandfather built, I was curious. I went to the Naval Academy Museum to see if I could find anything about the history of boats, schooners, and bugeyes on Chesapeake Bay. I happened to run across one that said it was built in Galloways. That was the name of Galesville before it was named Galesville. It said where it was built and its size and I said it could only be my grandfather. Nobody else built boats in Galloways, at that time. So I got enough information from them and I carved a model about two feet long and that's on the wall in the museum.

There's a road not far from Annapolis called St. George Barber Road. The family of St. George Barber had this big yacht and they asked my father would he be the captain of it, and he did. They would have him take them to New York or some places like that once in a while. They also had a little pile driving vessel, a scow, and he built bulkheads and docks and things like that for them. Then they gave him the pile driver. 'It's yours now.' So he went into business with that for awhile. One of the Smith Brothers of Galesville, who are now well known for their pile driving company, wanted my father to come in business with him. So they formed a company called Smith & Hartge. They had only been going for several months when a much bigger yacht came along, the *S.W. Legrow,* and wanted my father to be the captain of that. It was 150 feet long. He would have my father take him up to New England, New York, wherever. So that was his main business for quite some time. He'd go from Florida to Maine for people taking their boats back and forth. Generally speaking he was the captain of a big yacht that one owner would have for maybe 10 years or so. He was at sea most of the time."

Philip Van Horn Weems Dodds

In 2006, I toured the property at Pleasant Plains Farm on the St. Margaret's peninsula with proprietor Philip Dodds. His family has owned the property since 1942. Pleasant Plains Farm is a rural farm which is still standing very close to urban Annapolis, thanks to the decision of Philip and his sister to put the property into a land trust. The designation protects the farm in perpetuity from large scale development. I talked to Philip Dodds before he passed away on October 6, 2007 about his life growing up on the farm, and about the legacy left by his storied relatives. His father and grandfather were both captains in the United States Navy. His grandfather was also an esteemed writer and inventor. Phillip explained the decision to protect this historic and desirable farm from the possibility of being subdivided and developed.

"We're standing in front of the main farm house in which I grew up, a three-story brick house with a wing that was built in about 1830. My grandfather bought the place in 1942 and we moved here in 1957. It's not as old as some places around here, but the land here was settled in the 1600's. This house was built by John Ridout, who is the grandson of another John Ridout, who was the secretary to Governor Sharp in the 18th century."

The main house overlooks Ridout Creek, which connects to Whitehall Creek, which in turn connects to Whitehall Bay, and the mouth of the Severn River.

"We're about a 10 minute boat ride out to the bay, which is gorgeous. The creek extends about a mile to the left and three quarters of a mile to the right. It's where, as a kid, I would spend my time either in the water or on it, fishing it or crabbing it. It's got really nice deep water just across from the neighborhood called Amberly, which used to be called Hog-neck because they would turn pigs loose in there to feed on acorns. It was also owned by our family until about 1951.

This farm and the adjoining farm, called Hollywood Farm, which is owned by my sister, was part of what was known as Providence, originally settled in 1649. It is an area that was settled before Annapolis. There have been and continue to be archeological digs here. It was very exciting a couple of years ago, because they found the footings of a settlement of houses in the middle of the field that I used to plow when I was young. In the basement of one of those houses they found a skeleton. It caused quite a stir amongst the archeologists, who then brought out forensic anthropologists. They carefully pealed back the dust from this greening skull, which was clutched in a fetal position in a semi-upright state, which was very unusual. The anthropologists quickly concluded that it was probably a European male. They could tell apparently by the teeth. They surmised it was either a Catholic or a Protestant settlement because the people would alternately come and kill each other off in that period.

We have references in the patent for this area, which we have a copy of, that date back to the 1630's. This area was populated very early on and it's been an operating as farmland for quite a few years. In the old days, back in the 20's, this farm was both a dairy farm with cows and, we presume, oats and so forth. After my father retired from the Navy, he was a corn farmer for 30 years. We had two huge barns that were located near the house. We also had a small herd of cattle, a lot of hay, plus, we boarded horses and had about 300 pigs."

We're looking at an old piece of wrapping for sausage, framed on the wall. At the top it says, 'Pleasant Plains Farm Pork Sausage, Home Grown, Corn Fed Country Style.'

"This was a wrapper that my father had printed up be-cause he loved to make sausage. We used to make the sau-sage in the basement and sell it by subscription each year.

And everybody loved it.

We're walking past a small brick outbuilding that was the original smoke house. This is the place that the hams would be hung and cured into bacon and other meats. We just use it as a storage shed now but you can see at the top there are holes in the bricks to let the smoke trickle out. We're hoping to restore it. The problem with the brick here is what some masons call salmon brick. Some of the brick has begun to slowly degrade. You need to use the old original oyster shell-based mortar to restore it.

We've got a good collection of John Deere tractors, which you'd expect, along with furniture stored and awaiting the next turn in the furniture hospital. I have a secret office where I can hide, and I do my day job, which is consulting for the Department of Defense on education and training. I also have my guitars and bass guitars and amplifiers. We used to have a band back when we were in high school at Annapolis High called the Irish Potato Famine. We still play just amongst ourselves off and on. In the original band there was Ken Eaton, Chris Brown, Les Weller and Bob Showacre, the once DJ 'Bob Here.' All of us were Class of '69. I have over here a collection of instruments—clavichord, and harpsichord. Over there is an old synthesizer called a Rhodes Chroma. It used to be called an ARP Chroma. That's an instrument that my team and I designed when I was in the business of making musical instruments."

You may have seen Philip Dodds before and not realized it. As a key technician and designer for the synthesizer company ARP, Phil found himself the on-site technician for director Steven Spielberg, during the filming of Close Encounters of the Third Kind. *Phil's expertise eventually landed him the role as the keyboard player in the film's climactic sequence.*

"The apple trees were here when we were growing up but they were old then," Phil said. "I used to go out and grab handfuls of apples and eat too many of them, many of them green, and then get stomachaches. They're all gone now simply because they were planted in the 20's and apple trees don't generally last that long. There was a farm nearby called Harmony Acres. It was run by a fellow named Mr. Grimes. Colorful fellow. He grew arguably the best peaches in the state and ran that single-handedly. He was a single man. When he finally sold the place he came and worked for us and lived in the cottage out here. He was quite a character because he had a strong religious bent. He would go into the barns and work all by himself and he would preach when no one was around. He would just give these resounding sermons echoing through the barn. We kids would always just stand outside of the barn and giggle.

A big bell was the way that my parents would keep me in control over the 350 acres that comprised the farm. Whenever it was time to come home, for whatever reason, usually dinner, they always reminded me that 'the bell tolls for thee.' That bell would peal for five or 10 minutes and I could be a mile and a half away and I would hear it. I would be in very, very deep trouble if I didn't get home quickly.

We completely rebuilt the support building for the dairy, inside out. It used to have big stainless-steel tanks for processing milk, and the pipes ran underground over to the dairy. In later years, this was the place where my father had his workshop, and he had a big wood stove in the corner. Every morning all of the farm crew would gather around this thick gooey coffee that he would brew, being Navy. And he always had burnt bacon and biscuits for everybody. Everybody would stand around and visit for about an hour and a half and plot out what we would be doing on the farm that day. And I don't think I've run into anybody from that period who didn't remember the times sitting next to that fire and that stove and drinking that bitter coffee. They enjoyed it.

There's a picture of my father standing on a tractor and there's another tractor behind it. You'll see that he has a tie on. After 20 years in the Navy, he was also a captain, he just found himself uncomfortable without a tie. It was not a pretense. It was just that he found a loose collar uncomfortable after 20 years of having one, so even working around the farm he usually had a tie on."

We move to another of the small outbuildings, and enter a room overwhelmed with very old books.

"We restored this building and are turning it into a library for my grandfather's books. My grandfather was Captain Philip Van Horn Weems. He's the founder of Weems and Plath, which is still operating and prospering in Eastport. We're very good friends with the current owners. My grandfather was a very famous navigator and inventor, with many patents. The whole wall of books that I'm standing next to here were all books that he wrote. He knew many of the early explorers. And he created a lot of the basics for improved navigation over his period. For example, my grandfather taught Charles Lindberg how to navigate. He was Naval Academy Class of '12. He was recalled to active duty twice and served three times. He was very well known."

Phil shows me the original recording device that his grandfather used to dictate his books.

"It uses a sort of a floppy record—Autograph is the brand of the dictation machine. This dictaphone has a needle on it and it actually cuts a record into this thin plastic which then plays back just as a regular record. He would dictate into this machine and all of his writings were then transcribed by a secretary. I think I have every letter he ever wrote and have been able to transcribe some... it's so nice to hear his voice again.

My grandfather served as an engineer and navigator through much of his career. If fact he was very proud that he had his master's certificate for all oceans, a navigation certificate, and an engineering certificate. In World War II, when he was recalled to active duty, my grandfather was rapidly promoted to captain by James Forestall who was CNO at the time.

He was a convoy commodore taking convoys to North Africa. I think he took about 36 of them. My grandfather's first command was the *Hopkins,* which was what they called a four-stacker, I guess. It was a steam destroyer from World War I.

The second time my grandfather was recalled to active duty it was in my memory. It was in the 60's, when he was asked to form a class in space navigation. So he actually was responsible for putting together a year-long course on how to manually navigate through space. He helped develop some of the techniques that made sure that *Apollo 13* actually got home, because he worked out how you can visually navigate against objects. After the *Apollo 13* got in trouble they had to take a visual site and navigate the firing of their rockets to get the ship into an orbit that they could recover from. So he started with sea navigation, then air, then space. Right as the Mercury programs were starting, just as they were about to be launched, I remember our family went with him to the National Geographic when he was being awarded the Gorse Award. And he introduced me to John Glenn and Jacques Cousteau, who were also award winners there. I was mightily impressed. I think I was probably about 10."

The St. Margaret's area near Annapolis, just off of Route 50 near the Chesapeake Bay Bridge, like many areas surrounding the Chesapeake Bay, is a peninsula. There is one road to get in and out. Large-scale develop-ment on these peninsulas is a highly questionable propo-sition. Nevertheless, economic forces can severely pres-sure landowners and government officials into making unwise planning decisions. Overall quality-of-life issues and limited infrastructure options are pushed aside by aggressive developers intent on fabricating houses in precarious places by the tens of thousands. Phillip and his sister Thackray Dodds Seznec, along with then County

Executive Janet Owens, arranged to put the family estate into a land trust to preserve it.

"In the early days of this farm, certainly in the 18th century, this was quite remote and most of the traffic was by water. It was easier to get to town by water because there weren't bridges across all the little inlets and whatnot. By the 19th century, there were more roads and they were somewhat more connected but some of the Broadneck area was still farmland. By the 1920's things began to change pretty rapidly. If you were to look down on us now, if you do a Google World search, for example, or fly in an airplane over this part of Broadneck, you can look down and see one big green area and then housing all around it. Well, the one big green area is what's left of this farm. We were fortunate that the County Executive introduced us to a program, an open space program, to see the development rights to this farm such that it will never be subdivided, it will never have new housing on it. What you're seeing will be permanently all that's here. You can upgrade it, you can fix it up, but we can't build new houses. And we did that on purpose. We didn't really ever want to see the farm subdivided. The pressure to do that is very, very high. And the county had created a program where they would actually give you an annuity payment out of bonds that would compensate us for the loss in value. So basically the county is paying us to do what we would really like to do, which is to protect the land and make sure it's in agricultural or woodland use only. And we've got enough income from that to make sure that we can maintain the place.

I don't think people recognize how much land is at risk and we're losing, how much the density has just exploded in this immediate area. And you can't go backwards and restore it once it's developed. This will not be developed."

8

Gone Fishin'

Captain Rip Delaudrier

If there is one word that is synonymous with Chesapeake living, it's fishing. So I lucked out when I moved next door to Rip Delaudrier, a guy who loves to catch and eat fish.

I went fishing a number of times with Rip, who would give me the customary "arrgghh" pirates' snarl when I got the lines tangled, which I did often. One of the most memorable experiences I have of fishing on the bay is hearing the sound that croakers make. A croaker is a fish that purrs like a cat but with the tone of a frog. It is endearing. We sat and talked about Rip's favorite subject back in the fall of 2003 at his Annapolis bungalow on Waveland Farm overlooking the scenic Severn River.

"Fortunately I've been able to fish the bay, crab the bay, and I've enjoyed every minute of it. My grandfather fished and my dad fished, it kind of rubbed off on me, I guess. I've just kind of carried on the tradition. I'll tell ya, I couldn't think of a better endeavor. I've always said that I'd probably fish seven days a week if they'd let me.

I grew up on Mill Creek, which is right off of White Hall Bay, near Annapolis. You have the Cantler family and the James family there. These people have been hardworking people since day one. They're the kind of people that work 15, 16 hours every day, four seasons out of the year. They know what hard work is really about. The Cantlers not only crab, but they oyster in the wintertime when its freezing cold out there and you gotta make a living. They go out there and work their butts off oystering in the wintertime. It's been a pleasure to know these folks because they're kind of like the farmers of the sea. It's a tough way to make a dollar but it's a good life. You come home at the end of the day and you've supported your family and you're doing what you like to do.

Cantlers' Restaurant is over on Mill Creek and fortunately for my friend Jimmy, he had the opportunity to buy it in the 70's. He's been at it there for about 28, 29 years now. It's off the beaten path but that's kind of the mystique about the place. Some people like to seek out something different. To get over there to Cantlers' you got to go across the Naval Academy Bridge and you go up the hill there, and all of a sudden you make a right. There's a fork in the road there and you make a right and then you take another right and you zigzag back through this community and all of a sudden it comes out at this wonderful restaurant on the creek. I couldn't think of a better place to eat, you know, you're right there on the water. You can literally spit and hit Mill Creek. There's crab sheds so you're really in the atmosphere where the crabs come in. Of course, after all these years of cooking crabs and seafood, they've got it right. They know how to do this, ya know, cooking soft crabs and cooking hard crabs. They've got a winning formula there. There are certain nights when the locals come out of the woodwork and they exchange ideas. It's kind of like a fraternity where everybody helps each other out, where the fish were biting that day or whatnot.

Fishing is one of those variable things, it changes from day to day, just like the weather. The fish may be in one spot and then gone to another spot the next day. We go down and talk about where we caught fish that day and what technique we used.

Most of this year we've been chumming here. Chumming

is a term for grinding up alewives, or baitfish. You grind them up and take a chum bag and hang it off the stern there with the ground-up fish. It's smelly and it's messy but, you know, that's just part of the fun. You drink the right kind of beer and wish for the fish to show up, and then all of a sudden it happens. That's the way fishing is. Some days you load up the boat with a bunch of fish and everything's groovy and then the next day you go out and the wind's blowing and everything's different. The weather has a lot to do with it. It can shuffle the deck drastically, like this hurricane we just had. Fishing was really good up until the hurricane. I talked to a lot of cohorts here and they said the same thing. But I'm really confident that the fishing's gonna pick up here soon because in the fall the fish they need to get a feed on. They need to start eating before the cold weather settles in.

With the migration of the rockfish, there's a certain percentage of them that stay here all year round. They just dig in, and from what limited knowledge I have, I think they're the smaller fish. Your bigger fish that go over 15 to 20 pounds go out into the ocean and they migrate and go up and down the coast. They go all the way up to New England. In the wintertime they settle down there off the Carolinas somewhere, from what I've been told. But there's a certain population of rockfish that stay here all year round. The people that know how to catch fish know where those fish hide out and know where to go.

This is kind of like a transition period right now. It's no longer summer but you noticed we haven't had any frost nights yet. All the farmers know this. Normally what happens this time of year is the fish start to group up a little bit and they form schools. Because, you know hunting is a lot easier with strength in numbers. But that hasn't happened quite yet. All the buddies of mine that I fish with have indicated that there's been a few breaking fish out there in schools but they've been mostly the small fish. The big fish haven't really hooked up yet. But that'll happen within the next several weeks here. As soon as we get a little bit of frost and a couple of those cold and chilly northwest wind nights the fish are gonna start to bunch up and get hungry and do their thing and start feeding. It's just going to hinge on the weather.

Fortunately, I had the opportunity to study under one of the best. Most of the people in this area will acknowledge that Ed Darwin, who has a boat out here on Mill Creek called the *Becky D,* is one of the grand old masters. Everybody looks up to him with respect. He knows what he's doing as far as rockfishing goes. I had the opportunity to mate for him for a couple of years and, I'll tell you what, I had fished for 35, 40 years and I thought I knew what I was doing. I learned a whole new dimension of fishing from Ed. He's been at it for quite some time and fishes every day and fishes hard. He's a very successful fisherman. He trolls and he chums and he casts around the bridge. But the trolling method, it's very scientific. It's not one of these deals where you go out there and throw out five or six lines and drag them behind the boat and hope you catch fish. It just doesn't work that way.

He's pretty darn scientific about it, being an ex-school teacher that's the way he conducts his business. He is very specific about how he does things. Being a mate, he told me, for instance, if we had six lines out trolling, to let certain lines out at a certain length—90 feet, 100 feet, 120 feet, 150 feet. You're covering the different depths out underneath the boat. When the fish start biting at a certain depth, you know you better adjust your lines because that's where the fish are hanging that day. That's usually, but not all the time, determined by the thermal layer of the water column. In other words, in the fall the warm water is usually closer to the bottom 10 to 15 feet, whereas in the spring the warm water is on the surface. Things change throughout the year but in the fall, because the warmer water is down below, you have to adjust your gear and use heavier gear and more weight to get down to the bottom where fish are hanging.

You can't get too specific about this stuff because right when you think you know everything about fish, it changes on you. But usually the fish like to bite around the tide. If you can time it on the tide chart to go for, say, the last hour or hour and a half of one tide and the beginning of the next tide, that's normally when the fish like to bite. It seems like when that tide is racing real hard and it's moving along at a rapid pace they just seem to shut down a little bit and take a siesta or whatever. But if you can get that tide to slow down at the end of one tide and the beginning of another one, the fish seem to turn on and that's just the way they are. That's their habit.

For tackle, trolling-wise in the fall, your charter captains start using what they call a bucktail, which is made from a deer's tail and a leadhead. They put a couple glass eyes in there, drop it down deep where the fish are, and that seems to work. What it does is it represents a baitfish, the same profile as the alewives, or the bunkers, that the rockfish normally feed on. In the fall that's what these charter captains are dragging. There are several other techniques too but that seems to be the most successful one in the fall. In the summertime and in the fall here the charter captains are using ground up alewives and bunker. That seems to be working very well but that technique may change in a couple of two or three weeks according to the water temperature and the weather conditions.

Usually the spring and the fall are the best times for fishing. You will catch some fish in the summer time but they get sluggish, they get lethargic, they don't eat as much. They kind of lay low, like human beings to a certain extent. When it gets that hot you're not really that energetic and that hungry. But in the fall again when it gets a little cool they get hungry again and they want to bite. So actually the best time is early spring through June, and then again in the fall it picks up in September and October. We were fishing last year all the way until the end of the rockfish season which was around Thanksgiving, end of November, and catching some big fish. We caught some fish that were over 40 inches. I'm sure that most of the fishermen out there that are avid and hang in there will acknowledge that the big fish like to bite late in the fall. It's kind of neat 'cause most of the traffic's gone and you kind of have the bay to yourself there. You're out there catching big fish and life is good!

This has been kind of a strange year. Basically it's been due to the weather with lots of rain and the salinity in the water is not normal. You've got a lot of species of fish that didn't show up as a result. But it was a very good year for croakers. They're a very fun fish to catch. Pound for pound they battle as well as any fish around. There's a plethora of white perch. That's one species that has really survived really well through all the hurricanes and throughout the years. There's plenty of white perch and a lot of people out here on the Chesapeake will say to you, pound for pound, the white perch is the best eating fish around. But because of the rains and whatnot the sea trout didn't show up as well as they normally do. And I personally like to catch sea trout. I think they're a lot of fun. The same thing with the bluefish. It's been a slow year for bluefish. There have been smaller bluefish, you know, the 10 to 12 inch guys, up to about three or four pounds. But the big bluefish haven't shown up. Then again, it's a give-and-take kind of thing. Some species survive better with less salinity and some don't. Hopefully things will balance out in the long run, in the next five or 10 years and we'll have a little bit of everything."

Captain Ed Darwin

During interviews for the Voices *project I've asked a lot of people, including Captain Rip, "Who's the best fisherman in the Upper Chesapeake Bay?" The same name kept popping up—Ed Darwin. When I finally got the chance to meet Ed Darwin a few weeks before the opening of the trophy rockfish season in 2007 I thought I'd be running head on into a crusty old hardhead, kind of like the shark fisherman from the movie* Jaws. *I couldn't have been more wrong. We sat at his kitchen table with a view of Mill Creek on one side and a wall of hand-carved fish on the other. Besides being a brilliant fisherman, Ed is a brilliant carver. But instead of carving waterfowl, he's chosen to carve likenesses of many of the fish he's encountered over the years.*

"I've been down here since 1949," Ed said. "I've run fishing parties on the Chesapeake Bay since 1960. So this'll be my 48th year of fishing on the bay. It's been a wonderful life. I really count my blessings just being out on the bay. It's a good thing for me. I think you can appreciate nature by just being out there. Sounds kind of trite, but I can't think of anything better than going out on the bay in the morning with the sun rising on Kent Island and watching it come up. Then we can have the pleasure of fishing the rest of the day.

I grew up in Baltimore, or as they say Bal'mer. My family insisted I was the wrong child because no one had ever been on the water. But I was born just loving to fish. My father was just a working man. He died very young. I was 15 years old when my father passed away. But fortunately there was a man who lived down the street from me that owned a bait business. I used to get up at four or five o'clock in the morning and go with him down to Rhodes River and catch grass shrimp. Grass shrimp is a small shrimp that's in the grass in the creeks. You push a roller net and catch these. I did this all through high school and we were selling them for bait. I did that for summer and it helped pay my way through school. In those days we got three dollars a gallon for shrimp. It didn't sound like much but I think ice was something like a quarter for a 100 pounds and gasoline was 11 cents a gallon. So I probably had more spendable income then than I do now.

I graduated from Forest Park High School, then I worked at a research lab. It was wonderful and I really learned quite a bit. They were doing highly secret work at the time. We developed a chemical-type battery that was used in rockets and ejection seats on planes. Then I got drafted. Went into the Army and ended up on Lake Erie. I was right between the Korean War and Vietnam. I flew radio-controlled airplanes. That was a great adventure in itself. We flew these drone planes. They had anti-aircraft crews come in from Pittsburgh and Detroit and they tried to shoot these little planes down. They weren't very successful at doing it until the advent of radar. Once the radar came in you had trouble keeping the planes up. They could knock them right out of the sky. I guess I was very fortunate. They could only fly in the midwinter because it was a hunting and fishing resort. You couldn't fly during the hunting season or the fishing season. It was cold on the lake but it was pretty interesting to do.

I didn't have much chance to ice fish there because that's when we flew. But I fished there in the summer time. I helped a netter there and we caught yellow perch and catfish. That was before Lake Erie became polluted. The big fish there was the walleyed pike. I had a little boat and it was great. They're good eating, too. They weren't very big compared to what we catch here but we didn't know any better. That was 1955 through 1957. I got out and went to night school for 12 years. The only job that I could find where I could fish all summer long was teaching, so I became a teacher. All summer off and it was great. I retired from teaching in 1987, and I've been running full-time fishing parties since.

My true love is the Chesapeake Bay. It kind of hurts me sometimes seeing what's happening in the bay. It's still an excellent fishery. Crabs are good. The oysters are not as good as they used to be. But last year was one of the better years I've had for catching big fish. Normally we'll catch big fish, the ocean run fish, in the springtime. Then it tapers off and we catch small fish. Last year for some reason we had big fish here almost the whole year—striped bass, rockfish. It was good until the late fall when for some reason the fish left early. In fact, it got so poor in late November that I cancelled my last eight parties. But I'm looking forward to this year. It was a good year down at the mouth of the bay. That's usually a pretty good indicator of what we're going to get here in the springtime when there's massive numbers of big fish."

Why do you love fishing so much?

"I think it is innate. I think I was born this way because even when I was a small boy there were some streams up in Baltimore, and I would fish there any time I could. My family thinks I belong to someone else. They got the wrong baby. But once you've spent enough time on the bay, you've got to be here, I think. There's just something about it. It's more than just fishing. Fishing is secondary. It's all the things that go with it. I can go down on my pier and sit out there and catch sunfish or perch or pickerel. Or we can go crabbing. Grandchildren can come down and swim on the pier. It's just a paradise.

The bay has been kind to me. I've seen a lot of fish come out of this bay. I've seen a lot of people come and go too, in this business. I've been married for a long time. I have a son that's a doctor at the University of Maryland. I have a daughter that's a computer analyst. She gets upset when I say that. She's way above that and I don't really know the terminology. I have two granddaughters and three boats. One's the *Becky D.* And my son has a boat down here, so we have means to get out on the water.

Right now, the way I look, I have clothes on with paint all over them. I've been painting my boat today and getting ready to fish this year. I'm 76 years old. I'm just touching it up! Somebody's got to do it. I guess we've got to thank the good Lord. I feel good and I'd like to keep fishing. But I've told most of my parties now that in another 25 years I'm going to quit so they better find somebody else.

This season I think we're going to have another super year with rockfish. We get sort of an idea of what's in the bay by what the netters do in the wintertime. They were catching mostly big fish this winter. They were having a tough time catching the small fish because there were so many mud shad in the bay this year. When you set a net it would just fill up with the mud shad and you'd spend hours and hours and hours picking these mud shad out, and you get nothing for it. They don't really have much use for them and there's no market for them. I understand even the crabs don't bite them very well.

But there was a lot of fish outside. There was a lot of fish down the bay, and they come up the bay here to spawn. They're the migratory fish that are here just in the springtime, and they leave usually about the second or third week in May, when they're finished spawning. If they get a real warm spring they'll leave early, and that's not too good. We'll start on April the 21st and then fish until May the 16th for these migratory fish. Then we get our resident fish which are smaller. They'll be here until December.

The largest fish I've caught was between 75 and 80 pounds. It would have been a record rockfish, but it's a funny story. The man that caught it fished with me regularly. He still does. This was probably back in 1965, I'm not sure of the exact date. He got on the boat that day and said, 'What'd you do yesterday?' And I said, 'Well, I caught a couple fish over 50 pounds.' He said, 'What'd you do with them?' I said, 'I was hired by the Department of Natural Resources and we caught some over 50 and some over 45 and we threw them back. That's really the thing to do because they're all full of roe.' He said, 'If I catch a big fish I'm going to throw it back, too.' So we caught one that we measured and it was 56 1/2 inches long. I've forgotten exactly what the girth was, but it would have been a crime to kill something like that. It was ready to spawn. He looked at it and he said, 'Do you mind if I throw it back?' I said, 'No. I think you should.' So he threw it back, and that's the biggest fish I've ever caught. I've seen them bigger.

Usually the female rockfish are first and the males come later on. But they all get together at the same time somewhere. Some years you get really supersize fish here. This year (2007), I don't know if you're aware of it, but the last two years fishing has been so good that we've caught too many fish. Maryland's on a limit. It's really not very equitable because the other states are not on a limit. We were allowed to catch 30,000 oversize migratory fish, and we caught 60,000. We caught way too many and now we're going to be penalized. This year we're going to have a slot limit. It appears it's going to be 28 inches to 37 inches and then anything over 37 inches to 43 inches you have to release. You can keep one over 43 inches. But most of the people who fish for rockfish with me would rather let these big fish go. I personally would rather release them. I don't like eating a fish that big. They reproduce so many fish, so many young, so many eggs that I think it's a crime to keep them. If the party insists on doing it, they're welcome to keep them.

It's a thrill to catch something like that. They're not equal to a marlin but they're better than a catfish. Rockfish are a good fish to catch. They're considered a game fish. They don't have the stamina and they don't break water, jump, like a lot of other fish do, but they bite well and they do give you a pretty good tussle.

In the summer time I don't troll. I only troll in the spring. I would rather never troll. We use heavy tackle for trolling compared to what I like to use. We use wire, and now we use a lot of this braided material. The trouble with using wire is that it kinks and it breaks. The advantage of using wire is that you don't have to use as much lead. Your lines will go down a lot further. Most of my people, I've built my business fishing with light tackle. So we use spinning rods, light tackle. I don't have as many parties in the springtime as I would like because my regular parties won't troll. They feel that the boat's catching the fish, they're not. Whereas with light tackle you catch the fish, whether you jig or fish bait, you're catching the fish. When the boat's moving along the lure is catching the fish. They pull it in, but there's just not the skill required so my regular people don't want to do that. I'm in business, I like to go. But I prefer to fish light tackle. I like the jigging, that's my favorite way.

Jigging, we use a feather lure. It's just a lead head with dyed chicken feathers on it. The motion you use, you reel and jerk at the same time. If you get the right motion it looks exactly like a silverside minnow trying to escape. It's got to be as productive as any other kind of fishing that I know of. We catch everything. Any fish that swims in the bay here will eat a jig. They even catch a toad fish once in a while. I've caught fish at well over 30 pounds with one of these jigs.

I've been kind of a maverick. I don't fish like most of the other boats in the bay. For years and years I fished nothing but soft crabs. The good thing about fishing soft crabs is that if you don't catch fish you can eat the bait. You can't say that about worms. For some strange reason, the year before last, fish became sort of finicky and they didn't want the soft crabs very well. Last year you couldn't catch a fish on a soft crab. They wanted live bait. So I fished live spot and live white perch. That's really a picnic. I've been doing that for about 10 years on and off with the perch. And now this past year, all the other boats caught up with me; now they're all fishing live bait. It makes it exciting and interesting to do it. The difference is that when you have a live fish on there, and you feel the other fish pick it up, I mean there's a distinct feeling when he grabs it. You have to hook those fish. It's not instantaneous. You have to open the bail, give it a time to turn the fish around in his mouth, because he swallows it head first. If you pull it too fast you miss them, if you don't pull it at all you miss them, so it's a matter of learning how to feel it and catching him just at the right time. The irony about fishing with white perch for bait is that I guess 90 percent of the rockfish you catch are not even hooked. They swallow the perch, which has spines on his back. That gets lodged in his throat and if you try to hook him too hard, or you pull him too hard, or you lift him out of the water, you lose them. So, it's a kind of finesse thing. You get to know when. It's a hard thing to describe. You can just feel when the fish is on there, once you learn how to do it. The novices on the boat, they'll have a difficult time. But they catch on pretty fast. We have a lot of fun with regular people on the boat. They give each other a real hard time when they lose a fish. So do I! That's part of the game."

I ask Captain Ed about his infamous neighbors, the Cantler family. I loved hearing stories about these rough and tumble fishermen; there's a mystique about them that's just irresistible.

"The Cantlers consist of 19 children. They're watermen through and through. They have got to be as hard a working people as you've ever seen in your life. When they were young they played just as hard as they worked. I remember when they were little boys. I could tell you stories and stories about them! Jimmy Cantler is the one that owns the Riverside Inn, but he had a brother who's passed away now, Carroll. And he has a little brother, Eric.

When they were little they had a rowboat that Leo James had, the waterman across the creek. They would go out and fish around the Bay Bridge. In those days there were a zillion fish around the bridge pilings. One day we were fishing piling 16 and Carroll hooked a big fish on a rod and it went around the piling. Well, Carroll jumped overboard, and swam around the piling! I swear... ask Jimmy, he'll tell ya. Swam around the piling, got on the boat on the other side, and they took off down the bay afterward. They would do things like that all the time. You never knew what they were going to do.

I'll tell you another funny story that happened to me. I was fishing around the Bay Bridge, we call it the bumper. It's the abutment there in the center span. We were catching a lot of big fish using soft crabs. I came up there after a day of catching a lot of fish and there was a Rock Hall boat there. He had anchored on a spot next to where I had been fishing, but he was on the wrong corner of the piling. So I anchored on the right corner. You always had to put out a bridle; now a bridle is two anchors that are 180 degrees apart. Then I tied the boat to the piling. I got three ties holding the boat in, because these fish there at the time, you had to be right exactly perfect. If you weren't you couldn't catch these fish. You had to count how many feet of line you went out. There was a science to doing it. Well anyhow, the tide got off real strong and one of the Rock Hall boats who didn't know any better slipped behind me and he got his anchor on my wheel (propeller).

My son was working for me at the time. He went over-board to cut the fellow's anchor line off the propeller and one of the other Rock Hall boats called and said, 'We just saw two big sharks in the water.' He said, 'Get your boy out of the wa-ter!' My son heard this and he came right over the stern of the boat without any help. About five or 10 minutes later I hooked a rockfish, and a shark rose up and bit about a 20 pound rock-fish off in one bite! I came in with nothing but the head. So I came in here and told Carol Cantler about it. He went out that night and set a net—and we caught a 540-pound bull shark, right there at the bridge. We hung it up at Riverside Inn for two or three days 'til it got too bad and then we took it back out in the bay and let it go.

I haven't seen sharks in quite a few years. When we had those big massive schools of rockfish around the bridge, they would appear here usually in the last week of July and stay 'til about the second week in September. We knew they were here because I fished the bridge every day and I would anchor on the western stone pile or the Eastern stone pile and you could see the big rockfish swim around on the surface. And every once in a while a shark would splash and catch one of these things. My parties liked going there and just watching this. It was something, but I haven't seen them in a few years. That's the only kind of sharks that I've ever seen here.

Three years ago, believe it or not, we saw a whale up here. No, that's not true. We did not see a whale up here. But it was very, very calm and we could see it blowing. We could see the waterspout go up and we could see giant swirls. We stayed with that thing for maybe a half hour, following it up the bay. We first saw it right at the bridge by the western stone pile. When we left it was almost up to Baltimore Light. That's the first and only time I've ever seen one in the bay. But of you spend enough time out here you see a lot of things. We used to see file fish out here. They would lie on their sides, and had beautiful colors. Years ago we used to see those things out here all the time. You see some sea turtles once in a while. I'm not sure if they're loggerheads or green turtles, leatherbacks, I don't know what they are. But you do see them. It's an interesting thing.

I don't like killing anything, believe it or not. If I had my way, I'd release everything. Some of my parties feel like I do now. We catch them for fun. I think they're kind of majestic. It's just nature. I really feel bad about killing something. I guess somebody would say, 'Well, why are you in this business?' Maybe I wouldn't feel that way if I wasn't in this business. But I've seen so many of these fish come and go and I'd just as soon catch them and let them go.

I think there are water-quality issues, there are so many more people, there's so many more fishermen. I think we've lost a lot of spawning habitat. All these things count. But the positive side of it is that people don't act like they did years ago. Most of the people that fish with me are very pleased to take just a couple fish and throw the rest back or stop fishing. We'll never, certainly in my lifetime, see it like it was in the 50's or 60's. We had an abundance of fish and I'd go out and if we didn't catch 75 keeper fish in a day I'd apologize and say it was a bad day. Somebody said just the other day at one of these boat shows that when he was a boy you used to use four rods to catch 40 fish. Now we use 40 rods to catch four fish."

Bill Burton

I first heard about Bill Burton after reading his column in the Bay Weekly, *a forward-thinking free newspaper that circulates throughout the region. Bill Burton is another legendary character from the Chesapeake Bay region; his name comes up whenever you talk fishing. A former reporter for the* Baltimore Sun, *Bill came to Maryland from hither and yon and fell in love with the area just like I did.* Voices *interviewed him in 2002 at my home studio on Waveland Farm.*

"Don't know if you'd call me a Marylander or not," Bill said. "I was raised in Vermont where we had no tidal water, but we had Lake Champlain and a lot of great trout streams. I came here from Alaska, where I had lived for a year. I was a newspaper man. Still am. I sort of liked it here. I came here for six months and stayed. The Sun had an opening for an outdoor editor in 1956, and I took it. I told them I'd be leaving in about six months, and I retired from the Sun in 1992. I'm still here in Maryland.

I've been a newspaper man since 1947, full time. First job was with a radio station as a news editor. I was told by an old Vermont country editor that you never worked at a place for more than six months or a year. You moved on. I did that until I came to Maryland and I just didn't feel like moving on. Whether it was the job, 'cause all I had to do was write about hunting and fishing, or whether it was the fishing itself, I don't know. But I just stayed and was reluctant to leave.

I live in Rivera Beach, which is in the Pasadena area in the north county. I have a wife Lois, she works at Anne Arundel Community College, and I have six kids, one son and five daughters. Curiously, my son doesn't fish and my five daughters do. I'm from a farm background. We were farmers and I was raised in the Great Depression. Farmers had a curious life. If the strawberry and carrot crops sold well we had a little money and ate a lot of different things. If they didn't sell well we ate a lot of strawberries and carrots. But we spent a lot of time outdoors and I, of course, liked it. I'm a country boy.

I served in the Pacific during World War II and was in training for the invasion of Japan when it ended. I came back and spent much of the summer, almost all of the summer, hunting and fishing before I went away to start college. I only went to college for a year and part of another semester when the radio station opened in Montpelier, Vermont and I took the job. I've been on that route ever since.

I started fishing when I was four years old. I was five, my sister was four, and we had sneaked off to go fishing. We actually used a bent safety pin with string and a pole. I can remember my mother seeing us and coming down with a much lighter pole...the switch, because she had caught us. We weren't supposed to go near the water.

There is great fishing here in the Chesapeake and I like fishing. It's my life practically. But I sneak off quite often to go to Western Maryland because the mountains out there are pretty much like home, with their trout streams and people. I like mountain and country people. Western Maryland is a curious place. It's got Deep Creek Lake, and Deep Creek Lake to Western Marylanders is like the Chesapeake Bay to those on the Western and Eastern Shores. It has got an awful lot of great fishing. It's picturesque, and there's a funny thing about Deep Creek Lake; they don't have any insects. You don't get bitten by mosquitoes and you can go out in the evening and it's pretty much insect-free. And it's cool, and I like cool weather. The lake is the biggest in Maryland. It's an artificial lake. Maryland is the only state in the Union that has no natural lakes. Deep Creek Lake is manmade, a hydroelectric facility. The menu is really diversified. They have perch, pickerel, northern pike, large mouth bass, small mouth bass, blue gills, crappy, and trout. Walleyes are quite popular out there. They're great freshwater fish. Walleyes are from cold water and they taste very good. They come big. Deep Creek Lake has probably more records than any other body of water, other than the bay, in

Maryland.

When I came to Maryland in '56, Deep Creek Lake was considered pretty much of a problem area. The state had tried stocking it and tried different management techniques but nothing seemed to be working. But then, for some reason or another, everything changed. Everything got better and the fish prospered. Now it is a great, great fishing place. There are many bass tournaments held there. The distressing part of Deep Creek Lake, well, we see it on the bay too, is development. There are just oodles of people and everybody wants to build houses on the mountain overlooking the lake. They're clearing the forest to build these developments. Everybody's clearing so they get a better view of the mountain, and on the other side of the valley there's somebody doing the same thing, so they're just looking at each other's houses now.

Fishing has been good to me. I fished with two Presidents. I got to know Eisenhower a bit because he was a fisherman and we talked about it at times. Things were much different in those days. It was more relaxed and the press mingled with the candidates because we were on a train. I told him he ought to mention fishing sometime in his campaign, but he said that fishing was too personal of a thing to talk about in a campaign. Eventually, when Eisenhower got to Gettysburg after he retired, he invited me to fish. He was not a great fisherman, but you don't judge fishermen by how much they catch; you judge them by how much they enjoy it.

When I retired from the *Sun,* I got a call. I hate to tell you what I said. It was a telephone call and it said, 'Is Bill Burton there?' I said yes and he said, 'Well, this is the President.' You know I'm a practical joker myself and I said a few things I shouldn't have said, and then I realized it was the President. I had met George H. W. Bush fishing in Lake Texoma at the Oklahoma/Texas border. I had known him and he was a reader of mine because he liked waterfowl hunting and I did a lot of writing on waterfowl. He said, 'Well, I see you're going to retire and I'd like to give you a gift. Take me fishing.' So we went on the Potomac. I can't imagine being President because you can't get away to fish. We were in the middle of an armada, a fleet of Coast Guard, Secret Service, all kinds of boats around us. We couldn't do anything and we had to get cleared for everyplace we went. But we each caught a fish, so we had a good time. We each caught a bass. I have an autographed dollar from him. We had a bet on a fish. He was a good fisherman. We didn't have to untangle any lines. And, you know, we went at five o'clock in the morning. I met him at five and he didn't wear long winter underwear. It was early April and it was exceptionally cold. He had said that Barbara had been outside and said it wasn't too cold, but she was in the protected area where the winds weren't hitting her. We were out there and he stayed with it, and I said, 'Mr. President, it's going to be bad today. It's freezing and the wind is blowing very hard.' He said, 'I don't care, I just want to go fishing, so let's go.' And I always remember I was thinking somebody would always be around him, carrying everything for him. I was waiting in the White House—we were going to have breakfast—and he called down and said to meet him down at the entrance and we would have some hot buns and coffee instead because he wanted to go fishing. He came down in the elevator all by himself and he was carrying his two tackle boxes and two rods, carrying it all himself. That was probably one of my most enjoyable fishing trips because he is a great, great man.

You know, people think that fishing, you have to have something. You have to have some special technique there. There's a mystique about it. And there really isn't. I keep emphasizing that because people think there is. You have to basically think like a fish. A fish wants comfort, it wants oxygen, it wants waters at the right temperature, it likes clear water, and it likes a place where it can hide. Many species, of course, have to hide because they're small. So you just try to think, if I was a fish where would I be and what would interest me?

Fish don't always feed. They go on feeding sprees. At other times they don't eat, and you have to just try and figure it out. There is no mystique about it. It's just using common sense. Some fish eat best early in the morning, sometimes late in the day, but not always. Tides make a difference. Flood tides, especially if you're fishing from shore in the surf or something like that. Flood tide comes in and washes up things that fish can get to. There are so many things but you just put it all together. Anybody can catch fish.

You know Herbert Hoover, of course, was our President and he was the first President I can remember. Herbert Hoover was a great fly fisherman. He wrote a book and I had a copy of that book autographed. I had a leak in my office roof, and nothing was damaged—except that book. But in that book he said something people should remember. He said, 'All fishermen are equal before fish.' You can be a king or you can be a ditch digger, or whatever—it doesn't make any difference to the fish."

Capt. Lenny Rudow, Author,
Rudow's Guide to Fishing the Chesapeake

Lenny Rudow is a firecracker of a fisherman. He's fired up and ready to go. His book Rudow's Guide to Fishing the Chesapeake *brings together wisdom and knowledge from many of the Chesapeake's finest anglers, and those who want to catch fish would do well to have a copy onboard their boats. Lenny is also Senior Technical Editor for* Boating Magazine, *a writer for* The Fisherman magazine, *and the founder of Geared Up Publications. In the spring of 2006, just after the publication of* Rudow's Guide to Fishing the Chesapeake, *I sat down with Lenny at his Edgewater home and wondered aloud if he ate a lot of the fish he catches.*

"Eating is certainly a part of it, but it's not the end all be all of fishing," Lenny said. "It really is the challenge, it's man against nature, it's can you get out there and can you fool those fish. They're a heck of a lot smarter than we all think sometimes.

I grew up on the bay, born and bred in Baltimore. Since before I was born, my father had a boat on the Chesapeake. We always ran out of Pasadena, Maryland. Through the years we've run through many different boats. Currently my father has a 28 foot Bertram that we still fish on together, but we started out on a 16 foot Whaler and went through many boats over the years.

I can actually remember the first fish I caught. I was two years old. My father made a cast, the bobber danced around, went under the surface, and I got to turn the crank and reel in a little bluegill. The next morning my mother cooked it for breakfast. That was on the northern bay, where there's a whole lot of freshwater going in and you have a lot more freshwater species. When it came time to go to school and pick a career path, my father always told me, 'Fishing is a great thing. It's a wonderful way to relax. But when you get to the bottom line you're never going to make a living doing it. It's fun, its recreation, but don't spend too much time working on it because it's not going to be a career.' I take great delight in having proved him wrong, which is an extremely rare event. In my experience he's been wrong exactly twice. This was one of those two times.

I came out of school and immediately started writing for *The Fisherman* on a freelance basis. I hooked up with *Boating Magazine,* started freelancing for them and just started doing as much writing as I could. After about three and a half years of that, I got hired full time as writer for *Boating* and two years after that I took over as fishing editor, and then just branched out from there."

What is your best advice for becoming a great fisherman?

"Learning fishing is all a matter of experience. It's all a matter of how much time you actually put in on the water trying to catch fish. There's also a lot of value to documenting your experience. Everybody says, 'Keep a fishing log, keep a fishing log!' And for many, many years I didn't. Then when I did and I started looking back at what I had recorded, these tremendous patterns started jumping out at me. A lot of those are related in my books. I looked at 10 years of catch logs and saw some striking factors that went from year to year to year that always held true. What it really allowed me to do was analyze that data and to realize that during particular times of the year in particular places with particular species you can actually make a pretty decent prediction of when and where the fish are going to bite.

There are a lot of different ways to do it. The old standard is to have a notebook and just write down what happened when you went fishing. I find it's a lot more helpful to actually bring up a tides and currents program on my computer, which will put the tidal patterns into a bar graph. It separates each bar by 15 minutes throughout the course of the day. I can print out one of these bar graphs after every trip and mark what happened on which bar. I can mark down the water temperature, the depth, the type of fish, the time and the methods used. The printout will have the date on it. I'll put that into a file and I'll have files for every different fishing season.

Anybody who fishes regularly, even among the best of us, there are days when you just can't catch a fish to save your life. The real thrill comes when you're out in those kinds of conditions and you manage to fool the fish somehow, you manage to figure it out, and you turn a downer into a spectacular day. It's really a great feeling. The worse the conditions are, the greater the victory is. A lot of people, when it blows or when it rains they don't want to fish. That's my favorite time to fish. If I can get out when nobody else can and suffer through the conditions and actually fill the fish box, man, that's great."

You crammed so many hot spots into one book, and many of them came from other people. How did you get so many fishermen, who are usually so tight-lipped, to give up information about their favorite fishing holes?

"I always say that no one man can know the entire bay. It's just physically impossible. If you spend your entire lifetime doing nothing but fishing the Chesapeake Bay you would never learn every inch of it. There's just too much. It's just too massive. I consider myself plenty knowledgeable about the Middle Bay, pretty knowledgeable about the Upper Bay, somewhat knowledgeable about the Lower Bay. I pretty much know the common spots down there. But when it comes to knowing the nitty-gritty, like, where is that secret catfish hole on the James River? For that kind of information I had to go to a lot of different friends—charter boat captains, die hard fishermen—up and down the bay. There are probably about 15 or 20 different captains and diehard anglers that really treated me very well, by agreeing to give up some of their hotspots. Fishermen are great liars and they are not great information-sharers. They hold their cards close, for sure. Actually I cross-referenced just about every source for the book that was not a good buddy that I really trust.

The research for the book, it took me over a year to do it. It wasn't just talking to people. I also did a lot of research in fishing report histories. I went back 10 years through fishing reports to see what places were regularly hotspots, at what time of year, for what particular fish. I used my own catch logs. I used interviews with captains and friends. I would make a lunch date with an acquaintance who I knew, a charter boat captain or a friend, and I would show up with my chart book and a magic marker. I'd say, 'Do me a favor. Just give me five hotspots on this page of the chart book.' That was how I accumulated many of the different spots—there are over 550—that are in the book.

Here in the Middle Chesapeake, we have some of the most popular fishing areas in the Mid Atlantic region. Are there more fish here in the Middle Chesapeake than there are anywhere else? No, but this is closest to where all the people live. The downside of this is that if you go out there on a Saturday in the summertime you take your life in your own hands because there are a million boats going in every direction. One of the pieces of advice I give on fishing the Chesapeake Bay Bridges, for example, is to only go there during the week. It can be kind of hairy there on weekends, particularly around the rock piles. The rock piles hold some great fishing in the fall. Often rockfish, sometimes weakfish, sometimes bluefish, there can really be some tremendous fishing going on around those rock piles. But if you go there on Saturday morning at nine a.m. you stand as good a chance at catching someone else's lure as you do of catching a fish. There are so many lines in the water there, it's just saturated with fishermen.

Another thing you have to remember about fishing the Bay Bridges is that it's right next to Sandy Point State Park. We Anne Arundel County, Marylanders, we sort of have a curse and a blessing here for water access. The curse is there is very, very little public access to the Chesapeake Bay. It's microscopic. The blessing is we do have Sandy Point. That's our one spot. And, guess what? That's about the best launch facility on the entire East Coast. It has over 20 ramps. It has tremendous access. You can go there and there can be 100 people using that facility and you can still get in and out in short order. The piers are in good condition, the ramps are in good condition. There are all kinds of facilities right there. The DNR has presence there, so it's a safe place to be. Everything about it is good. For the magazines that I work for, I've gone up and down the coast to just about every state on the Atlantic seaboard and I've seen most of the public launch facilities and really none of them hold a candle to Sandy Point. It is the best that I've ever seen."

What about the fishing conditions in the Lower Bay, down around Tangier Sound and further south to the Chesapeake Bay Bridge Tunnel?

"Boy, do I love Tangier. The Tangier Sound is just an incredible place. It's where you leave behind the dirty water that you sometimes have to deal with up north. It's where you look over the side of the boat and now you can see your lure, your jig falling five, eight feet down. The water really clears up tremendously. The fishing gets great. The Honga River has some great areas to go light-tackle fishing. You can start to pick up some of the species some bay anglers might consider exotic, like speckled trout. The guys out of Baltimore don't see speckled trout very often. Well, if they make it down to Tangier they will. You also start to see lots and lots of flounder. The fishing becomes much closer to the ocean and much less like the freshwater. The flipside of that is you lose the great bass fishing you have in some of the northern areas of the bay. You lose the pickerel. You lose the catfish out in the Tangier Sound. But, you might catch sea bass and you might even catch cobia. There are a lot of fish that come into the Tangier that you just don't find farther up the bay. Before I had kids I used to go down there all the time. But boy...having little kids will put a crimp in your fishing time.

If you have a boat on a trailer it's not a bad run, it's just like going to Ocean City. Now, if you're running your boat down from the northern areas it's a good haul and it'll cost you some fuel, which everybody's concerned about these days. But the Tangier Sound remains one of my favorite places to fish, just tremendous water.

The CBBT, the Chesapeake Bay Bridge Tunnel complex, is another just astonishing area. They have a longer season down there. That's also where you can really get into serious cobia fishing. Black drum are around for a much longer duration than they are up the bay, where we have a month-long run, max. Flounder fishing is just incredible and of course bluefish and striped bass are all over the place. You know, it's where the bay meets the ocean and there's tons of structure, thanks to the CBBT. You put those two factors together and it's no surprise to anybody that fishing is just great. But, it's close to Norfolk and Hampton Roads and meanwhile plenty of people also haul their boats down from this area... so these days it gets crowded even down there.

The neat thing about the cobia and the black drum is now you're looking at the potential of catching 100-pound fish in the Chesapeake Bay. There aren't many species you can say that about these days. I guess you could put shark in there, too, if you're fishing the Lower Bay. Middle Bay anglers have a shot a black drum, usually during the last few weeks of May and the first couple of weeks of June, at the Stone Rock, at the mouth of the Choptank River. The drum run up the bay in tight groups and you can have some really thrilling fishing. You can regularly catch fish that are 50, 60, 80 pounds. And if you get lucky, you never know, you might get that magic 100-pounder.

Unfortunately, fishing's not as good as it was a few years ago. When I was a kid it was okay for blues, but during the 90's it was absolutely world-class for rockfish. Striper fishing was amazing, you could almost plan on catching limits of big fish on every trip. But then we had some rainy springs, and all the chemicals and garbage that had collected on land flushed into the bay. That's what I think happened, anyway, because when we started having rainy springs again after a long drought, the fishing got worse and worse. It changes from place to place and from week to week, sure, but generally speaking it's all been in decline for six or seven years now. The stripers, the trout, and even the bluefish. Every winter, I think 'Maybe it'll turn around this spring.' And next year, maybe it will!"

9

Farming

David Harper, Rolling Acres Farm

Two distinctly pleasurable experiences that struck me after moving to the Chesapeake Bay region were the feeling of open space on the Eastern Shore and the fact that some sort of waterway was around just about every corner. Creeks and rivers flowing into the Chesapeake Bay are the veins and arteries providing the freshwater that makes farming here such a big industry.

It's important to know just where our food comes from and how its production impacts the environment around us. Just as the Midwestern states are the heartland of America, the Eastern Shore is a highly productive American bread basket. The Maryland Department of Agriculture reports that agriculture remains the largest single land use in Maryland, with 2.05 million acres, or roughly 33 percent of total land area, used for farming in 2004. Approximately 350,000 people are employed in some aspect of agriculture, making it the largest commercial industry in the State. In 2004, some 12,100 farms averaged 169 acres each. The majority of farmland in Maryland is located in the north central part of the State and the upper Eastern Shore.

Family farming is an endangered occupation in our country. There was a time when family farms thrived and the countryside bustled with privately owned canneries and granaries. The bigger farms now are conglomerates and corporately owned. One of the surviving family farms on the upper Eastern Shore is Rolling Acres Farm, run by the Harpers in Preston, Maryland. David Harper is the principal farmer with help from his wife Brenda and son Dave, who now works full-

time as a teacher. The farm has been in the Harper family for over 60 years.

"My uncle, Mr. A. T. Blades, purchased this farm back in roughly 1945. It's called Rolling Acres because where most of the Eastern Shore is flat, the land actually rolls here. It's about 380 acres and it's located on the Choptank River. I think it's maybe an average size, but a lot of the farmers today, because they own many farms, their actual total acreage is much greater. Harriet Tubman's parents supposedly lived on this farm. Right now, the Caroline Historical Society is undergoing a lot of study about this property and about the main house. Back in that time I think it was called Poplar Grove because of all the poplar trees that were here. The farm was purchased to run a logging operation and it's been passed down through several landowners. My uncle bought it from a Captain Carmine. It's been in our family since the 40's and we will pass it along to our kids.

I worked here as a kid, starting when I was 14. Then, it was strictly dairy. We milked about 125 cows and we also had the dry cows, the calves and the heifers. Everything that was grown here at that time stayed on the farm. All our production was geared toward the cows. By 1965 it was becoming more and more difficult to obtain farm labor, both farmhands and people to do the milking. So, at that time, my uncle decided to go strictly to grain farming and that's what it's been ever since, with the exception that now we grow seed for Southern States and some of that seed is used to grow beans for Japan. We've tried to have a bit more of a value-added situation to make the farm more profitable, and hopefully we'll do more of that as time goes on."

How many crops does a farmer have to grow these days to be able to make ends meet? How do American farmers remain competitive in this day and age?

"Grain farming today, with the prices, has become extremely competitive as far as being able to even make a living. Some farmers use vegetables to earn a better living and to be able to support themselves, plus keep the farm in the family. Value-added products would be most anything that we could use to get a higher income. We've been working some with Chesapeake Fields and they want to start growing crops that will produce snack foods, popcorn being one of those. I haven't grown popcorn for them but some of the seed I do grow for Japan goes to farmers growing popcorn. That in turn gives us extra value and allows us to keep farming.

It's just so expensive. If people actually stop and think what they're paying for food in the United States, it's probably the cheapest in the world. Where does that leave the farmer when his equipment expenses are going up? His fertilizer expenses are going up, so are fuel and chemical costs. He has to do something in order to make a living. And therein lies the problem. We have to constantly search out ways of making a better income. Some of the boys grow potatoes, and those go for potato chips. Some grow cucumbers for pickles, and sweet corn.

They're finding so many uses for soybeans. There are soy snacks and roasted soybeans. They're finding that soybeans can be used for diesel fuel. They're going to keep looking for every avenue there is to give the farmer extra benefits for their crops, because there is a lot of pressure from overseas to take over the markets that we presently have here. So we have to keep looking further.

Brazil is one of our bigger competitors, as well as Argentina and Australia. Labor is a lot cheaper there. Also, what people don't understand is that sometimes we have even more expense. Take what we call Round Up Ready Soybeans, which has a gene that's added to make the crop able to withstand a chemical we use call Round Up, which most people probably even use around their house. This chemical can be used atop the bean to give greater weed control. We have to pay a premium for those beans in the U.S., but Brazil and the rest of the countries are not charged that premium for that seed. And we're not allowed to keep the seed to use for next year's crop, but they are. So not only do they have cheaper labor, but they pay less for the products that they buy. So their cost per acre for production keeps going lower than ours.

This is the same thing that's happening in the prescription drug industry. You can go to Canada and pay half for the same drug that you would in the United States. And that gives them the benefit of taking our markets. That's what has happened to a lot of our soybeans. We keep looking for other avenues so that we can use our crops here at home because we certainly are losing our market share overseas."

There must be a strong case to be made for selling out the family farm operations to the corporate mega-farming operations. So what made the Harpers stick with the family run operation on Rolling Acres Farm?

"Rolling Acres Farm is strictly private and I'm hoping that we can always keep that way," David said. "Corporate interests have one thing in mind, and there's nothing wrong with making a profit. Everybody has to make a profit to survive. But the minute that corporate interest is not turning a profit, they'll shed it off, and it will go into whatever use; mainly building. A lot of farms, beautiful, productive farms, have been sold to developers. And I can understand. It gives the farmer that's aging an income to retire on, and he needs that. But I think it's very sad that it has to come to that. Because sooner or later, if we keep importing more and more and more of our foods... look what's happening in the oil industry. Once they get a stranglehold on you because you're not producing your own, you're going to pay more.

And why worry about just your own generation? You might say, 'Well, we've got enough to last us for our lifetime.' You can't do that. You have to look at what is going to happen to your children. I don't believe in just putting my head in the sand. I think we need to worry about each other. And we need to worry about the future, and not just one generation, but as far ahead as you can look."

Rolling Acres Farm is stunningly beautiful, situated directly on the picturesque Choptank River, making it prime real estate for eager developers. The Harper family has grown up working and playing on the river. Perhaps it's this complete connection to both the farming and aquatic lifestyles that caused the Harpers to put Rolling Acres Farm into an agricultural conservation easement, similar to the arrangement made by the Dodds family.

"We're located on the Choptank River and I suppose we have roughly three-quarters of a mile river frontage," he noted. "It's on a nice, wide part of the river because we're located right outside of the town of Choptank. There's also Skeleton Creek, which takes up, let say, one side of the property. Skelton Creek backs up to a pond that we have that's around six and half to seven acres, so we have water around a great deal of the farm. So it would be advantageous for a developer to come in here. However, we thought about that and we decided some years back to put this farm in AG preservation through a conservation easement. This farm will stay in a conservation easement, which means it is not to be developed. Ours is in perpetuity, which means that even if I should have to sell the farm at some point, for some reason, whoever buys it must carry on. They cannot do a buyout and get the farm back so that it can be developed. That probably has hurt the value of the farm, but now I'm 56 and I've been working here since I was 14. It's just too pretty to see it get built up with homes. It would just destroy the land. I don't think we need that. I think we need to keep some of the farms just as they are."

Agricultural runoff is considered one of the major sources of pollution in the Chesapeake Bay. Being so close to the water, how do you control the use of fertilizers and chemicals which might run off into the river?

"We are in a state-mandated nutrient management plan. We do a soil sample for nutrients in every field, every year. It goes through a laboratory that does strictly soil samples for farms and they also do leaf tissue testing, which is another way we have of deciding how the crop is using its fertilizers. Have we given it enough or is it too little? And some years we'll also do stalk testing on corn to see how well it's used up the chemical fertilizers that are available to it. And all this helps us refine how much we are applying. Because each crop, both corn and soybeans, they each use nutrients at a different rate to produce a certain number of bushels. Soybeans, actually at a point, will produce their own nitrogen. Corn won't. Corn is a huge user of nitrogen. So, we will start by getting our soil samples in line and decide where things will be planted.

We send the fertilizer, manure, out and have it sampled to see what's in it. We then take that figure and apply it according to what the soil test shows and what the nutrient plan says we are allowed to use. At no time on this farm do we over-apply either chemicals or fertilizer. The margins of profit are so small, you cannot afford to do that."

What kinds of programs and techniques do you use to slow down or stop runoff into your river and creek? Do you plant buffers and use the no-till technique?

"We are right on the Choptank River, so we would probably have more chance of polluting than a farm located a number of miles off. But we do use buffer strips, which set us back. In our case, we set back 70 feet from the river. We did that even before the state and federal government came out with those programs. They allow us to plant certain grasses around the borders next to ditches and also next to the river. Most people would probably refer to that as buffer zone.

My uncle was very forward thinking and because our land is rolling we have used no-till to conserve soil from erosion. We've no-tilled full-season beans and corn now for probably 35 years. And we didn't always get the bushels per acre when we first started doing conservation tillage, but as time goes on and we've been able to refine it down, our bushels per acre have gone back up to where they should be.

A lot of people think that as farmers, we just apply fertilizers and farm chemicals on a whim without regard to the volume. While that may happen in some cases, it is not the rule. Number one, we do not want to pollute the bay or the rivers or its tributaries because there are fishermen that are farmers of those waters. It wouldn't be fair to them to destroy their lifestyle and their work. Also, the chemicals are so expensive you're driving your cost per acre up by using indiscriminately. So we wouldn't even consider doing that.

We also use the best management practices that allow us to only treat what is necessary and at the rate that's necessary when we have problems. I'll take this one particular weed chemical that we use to control noxious weed, called Canadian thistle. I haven't bought any for about two years, but the last time I bought it, a quart cost me a $125. Now, it's used at a very low rate, however, you just cannot be indiscriminate about what you're doing.

I understand why the regulations of today came about. But I think that once farmers are taught about the problems, and they can see the dollars and cents of it, they're just not going to travel that road. No matter what the profession, there are always going to be some renegades who are going to do what they want to do. They might say, 'Well, this field tested that it needed a 100 pounds nitrogen so I'll put it on the other one in that amount too.' Well, we don't do that, it would behoove them not to do that, and I think most of them don't.

It's just that it's a perception that we have been using a lot of chemicals. Some days I look out here in the early mornings on this river, 'cause I get up around five, five thirty, and I can sit here and look out my window. I can see stuff floating down that river that you don't see at any other time of the day. It's there early in the morning. I'm downriver from a discharge plant... there's no need to get into where it's coming from. Why is it only in the early morning that I'm seeing that?

I have asked at research center meetings if they do actual tests of runoff from suburban areas where people are keeping their lawns as green as they can be. They have people that treat their lawns because they have to have that beautiful lawn. Have you done tests through storm sewers? The answer is no. I think that when it comes to runoff and pollution, the farmer is the little guy. I think people have a tendency to attack problems through the little people first because they can only scream so loud. I hate to have to say that, but I feel that is the case sometimes. This testing should be done across the board, equal for everybody, and everybody working together. Whether it's us or it's suburbia. Look at the lawns. Look at industry. Work together."

Russell Brinsfield and Kevin Miller, The Harry R. Hughes Center for Agro-Ecology

The Harry R. Hughes Center for Agro-Ecology is part of the University of Maryland's Wye Education and Research Center. The Center is located near beautiful Wye Island, adjacent to the eastern branch of the Aspen Institute.

The Aspen Institute is dedicated to fostering enlightened leadership and open-minded dialogue, a gathering place for thinkers, leaders, artists, and musicians from all over the world. The Institute allows participants to step away from their daily routines and reflect on the underlying values of society and culture.

One of the ways of accomplishing these goals is through a program presented by the Aspen Institute called the Executive Seminar. This seminar, aimed at corporate and business leaders, was inspired by philosopher Mortimer Adler's Great Books seminars and is based on the writings of great thinkers, past and present.

"The Executive Seminar was not intended to make a corporate treasurer a more skilled corporate treasurer," said Institute founder Walter Paepcke, "but to help a leader gain access to his or her own humanity by becoming more self-aware, more self-correcting, and more self-fulfilling."

The Aspen Institute was the location for the 1998 summit meeting between President Bill Clinton, Palestinian Chairman Yasser Arafat, Israeli Prime Minister Benjamin Netanyahu, and King Hussein of Jordan, which produced the Wye Accord for Peace in the Middle East.

I've always been a lover of the visionary work of Mortimer Adler and a believer in the dialogue approach of the Aspen Institute. The work of the University of Maryland Agro-Ecology Center, I believe, runs parallel with the Aspen Institute, bringing together stakeholders from seemingly diverse backgrounds and points of view. Here, the farming, forestry

and environmental communities come together to find com-
mon ground and explore common outcomes.

Russell Brinsfield is a family farmer from Vienna, Vir-
ginia. He also happens to be the town's mayor. On top of that,
Dr. Brinsfield is the Executive Director of the University of
Maryland's Harry R. Hughes Center for Agro-Ecology, and he
earned three engineering degrees at the University of Mary-
land. Kevin Miller was the Assistant Director of the Center. He
received his masters degree in journalism from the University
of Missouri, and a masters degree in biology from St. Louis
University.

"I came here at the urging of Governors Hughes and
Russ," Kevin said. "I remember very well crossing the Bay Bridge
for the first time and seeing the estuary. It was locked into my
mind from the moment I crossed.

If you think about the cultural and historical heritage of
the upper Shore you think about agriculture, you think about
tourism, think about bay-related activities, sailing, biking, and
hunting. Our future is linked to those 'clean industries.' That's
something we ought to be celebrating and expanding. Clean, I
think, in the sense that they use our natural resources in a very
environmentally compatible and friendly way."

Russell said, "In so many ways the Chesapeake Bay region, and particularly the Eastern Shore, is the heart and soul
of what emanates my value system, having been raised here.
Actually, I was sort of taking it all for granted until I left. Then
I had the opportunity to come back and see it from a whole
different perspective. With my background as a scientist doing
research, looking at bay-related issues, it's given me a greater
appreciation for what we have here, and how important it is
to find ways to protect it. But at the same time, we need to
address the environmental issues that are facing industries
so that they can survive in an economically sustainable way.
Being raised here on the Eastern Shore this is particularly important to me, because this is where I plan to spend the rest
of my life.

You know, it's really interesting that I didn't appreciate what it is here until I left and had the opportunity to come back. You take it for granted, the geese flying and the fish out in the rivers, and paddling around as a kid. You just figure, well, this is the way everybody lives, but that's not the case. And I think our challenge here on the Shore in the face of development is how to find the balance to make sure you protect what makes this place unique, but afford opportunities for folks to come here that haven't had the chance to enjoy it yet. To determine what it is that we want this region to look like and how we're going to be able to accommodate the growth and still retain the character—that's going to be the real challenge. I'm not sure we can find the balance."

Kevin agreed, adding, "I guess when I think about that, that's what really comes into my mind too: striking a balance. You know, farmers and foresters are all driven as business-men to make economic decisions. Environment comes into play in those decisions they make, just as it does for a hom-eowner when he puts Turf Builder on his lawn. I think farmers are inherently good stewards. They want to be. Their liveli-hood depends upon the soil and the resources on their farm. I don't think any steward, any businessman, would want to degrade those intentionally. It doesn't make sense to destroy your greatest asset. So farmers are faced with tough decisions every day, and certainly much stronger societal pressures, es-pecially since pfiesteria."

Pfiesteria (phiesteria piscicida, pronounced 'fist-ear-ee-ah') is a microscopic aquatic organism that is believed to produce toxins that injure or kill other marine life, particu-larly fish. However, these toxins have never been definitive-ly identified. Some scientists also believe that phiesteria can cause temporary health problems in people who breathe in the toxins, or get them on their skin. Phiesteria was at one time blamed on the poultry industry for overuse of chicken manure and excess runoff into the Chesapeake Bay. These claims were never substantiated but the farmers took a direct hit from the allegations.

"I was fortunate enough to be working in Paul Sarbanes's office in the summer of '97 when pfiesteria hit," said Kevin. "I made quite a few visits to farms, and to the Pocomoke and other waterways that were affected by it. Talked to a lot of farmers, a lot of people who are members of our board, for example, who said, 'I feel like I got a stick put into my eye when pfiesteria hit, because farmers went from being good stewards to being the bad guys.' They certainly feel that way. And they don't feel like their numerous positive efforts, you know, conservation reserve programs or grass buffers or soil conservation, were really taken into account. You know they've been doing those things for 40, 50 years probably in this area, at least. But they feel that all of a sudden, overnight, because of one dinoflagellate, they were suddenly the evil people.

In the broad context in terms of trying to deal with issues facing the future in agriculture and forestry I think growth is central, that we need to get this resolved. In spite of all the good efforts in trying to direct growth, if we look at where it's actually occurring, over half is in areas that are not designated as high-growth areas. It's on farms where the farmers are selling out. The average age for a farmer in the State of Maryland, I believe, is about 57 years old. The same thing is happening in the seafood industry. There's no next generation to take over."

How did the poultry industry grow so strong and how do the grain farmers and the poultry farmers coexist so well on the Eastern Shore of Maryland?

"The poultry industry needs more corn and soybeans than can be grown in the region," explained Russell, "so they encourage farmers to grow grain and pay them a premium. Most of the time farmers in Maryland, and particularly on the Eastern Shore, can get 10, 15, up to 20 cents more per bushel for their corn and soybeans than say, farmers in the Midwest.

That's tied to the transportation costs that it would take the poultry industry to move that grain in from the Midwest. That really gives us an economic boost. If something were to happen to that poultry industry, in the short term we would have some real serious economic problems.

The poultry industry has been around for some time. It really started gaining traction probably in the late 60's, early 70's. The industry is quite large, and it's quite important. As a matter of fact, the Center commissioned a study by an economist that looked at the economic impact and the economic value of the poultry industry, not only to the farming community in Maryland, but also in the context of the State of Maryland. You know, the percentage of the revenue that comes into the state coffers associated not only with agriculture, but with poultry itself. It even surprised the authors of the study that about 45 percent of the total agriculture sales in the State of Maryland are tied directly or indirectly to poultry. On the Eastern Shore that number is about 60 percent, and in some counties on the Eastern Shore, like down on the Somerset County or Worcester County, where poultry is king, sales related to poultry are 85 percent of the total. In addition, the poultry industry employs about 15,000 people directly, and another 15,000 indirectly. So you're looking at a major contributor. In a global situation it's not that large, but if you look at it locally, it becomes very important.

In another study that we funded, we had a scientist compare water quality in a situation where a farmer would be using inorganic fertilizer to grow a crop, versus if he were to use poultry manure, and ask what relative economic problems arise. The question is, can you apply those organic nutrient sources in a way so that farmers can benefit from that resource, yet minimize the impact that using those sources of nutrients has on our environment?

Farmers are willing to do things like plant cover crops, to reduce nitrogen losses to groundwater. People say to me all the time, 'Well, why don't farmers just do it on their own?' To the extent they can, they will. But the problem is that it adds another cost. You have a farming community that is already stretched in terms of economic viability, and then we're demanding that they spend another $25 per acre to plant cover crops. He plows that back under, or he kills it, and plants a crop into it. So in the short term, that's an added cost to the farmer. That's why we've worked in many venues to get cost share money for farmers.

Cost share money comes from either the federal government or the state government, to encourage landowners to put in place practices that in and of themselves would not be economically viable for the farmer to do. From an environmental and societal standpoint they're important. The farmer bears part of the burden, but society is also helping him to do the things that he needs to do to protect the bay, and doesn't ask him to do it out of his limited revenue stream. The last thing we want is to make the farmer go bankrupt, because then we have more sprawl. So we're trying to find the balance.

Ever since pfiesteria we've had varying amounts of money in the budget to support the cover crop program, and every year all of that money is used up and there's a demand for more than what we as a society have been able to afford. Recent legislation in Annapolis is called the 'flush tax.' My understanding is that 60 percent of that revenue stream will go toward educational programs, to upgrade septic systems, and to encourage homeowners to install new technology. The other 40 percent is earmarked to go to the farming community to help farmers in a cost share program to plant cover crops.

They estimated that there are about 400,000 septic tanks in Maryland, so that's about $12 million in revenue, of which about 40 percent of that, I think, would be about five million dollars. So that five million dollars can go to the farming community and that will plant cover crops on about 200,000 acres annually. We can say with a high level of assurance that for every dollar invested in that program, we can keep a pound of nitrogen out of groundwater. If you keep it out of that shallow groundwater, eventually you're keeping it out of the bay. Now that's good, but to put that in context, the most recent tributaries strategies update says that in order for agriculture to meet its goal of a 40 percent reduction, maybe more, we need farmers to plant 600,000 acres in cover crops annually. That's an enormous challenge. At least this money will allow the planting of a couple hundred thousand acres of cover crops, which is a major step in the right direction."

Rob Etgen, Executive Director, Eastern Shore Land Conservancy

Land trusts and conservation easements are set up by organizations such as the Eastern Shore Land Conservancy (ESLC) which works directly with farmers and homeowners on the Eastern Shore. Like the Harry R. Hughes Center for Agro-Ecology, the ESLC offices are located on Wye Island, not too far from the Bay Bridge. Rob Etgen and I met to talk about the effort to promote land trusts. His experience and dedication to this movement are directly tied to his upbringing along the Chesapeake Bay.

"I'm a lawyer; a member of the Maryland Bar and a forest ecologist. Two of my brothers have gone into conservation as well. I grew up in Severna Park, Maryland. There were five boys in my family and one girl. For all those years growing up, we were always in the woods and in the creek. I was just talking about it at lunch, remembering how we used to go out and dip-net yellow perch during the spring spawning run. I think they're coming back now but for a while yellow perch were almost extinct in the Magothy River.

We used to walk in the mud down there and soft crab all summer long. I grew up in Severna Park in the 70's and I watched the water quality of that area drop off the table so quickly, to the point where in the mid-80's there were awful red tides and green tides in the summer (algae blooms). The water was barely swimable anymore. I think that instilled an ethic in me of concern that, 'this isn't right.' We saw it happening almost on a monthly basis, because at that time they were building strip malls up and down Ritchie Highway. I remember very distinctly when they put in a huge parking lot and the very first rain we had ran off that parking lot and blasted right down through the woods, right down to the headwaters of the Cypress Creek, dumping all this silt and oil and garbage out there. So the connection between growth and water quality deterioration was very clear.

It's my opinion that we are in a window of opportunity that is fast closing, and that we maybe have until 2010 before things are really too far gone to come back. Too much development, we're going to have too much sprawl around. We're basically making our bed now. I mean, that's my feeling. I think we've got to deal with this now and if we don't, by 2010, with the given rate of sprawling development that we have, we may not be able to go back.

Maryland's land preservation programs are recognized nationally. There's a goal in the Chesapeake Bay Agreement to permanently preserve 20 percent of the entire bay watershed by 2010, and to reduce sprawl by 30 percent throughout the entire watershed by 2012. It's a work in progress."

What techniques has the Eastern Shore Land Conservancy successfully employed to preserve open space on the Eastern Shore?

"We were started about a dozen years ago out of a concern that sprawling development was consuming our waterfront areas, which are important for waterfowl habitat, and our prime farmland areas," Rob said. "To date we've preserved 140 properties on about 130,000 acres, using mostly different types of easements or development restrictions on land. A conservation easement is a deed that runs with the land forever, and puts a set of restrictions on land use. They prohibit that property from being developed, or for instance, if there's a bald eagle nest it'll put a prohibition against any kind of forest disturbance within a certain distance from the nest. If it's Delmarva fox squirrel, which is another federally endangered species, there will be different kinds of restrictions to protect those critters. It becomes a part of the chain of title and then we have a permanent responsibility to make sure those restrictions are enforced. We do own a series of preserves ourselves as well, and we've bought some land and given it to towns and others for parks.

Land trusts are the quickest expanding part of the whole conservation and environmental movement. There are right now about 1,500 land trusts in the country. Our bread and butter for our first eight or nine years was using gift transactions. Land's expensive, so in targeted watersheds like the Chester River we would go contact all the landowners on that watershed. It's kitchen table conservation, really. We spent most of our resources sending professionals to meet with landowners and encourage them to donate development rights to their property.

Preserving prime or important farmland is another aspect of our work. It's a really important piece of the history and culture here on the Eastern Shore. You know, we have some of the best farmland here in the country. And it's strategically located in the Mid-Atlantic to provide food for a lot of people in this country, and we need to protect it for that reason. The Mid-Shore here annually produces more than half of the top five crops in Maryland in total, just in this little area. It's overwhelmingly the most productive soil in Maryland and some of the most productive in the region. It holds moisture in the hottest part of the summer.

Any of the farms that we preserve, all of them are required to have buffer strips. The critical area requires a 25 foot buffer strip between farming and the bay. Our minimum is now 100 feet. So if it's in a preservation program it's going to have 100 feet of generally forested vegetation. You can keep the forest cut but maintain a shrub layer in some cases.

On all of our Eastern Shore Land Conservancy easement properties we give them a little sign to put on their gate that says, 'Farmland Forever: This farm preserved forever in a conservation easement held by the Eastern Shore Land Conservancy."

<u>10</u>

Kayaks and Powerboats

Tom Horton and Don Baugh, Circumnavigating Delmarva

I don't know when these two guys first met but it must have been a really nice moment. We search for our whole lives for a few friends that we feel at ease with, and Don and Tom seem to be the epitome of what we call 'best friends.'

Tom Horton recently retired from writing a weekly column and regular features about the Chesapeake Bay for The Baltimore Sun *newspaper. He's also the author of several books on the Chesapeake Bay including the award-winning* Bay Country, The Great Marsh *and others with photographer Dave Harp,* Turning the Tide: Saving the Chesapeake, *and* An Island Out of Time.

Don Baugh is the Vice President for Education with the Chesapeake Bay Foundation. His primary job is getting kids out on the bay to get their hands wet and their feet muddy. Don is a huge inspiration for the Voices *project. His motto at CBF is "If it isn't fun, why do it?" His latest work includes working as key coordinator for the No Child Left Inside initiative spearheaded by the Chesapeake Bay Foundation and the National Park Service.*

It's fitting that after kayaking the Chesapeake Bay together for a number of decades, Don and Tom would celebrate Tom's milestone 60th birthday with an epic journey around the Delmarva Peninsula. Voices *had the unique opportunity to chronicle this great story in January of 2006, when I met with Tom and Don at CBF headquarters.*

"It actually occurs to me now that every 20 years Baugh seems to change my life," said Tom. "Back when I was 40 I mentioned the need to hunt and fish more. I ended up leaving *The Baltimore Sun* for five years and living on Smith Island, working for him, running education trips. This year, with my 60th birthday coming up, he suggested that I needed some adventure in my life. He had thrown out several things. The trip around Delmarva was the first one I didn't think would kill me."

"He'd shot down every venture I'd thought of: around the world, anything Arctic or Antarctic," remembers Don. "Then all of the sudden it just dawned on me one day that this guy has spent his life writing about the Eastern Shore and the Chesapeake Bay. Why not paddle around the Delmarva Peninsula? The second it came out of my mouth Tom jumped on it and said, 'We're doing that.'"

Has this kind of trip ever been attempted before in kayaks?

"When we left," Tom said, "to our knowledge, we were the first people to ever do it. I knew a guy who had done it in bits and pieces, and I never doubted that someone else might have done it. We knew of one guy several years ago who did it in a speed boat in six and a half hours. It took us about 28 days.

After we left we ran into a fellow who is a little older than I am, who, I think, did it and did it faster than we did. I have yet to catch up to him and actually talk to him, but to our knowledge someone else did do this a year before. I knew people who had sailed around it. Going around it in a powerboat or sailing you have to stay far offshore for much of the time. You can't really follow the edge, which is where the interest is for us. I think it's hard to beat life at four miles an hour, which is about what we averaged. That's a brisk walk."

Just what is the Delmarva Peninsula?

"If you look at the Delmarva Peninsula from space it looks a lot like a conch shell," said Don. "The Delmarva Peninsula is the land that lies within the Chesapeake Bay, the Delaware Bay, and the Atlantic Shore. Delmarva is the contraction for Delaware, Maryland and Virginia. Not three political areas but one big geographic region. So the circumnavigation is up the Chesapeake Bay, down the Delaware Bay, and then down the Atlantic Shore to the mouth of the Chesapeake at Cape Charles. Overall it's a 445 mile circuit, more or less as the crow flies.

You can go a whole lot further if you want to do some exploring, and there are lots of opportunities for creeks and rivers that lure you in. At the same time, if you know that you have another 350 miles ahead of you, you've got to minimize the distractions along the way, try to stay on the main stem. So we looked at it, and we punched in a little map program and it said 445 miles. I think we gulped a pretty good gulp and then said, 'Well...we'll give it a shot.'

A computer program was very effective for us. It allowed us to plot the distance for each day. I carried a laptop, mostly so I could communicate with a daily web entry. We loaded the map software, the tides and currents. Both were critical for allowing us to know how far a given day might be. In a sense, there's also a lot of physics. We could push the kayaks about four miles an hour. A 10 mile an hour wind would push us plus or minus one mile an hour; a 20 mile an hour wind would be plus or minus two mph, and 30 would be plus or minus three. The tide would run about a mile per hour. So it was just a quick little math formula to say, 'Okay, today we can do 40 miles, or today we can do no miles,' because at some point there are diminishing returns. You don't want to put all your energy into a day and get one mile. You've got to wait until the conditions are a little bit more favorable."

How did you hold up physically to the challenge of such a long trip?

"This is the first trip of any real length I've taken," said Tom. "It's interesting, things like an ache or a pain or a blister, on our normal two or three or four day trips you don't worry about. You say, 'I'll be home in a day or two,' and you tough it out. On this trip you'd start to think, 'Whoa, this could be a showstopper. I'd better attend to it.' So you end up powdering your butt with talcum powder, doing things that you don't normally worry about, to make sure you don't get stopped.

I had spent the previous two weeks on a bike trip. I wouldn't recommend this as training for a month-long kayak trip. It doesn't do a thing for your shoulders. I was hurting and taking the Ibuprophen the first few days. But the gratifying thing, especially gratifying when you're 60, is even after paddling to exhaustion early in the trip, I really rebounded quite well the next day. That night it was like, 'I don't see how we're going to paddle tomorrow,' and then the next morning it's, 'Hmm, I don't feel too bad.'

We were really fortunate, we had a good friend, Turney McKnight, who dedicated about three weeks of his life to running a support boat. He had a new 19 foot skiff that he had just bought. Turney spent a good bit of the trip scouting out ahead for campsites, and that enabled us to do away with things like freeze-dried food and go for things like cold beer, when we got to camp at night. We owe him an eternal debt for his support. It was a birthday party after all, so what are you going to do, expose yourself to hardship? We had it pretty good from an eating standpoint. I never appreciated Don's organized mind because he comes across as a what-the-hell kind of guy, but in fact, he's extremely organized. He had actually pretty much planned the diet to be like 60 percent carb, 30 percent protein, 10 percent fat; not religiously but we ate pretty healthy. Despite eating all I wanted, including chocolate bars and stuff, I actually lost about eight or nine pounds on the trip. I was surprised."

How did you decide when would be the best time of the year to make the trip?

"We had looked at the entire calendar year and tried to figure out when the best time to do it would be. In the Chesapeake and along the Atlantic seashore mosquitoes and no-see-ums are a big factor, so we elected for fall rather than spring. You could do it in the summer, but in the summer you're just going to have less comfort day by day. But by October the bugs are gone and the water temperature is still warm enough you don't have to worry about hypothermia. In the springtime, by the time the bugs appear, the water temperature is still 60 or so. The only downfall to the fall season is that you have such short days. The sun starts to go down around five o'clock or so and that really compresses the amount of time you have awake, and can see to pitch a tent and do your work. It's really only about 10 hours a day. Overall, I think we chose the very finest time of the year. The end of September and October are glorious times on the East Coast."

There was also the decision about which direction to start off in. Perhaps the tides played a role in that decision?

"We started our trip from Bishops Head in Lower Dorchester County, a place where CBF has a lodge. We went up the bay to the C&D Canal, through the canal, down the Delaware Bay, to Cape Henlopen and Lewes, Delaware, and then down the seaside all the way to the Bridge Tunnel. We came under the Bridge Tunnel, which was a great moment, and then back up the bay into Dorchester. We sort of divided the trip into four or five chapters. Once we got up the bay to the canal that's the end of chapter one. Now we're on the Delaware Bay.

The lower Eastern Shore, the middle bay, the upper bay, those are three different worlds. You get over on Delaware Bay and that's another place entirely. The seaside in Virginia, that's another universe. I think that's the wildest territory you can paddle through between Maine and the Carolinas, really. The Nature Conservancy bought nearly 70 miles of Virginia seacoast; beautiful barrier islands and a lot of land on the mainland. That's a true Mid-Atlantic wilderness, and there aren't many Mid-Atlantic wildernesses anymore. We saw a huge diversity of places. One peninsula but several different worlds."

Don added, "Dorchester County, for those who haven't had the privilege of being there, is adequately coined 'Maryland's Everglades.' It's flat marshland. People think of it as Blackwater. The waterside is rimmed with little beaches along the way, so you've got everything from sandy peninsulas to a lot of eroded shoreline around Taylor's Island, a lot of riprap, and a lot of construction. You've got an area that may be connected by a third Bay Bridge one day, but today it's mostly inhabited by eagles. Dorchester itself is a pretty exciting county to be a platform to leave from. It's basically you and the birds and the bay."

One wonders about the repetitive movement, the trance you get into when kayaking such a long distance for days at a time.

"Your kayak is like your shoe," explained Don. "You don't think about it. It's always there with you. You're not really thinking about the paddle stroke, and you're not typically thinking about your direction, because you know where your point is. It's ingrained in your mind enough that your mind is free to roam. Some of the time you're there, paying attention and looking for the eagles, and sometimes you're completely somewhere else, you know, solving all the world's problems. That's the beauty of self-propelled travel, particularly kayaking. It allows your mind to escape wherever you want it to go."

From the natural light and shadows of Dorchester Coun-

ty open space, Don and Tom arrived in the middle bay and saw some of the more developed shorelines they would see along their journey.

"I'd say that the first dramatic change of the trip is when you get up along Kent Island," Tom said. "Then all of a sudden you're seeing some nice houses and some of the most garish, oversized, overbuilt bayfront homes anywhere. It was interesting trying to pick the winner for most egregious, oversized home. Then you get to something unexpected. Once you get up above Rock Hall, that upper bay, partly because of Aberdeen, is really dark at night. Because it's a military reservation there's no development and there are no lights. Near the Canal we started running into a few little trailer parks along the water, but I don't think I had been prepared for the darkness of the shoreline and the very undeveloped look to a lot of the upper bay.

The Chesapeake & Delaware Canal is a nice ride because the current runs hard through there. We were doing seven mph, maybe a little better, not even paddling hard. That was a real sleigh ride. We were actually hoping to see ships and saw almost none. Only about 10 percent of the big ships using the port of Baltimore go through the canal any more, and it may be quite a bit less than that. This has raised some interesting issues. About 60 to 70 percent of all the dredging we have to do is for the upper approaches for the canals. With all the problems we have placing dredge spoils and the expense, how long do you do 70 percent of the dredging for 8 to 9 percent of the ships? In the whole approach to the canal we saw a few tugs and barges, maybe one big ship. It was pretty sleepy the few days we were up in that area."

What was it like in Delaware Bay, in contrast to the Chesapeake?

"When you come out of the mouth of the canal what greets you is a big nuclear power plant on the other shore, the

New Jersey shore," Don said. "What also greets you is the heavy ship traffic to and from Philadelphia. In a lot of ways it kind of underscores present day Delaware Bay. Delaware Bay is a very different system from the Chesapeake and always was. It's a short system. It's one big mouth. It doesn't have the rivers that feed it like the Chesapeake does. It appears that it never had the clarity or the grasses or quite the life that the Chesapeake had. It's a dynamic high-energy zone, and when you're in a kayak you and that energy bond, for better or for worse. It gets rough fast and there's a lot of current. The water's very turbid and choppy; it's not a kayakers dream. You just have to get through it.

Some days it would be absolute blissfulness and calm. Then minutes later it turned from heaven to hell with about 15 miles an hour of wind and a couple knots of current, and it would be a showstopper. You'd have to push hard just to make any forward progress. We saw a little religion one day on Delaware Bay when things turned against us. After a pleasing morning of paddling we had a very rough afternoon. Because of the wind and the tides we did a little scouting around the bushes, looking for where we might have to spend the night. At that point we were without a tent, without gear, without anything. We were also going to have to do without ground because the best that we could see was a little marsh stump that the waves lapped up against. Presumably we'd survive through the night, and we made it, but it taught us that we better get it done ASAP. So with the next weather window, we pushed hard and got into Lewes.

Lewes is a wonderful, beautiful, historic port, obviously there because it's at the mouth of the Delaware Bay. It was a shipbuilding center for 100 years or so. It serves a kayaker similarly, a nice port where you go in and everything is there on the waterfront—grocery stores, movie theatre, restaurants, hotels, showers."

"The best thing about Lewes is motels," Tom said. "That meant that for the first time our wives came down to spend the night with us, so Lewes was a good experience. That was the deal, you know, 'Let us know if you're near a motel, guys.' They weren't really looking for excuses to camp out with us. They've had too many opportunities in the past perhaps, and I guess maybe we weren't showering too regularly, either."

The final week of their trip Don and Tom didn't have the support boat, and they traveled with full gear. With the added weight their endurance was put to the test.

"The first three weeks when we had the support boat we could go very light," said Don. "That was very useful. It allowed our speed to stay up. Also, it takes a long time to pack a kayak in the morning. The last week we were un-tethered and so we carried everything. We probably had about 100 pounds of gear each, which would be a tent and a sleeping bag, utensils, your stove, your saw, all of your water, your food, your backup clothes, your rain gear and hats. It really makes a big difference, empty or loaded.

The last week that we were carrying the additional 100 pounds was the week we were obviously in the best shape. We might have felt differently about our prospects of paddling around during the first week if we'd had to endure that extra weight. It makes about a mile per hour difference. I guess we were probably keeping our average up around four, but only because we were in such better shape towards the end. Typically, I think the extra weight would push our speed back to about three mile per hour."

From the Delaware Bay into Indian River Inlet and out into the Atlantic Ocean, the varying conditions must have presented a real challenge.

"We went behind Rehoboth Bay, then went out into the ocean at Indian River Inlet. Those that have fished that area know it. It's like a big balloon. The balloon itself would be Indian River Bay, and the little neck of the balloon would be the inlet. You have all of this water just blowing through. I mean, to the point where the bridge is toppling over. They're struggling to put a new bridge in because the 40 foot pilings are now 100 feet. The water is scouring out around them and they're about ready to topple. That inlet just spews you right out, and all of the sudden you go from inland bays to the big, bad ocean.

We actually only paddled for one day in the open ocean waters. Tropical depression Tammy was forming in the south and we were well in advance of the storm. We saw Tammy way in the distance. In the meantime, we watched the waves build up and the weather build up, and then the weather leave us. But the passage on the outside was a very calm one once we got in the ocean and we got past the waves and currents generated by Delaware Bay. We stayed close enough in, really right behind the breakers, because to me that's the interface. That's where it all happens. That's where the fish are, for one thing, and it's a nice vantage point for looking at the Atlantic Coast.

We were followed by porpoises quite a bit. Sometimes you smell them from their exhaust. Sometimes you hear them and occasionally you see them. But they follow you when you're normally looking ahead, so to see them you have to turn around quick. Sometimes they'll escort you side by side, and at times they're a paddle length away. They're very unconcerned about kayaks, which makes kayaking with porpoises pretty neat."

Tom added, "I expect those porpoises are a little bit curious. They seem to like to get close to you. It's a little bit scary at first. You realize they have total control and if they wanted to upset you they would do it. They don't but, my gosh, sometimes your paddle's almost brushing them. You can smell the fishy smell coming out of their blowholes and sometimes you look around and, 'Wow, there it is right behind me!'"

"It really is kind of a fascinating ride as you leave the Delaware beaches and enter Maryland's beaches," said Don. "Maryland's high-rises in Ocean City are just a sharp knife-edge from Delaware, where they have a height restriction. So looking in from the coast you can just see the benefit of some visionary thinking years ago.

Then you just cruise down the Atlantic Coast in front of Ocean City and you see the shoreline erosion. There's a ship that's anchored out there 365 days a year trying to pump sand onto this barrier island, as the barrier island retreats, like they all want to do. Then you go round into the Ocean City Inlet, past the amusement park. It's kind of an interesting chapter of the trip because it's the developed coastline at that point."

"We'd had a fairly long day's paddle on the seaside coming down the Atlantic coastal island bays from Cobb Island down to Smith Island," Tom recalled, "which is the one that's actually named for Captain John Smith, right at the mouth of the bay. The northernmost stand of live oak (Evergreen oak) in the United States is out there. We came around through the Bridge Tunnel, turned the corner, and suddenly you've got traffic rushing overhead and big giant concrete columns—but that was totally drowned out. It was like a waterfall drowning out all the other noise, because of the tide rushing into the bay. There was a huge tide coming in there! We're trying to keep our eyes on everything, like the bridge pilings, which are rushing past. They looked very unforgiving, like they would win any tangle. Hardly paddling we got something like 6.8 mph on the GPS.

I think in both of our minds, even though we'd had a good hard paddle and, in fact, some of the hardest paddling of the trip ahead of us, it was like, 'We made it.' All the way around, all the way down Delaware Bay, all the way down the ocean, and we're back in the bay, back in familiar territory."

Home free... almost?

"The Chesapeake has a different tidal cycle than the Atlantic," Don said, "and a different tidal cycle than Delaware. When those chapters meet and those big bodies of water intersect you're going to have a lot of currents, a lot of velocity, and a lot of waves at times. Because it was the Chesapeake, because we were more or less raised here, it was home. But still, the lower bay is a different animal than the upper bay. Part of the paddling we had, the bay was 38 miles wide from shore to shore."

Tom added, "The other good thing about coming back into the bay is Don had just snagged a nice fat speckled trout just as we left the seaside, so we had a good fresh dinner on-board. Then, to get even better, we're up the bay about two or three miles and this bunch of clammers comes out on a boat. These are clam farmers; clams have become a huge aquaculture business in Virginia. They said, 'Are you the kayakers going around Delmarva?' I'm thinking, 'How the heck did they know that?' They had met our friend Turney in his skiff. They came out on the deck and handed each of us a cold beer. I wanted to drink it then, but figured we had about eight or 10 more miles to go that day and the wind was starting to turn, so we just stowed them. Don remarked, 'You know, we've been wet the last four days,' and one of these guys said, 'Hell, I've been wet for the last 11 years, man!'

Then, we had to paddle 14 or 15 miles up the Eastern Shore of Virginia against tide and with wind in our face. Eventually it got dark and a full moon was coming up. We ate a sandwich and took off across about 16 miles of open water for Tangier Island. After what I would have considered a heck of a days' paddle the first week, we did double that distance. We pulled into Tangier about 10 or 11 o'clock that night. It was a nice night, you know, a little bit rough out on the bay. The waves looked twice as big in the dark. But, my gosh, we started to see the lights of Tangier about eight or nine miles out, just little dots and then little streaks, and then finally the lights. I thought they would never, never come up to our kayaks. I said, 'Man, I've been looking at those lights for hours and hours,' and it had probably been about an hour and 45 minutes. My legs were cramping. That was a heck of a paddle. That was as close as we got to being exhausted, I think, that night. Once we got back to Tangier Island after the night paddle, at that point we were really back home. Tom and I have both spent a good deal of our lives in that area. We knew that no matter what God would throw at us at that point, we could make the last 30 miles in two days. As it turned out, God shined on us the last couple days, for what I call two days of a victory lap. It's just a wonderful place to paddle with Caribbean-like sandbars. And we finally really did hit the fish. The fishing was almost distracting.

We had a cumulative mileage counter on our GPS; 445 was our final tally. We had a small but very active welcoming committee. We were happy to have some company in our rejoicing. It felt like a real accomplishment in many ways. It was an opportunity to reflect on life, to participate so closely with nature, and then the privilege of being in this particular area. It was not just a trip on the water. This is the Chesapeake, Delaware, and the Atlantic Shore, and there's a lot of magic there. So we felt for 30 days that we were the magic."

Jake Flory, The Susquehanna Flood

Since the day he was born, Jake Flory has never dried out. He's a water person inside and out. From flying mechanized model seaplanes off a semi-sinking skiff, to sailing sloops from Annapolis to the Caribbean, Jake is most at home on the water. Flory grew up on Harness Creek in Annapolis on an old tenant farm they now call Wimbledon Farm, just across from Quiet Waters Park

"When I grew up there were farms everywhere," *he remembered.* "It was the best that it could be back then. You had all the water and all the land, you could run around. I'd leave in the morning and I wouldn't come home until the end of the day, unless I was hungry or something... Nobody kept track of you in those days. You just went out and ran around and played in the water all day long, and at the end of the evening you came home, ate dinner, and got up and did it again. My dad has told me several times, 'All you could see of Jake all summer long was his butt sticking up at the end of the pier.' That's 'cause I was crabbing all the time!" *One day in midsummer 2006, Jake relived two kayak adventures he and a friend experienced on the mighty Susquehanna, the mother river of the Chesapeake.*

"Somehow, about 10 years ago, I got into kayaking, which is a great way to get out in the water. A good mechanic friend of mine was into kayaks too. He's an adventurous type, like I am. Going for the weekend doesn't seem to excite us too much, but going away for a couple of weeks sounds like a lot of fun. In 2000 we took our kayaks and got somebody to give us a ride up to the beginning of the West Branch of the Susquehanna River. We got out of the car and loaded up our kayaks with all of our gear—food, water, supplies, camping gear—enough for two weeks.

The Susquehanna has two branches. The main branch

is the north branch which, if we're going backwards, goes all the way to Cooperstown, New York. That's the headwaters of the Susquehanna at Otsego Lake in Cooperstown, which is, of course, the Baseball Hall of Fame town. That's where the river starts, right there.

The West Branch goes much further west. It doesn't have a lake that it starts in. It starts in the bogs in the southwestern part of Pennsylvania and then it's fed by many rivers up there. It goes through a stretch between Clearfield and Lenovo, where my kayaking buddy was born, and that 80 mile stretch is uninhabited. There are no towns and the mountains are pretty shear on both sides. I think it's the most beautiful part of the entire Susquehanna River system. It's so raw there. But, unfortunately, man has put his mark on it. I'll never forget the day we were in this beautiful spot with big boulders, and deep water sections. We stopped and went swimming, and I said to my partner Chuck, 'It looks like the Caribbean here, with the color of this water.' We spent most of the day just swimming and fishing and having a ball there baking in the sun. Then we got in our kayaks and started to go down the river later in the day. We went around a turn and there was this big orange swath of stream coming down the mountain. It was just like somebody painted it on there. It was acid mine runoff. The river after that point was dead. There were no fish. The water didn't have that beautiful color. It was all murky and it was just terrible. That's from the mining. I guess they can't stop it. It was just an awful thing to see in this beautiful country where man had just torn it up. We went another 150 miles past that before the water started to get better.

We made our plans to kayak for two weeks during the last week of June and the first week of July, starting from the headwaters of the Susquehanna. We planned to kayak the entire river, and that way we could say we did it from the start to the finish. Our buddies took us to Cooperstown and we put in on Sunday morning around nine o'clock in the lake, paddled around the corner, and the river started flowing right there. By about two o'clock it started raining. It rained all day and night

Sunday, into Monday night, into Tuesday. That Monday night I remember we found a little island just big enough for both of our tents and our kayaks. We hacked our way on with our machetes, which was normally the way we camped. There are no nicely mowed places for you to put your tent on the Susquehanna. We were only about 18 inches above the water. My friend Chuck had a little stick that he was watching all night because the water came up about an inch an hour. By morning and the time we'd packed up, got our kayaks loaded and ate some breakfast, the water was floating our boats. We shoved off and then we looked back and the water was just starting to lap up over where we had been sitting. It rained all day. It rained so hard you couldn't hardly see the front of your kayak sometimes. It was pretty neat.

It's a very interesting thing to be kayaking in very heavy rain. All the ripples on the water go away and you can't see the current. It's hard to read the river; it disappears with the rain. But it was a wild ride on Tuesday. It was moving fast and it was a lot of fun. We'd go faster than anything floating. It's a somewhat rocky bottom but not a lot of rocks up in that section of the Susquehanna. It's more muddy than rocky. It usually doesn't get any deeper than your paddle, so we're talking maybe six feet.

On Tuesday we knew we were getting a lot of rain, it had been raining hard for three days. We weren't worried, we were just kind of wondering what would happen with the river. It was obviously swelling up and moving faster. We had no outside communication with anybody or anything. We had our skirts on our kayaks with rain gear and hats. We used our PFDs (personal floatation devices) for safety and also warmth. The temperature was right on the edge. If it had been two degrees cooler it would have been a little tougher. Staying dry wasn't a problem. My sleeping bag was dry and when we slept at night we were dry.

Five o'clock came by on Tuesday and we had the customary hour set aside to look for a place for camping. Chuck goes on one side of the river and I go on the other. The river's not so wide you can't holler over. I had been thinking for the first time about staying in somebody's little camping area, a fish camp with a trailer on it. They're usually handed down from generation to generation. I was looking for some comfort and I saw this one trailer as I was going by and I thought 'this is it.' We went in and it was about three feet above the water-line and we thought, 'this is the Hilton! This will be wonderful.' We went up and checked and found that nobody was in the trailer. I could see that there was a drive that cut through the woods and up to a road. So we put our campsite together and had dinner.

'Bout 11 o'clock that night, Chuck woke me up—and the water was about two feet from our tent. So, we figured we had to move fast. We got our kayaks packed with everything. We didn't take our tents apart, we just picked them up and we got everything moved up to the top of that drive, which was a service road that used to be a railroad. We had to hack into the side of the road for a place for our tents and everything. We got all set up and went back to sleep. The next morning we woke up and the water was right there, two feet away from us again. It had risen that night 20 to 25 feet. The trailer that we saw when we came in was gone, underwater.

The floodplain was several hundred feet on the side we were on. On the other side it was farmland and it was totally flooded. It was like football fields full of water. That morning we were pretty surprised. We talked about how lucky we were that for the first time we picked somebody's yard to camp in, because we had an escape route. If we would have picked an island to camp on I'm not sure how we would have dealt with that.

I don't know if we were scared. We were certainly awe-struck and very respectful of what was going on. I called it right off the bat, it was the flood of the century. That's what I started calling it. And low and behold, it was the flood of the century.

We were on the service road, so everybody and their mother started coming by on ATVs to see the crazy people with the kayaks camping on the side of the road. As it turned out there was a three-mile stretch of road right there which was flooded on either end. These people couldn't get out. So they all came by and said hello. They brought us food and they kept asking us what we wanted. That first night there was a fellow that was barbequing chicken at a friend's house, because his house was underwater. They made sure we came down and visited with them. They said, 'You're not going any-where.' Helicopters were flying up and down and we heard all these stories that they don't want you on the river. It's against the law to be on the river. We just camped and sat there for three days.

We went kayaking every day in the floodplain. We were kayaking over the top of people's homes. You'd look in the window and see the refrigerator floating. We saw animals that had been tied up and were on the leash floating. We saw half a house go by down the river, just floating by! You didn't know but then you'd look over and see somebody's chimney or the top of a flagpole. We kayaked over the top of all these people's lives, is what it felt like to me.

The water did not go down from Wednesday through Friday. And then on Saturday the water started to go down. By Saturday evening all the water had gone down. When the wa-ter receded, we looked and we could see where we had been kayaking. In one case we had seen a car and somebody said it was a '56 Chevy that was being restored. When the water went down, sure enough, you could see the car and it was full of mud and ruined. You couldn't help but think of New Orleans and seeing these people's lives all flooded out and just think-ing, 'Here we are in maybe just a square mile. Our little world was small.'

The last day, on Saturday when the water went down, we finally realized that there was so much muck that you couldn't camp if you were to go down the river. There was six inches of muck on everything. It's probably a good idea we didn't go because there was a lot of water in that river and it was rag-ing. We had a car in Wilkes-Barre, so we got a ride from where we were. As a matter of fact, the people that owned the trailer showed up on Saturday to check out their fishing camp. The water was still up, so we loaned them our kayaks and they kayaked down to it. They came back shaking their heads. But it turned out that they lived about five minutes from where our car was, so Chuck caught a ride with them and brought the car back.

It's 444 miles of river from Cooperstown to Havre de Grace. Chuck and I have never given up on finishing our trip."

Kathleen and Dwight Moxness, Pleasure Cruising

Dwight and Kathleen Moxness are the quintessential weekend boaters. They started sailing 20 years ago and later moved on to a common love for more comfortable powerboats, which provide the space to enjoy longer weekend trips on the bay. Dwight is an engineer by trade and also loves to play music on a variety of instruments. He met Kathleen in the high school that they both attended in Vienna, Virginia. A few years down the road he joined forces with her in a college rock band at Virginia Tech. After they were married they decided to live full time near the waters edge and moved to a lavish tree-house-like home in the Saefern section of Annapolis.

"We were in Annapolis, so you've got to be a sailor," Dwight began. "We bought our first sailboat having never really sailed before. We got some books, *Sailing for Beginners*. We read books about cruisers, you know, Joshua Slocomb, who sailed around the world alone, and Tanya Haybe, who was the youngest female sailor to sail around the world alone. We got inspired by people who had done that. Went out there and just learned it on our own."

"*Waimelea* is Hawaiian for water music," Kathleen said, "so our spirit was with Water Music right from the beginning. After our 23 foot Hunter, which had a little Porta-Potty and a small cuddy cabin, I figured that I need a bigger toilet and a little more room. So, we graduated from that to the 32 foot *Seventeen Year Itch,* celebrating our 17th anniversary. Fortunately, we were itching for the same thing. *Seventeen Year Itch* was probably the first time we cruised across the bay. We went over to St. Michaels to the Inn at Perry Cabin. It was pretty rough, and the bay's challenging for a small boat. We stayed in the Inn, we didn't stay on the boat... That's why now we have a 47 footer."

"The marina we're in here, our community marina, if you

look around there are many more sailboaters than powerboaters," said Dwight. "But we all get along pretty well together. Most of us have done both. I think sailing is a good way to learn how to be out on the water because it teaches you to respect the wind and the current. You have less maneuverability and it takes more time to get out of bad weather, so it's a good learning experience."

"One thing about boaters," Kathleen said, "is they change boats fairly often, because nothing's ever perfect. We were leaving the Chester River one morning, and we listen to the weather every time we leave because the weather's very important, and it just said some light rain, something of that nature. So we got out to the mouth of the bay and the Chester River and it started raining. And then the rain picked up a little more and it got dark and then the wind picked up. And we ended up to where the seas got to be five or six feet. Since the bay is very shallow that means that the waves are very high and they're short. So it becomes very rough. The boat was tossed all over the place. The rain came in so hard we couldn't see. We had nothing like a GPS at that time. We didn't know where we were. I was up on the bridge and the wind blew the Bimini cover off. It blew the rails off the top of the boat. And I decided I better put on a life jacket at that time.

We had a collie on board and first thing I did was put her life jacket on. Then I went up and told Dwight, 'Put your life jacket on.' He said, 'Oh, I'm alright.' And then I said, 'Please put your life jacket on,' and he did. That's not something we normally wear all the time on the boat. We got tossed about pretty good and after that we realized that we wanted every electronic known to man on the boat. I think the winds were almost 50 miles per hour. Believe it or not, we actually found a sailboat and we thought that they might know what they were doing, so we sort of stuck by them throughout the storm. It lasted maybe 20 to 30 minutes but it seemed like the longest time of my life. I remember we saw a little break and we saw the Bay Bridge. Dwight gave me the helm and I just started gunning towards it. He said, 'No, no, no, stay by this marker!'

And I said, 'No, I see the bridge and I'm going there. I see it.' I felt like at least that was something familiar because it was a horrible feeling being in such heavy rains and... I mean, even though the bay is the bay it feels like the ocean when you're out there in that kind of situation. And it's pretty challenging and it makes you realize how vulnerable you are and how foolish you are if you're out there and not prepared. There are more electronics than I ever thought I'd have in my life on this boat, and I'm grateful for that.

He so much as goes out on the dingy and I say 'take the GPS, take the cell phone.' He always thinks, 'Why do you need me to... I'm going for a quick ride.' But hey, what if our anchor breaks loose and I'm on the boat by myself? I want to be able to reach him. Sometimes the only way you become prepared is to be out there and have something happen that's a real slap in the face. I always love it when the Chesapeake's kind, and I respect it when it's not.

I'm really in tune to any sounds in the boat, too. When we're cruising, you know, we're running generators and air conditioners and there's satellite TV aboard. There's all this stuff and all these noises going on, so I'm always really in tune to any sounds that are different in the engines. And if I'm riding on the bow and I hear a slight change in the speed of the engines or something, my antennas are up right away."

"Even if nature can be tough sometimes," Dwight explained, "it's the one of the elements of boating we like the most: the beauty of the bay, the wildlife, the scenery, and the challenge of the weather. The other thing is the people. Probably the most interesting thing we do is stopping around different ports or places and running into people who have a similar lifestyle. Some who live on boats, some who have come from across the ocean, or are on long cruises.

We go to the Narrows every year for the Fourth of July, and there's energy around the marinas. There's a barbeque and parties and Harris' Crab House and the Red Eye Dock Bar, and there's a Buffett song on probably every third radio. It's a great feeling and it's almost like being at a concert. So the music's a big part of the bay too.

Just last year we took a fairly long cruise. We went down into the lower portion of the bay, down to the Potomac River past the mouth of the Rappahannock River, over through Tangier Island and Smith Island, which are very unique places. We stayed in Crisfield one night. In the lower bay we saw dolphins swimming. We saw rays and a lot more of the ocean-type wildlife in the water, which was very interesting. I think we put in about 3,000 to 4,000 nautical miles on that trip. We ended up going back and forth across the bay, sometimes to small towns. One of the more interesting towns we visited was Reedville, down in Virginia on the Northern Neck. Reedville is the last remaining menhaden fishing area with a processing plant. We stayed at a very small marina there and I was talking to the marina owner who was also the cook in the restaurant, and he ran the local inn. I said, 'Is the menhaden industry still running?' He said, 'Yes, there's a plant across the way. You'll know if they're cookin'.' Next morning we get up, the wind had shifted and it smelled very, very strong, very fishy. If you live in Reedville you probably know which way the wind blows. In fact when I took our cat out that morning to show her the outside, she got very interested because I think she could smell the food cooking in the distance."

"Annapolis is my favorite port 'cause its home port," said Kathleen, with an ear-to-ear grin. "St. Michaels is another favorite, and we love the Narrows. Rock Hall's a great town. We added a motor scooter for getting around on land. Dwight designed a davit system so he could pull the scooter onto the boat. It gives us a lot more flexibility. It's our land dingy.

We're known in the neighborhood as the people who use the boat the most. I'd say we come down to the boat every day. We have dinner and at least cocktails on it three times a week. We leave on Friday night every weekend and come back Sunday. We pick the boat up at the beginning of April and we take it back in after Thanksgiving. From April thru November you don't see us much unless it's in a harbor somewhere. We want to be on the boat every minute we can. We love being on it even if we're not going anywhere, just to sit and watch the osprey flying around. We've got a lot of great blue herons. Even baby Canada geese, a real treat. Being a bird lover I can just come down here in the afternoon. Instead of sitting at home I can come here and watch the birds and just enjoy where we live. We live in one of the greatest places in the country."

11

Professional Sailboat Racing

Gary Jobson, ESPN Commentator, America's Cup Champion

The Chesapeake Bay is home to some of the world's top sailors. Along with Newport, Rhode Island, Annapolis has been called "The Sailing Capitol of the World" for many years. Sailing is in a way like baseball and other sports, here in the bay region. Kids grow up as recreational sailors and compete at various levels throughout a lifetime. A chosen few go on to compete at the highest levels in races such as The America's Cup, or the grueling Volvo Round the World Race. Over the past seven years several of these world-class athletes have added their voices to the Voices *project, telling us what it's like in these extreme races and what life on the bay means to these dedicated and supremely talented performers. Joined by* Voices *volunteer Scott Weiss, I had the chance to talk with ESPN Sailing Commentator and America's Cup Champion Gary Jobson, at his Annapolis office about the 2001-2002 Volvo Ocean Race (formerly the Whitbread Round the World Race), and the 2005-2006 Volvo Ocean Race.*

"The essence of racing around the world is contrast," he began. "At times you're crossing the equatorial doldrums where it is 110 degrees and you're hot and parched and yet you've got to wear clothes and it rains and it's tough. At other times you're in the Southern Ocean. It's 25 degrees, blowing 50 knots. You're scared to death, surfing down 40 foot waves. The key to doing well is to handle the range of emotions, the range of conditions, and the range of human problems. You have to be resourceful. You have to fill in the valleys, knock off the peaks, and have kind of a steady attitude, steady mentality, just keep plugging as hard as you can, and take a look at the long term. If you get behind, don't panic. Just keep plugging away. Just because you're last in the Volvo Ocean Race on one leg doesn't mean you go in. You keep plugging."

Describe the most notorious leg of the Volvo Ocean Race, scaling the peaks and dodging the growlers (submerged icebergs) in the infamous Southern Ocean.

"The key to doing well in the Southern Ocean is not opening the throttle all the time. In the America's Cup the throttle is usually open. You push as hard as you can every second. In the Southern Ocean the key is to throttle back so you're not hurting people, you're not breaking things. Sailing at 90 percent you're probably doing a better average than being at 100 percent and then having to throttle back to 50 percent. That was the lesson that Captain Paul Cayard learned, and what he taught all of us was pace yourself well.

I climbed a mountain with the late great Alex Lowe. He said to me, 'Go up the mountain at any speed you want; doesn't matter how fast or how slow. But whatever speed you select, keep a steady pace.' So the secret to doing well on the Volvo Ocean Race is to keep a steady pace. Keep the watch routine going. Don't pull an all-hands-up 15 times a day because you'll burn everybody out. Those that keep the steadiest pace will probably be the ones at the top of the heap when they get back to the finish line.

When you're onboard the boat it's important to eat the food even though it's freeze-dried. Also make sure you have enough water and stay regular. Put sun cream on and wear the right clothing, so you don't fatigue yourself. I think it's the crews that learn to do that, which survive. The crews that can't handle it quickly get off the boat. Yes, it is again contrast. You're everybody's hero, you've got the limelight, you've got the media, you're eating well, and you're back on the boat. I actually think the race should look at itself a little bit. Are the conditions too hard for people? I noticed that we've had some injuries. I noticed that there's some dehydration going on. There are some heatstroke problems aboard the boats. There's been some frostbite. So maybe a little bit better living conditions, a little bit more normal food than freeze dried might be something for race organizers to look at in the future.

A two-gallon bag is all you get to put personal belongings in. It was reported that one guy wore the same T-shirt for 20 days. No freshwater showers, except maybe occasionally with the dump over the head of a bucket of clean water.

When I was in Antarctica we spent six weeks down there and we only had saltwater showers. Saltwater showers work, believe it or not, if you dry off right away. Hygiene is really important but everybody's trying to save weight. You're very limited in what you take. Luckily high-tech clothing, Gore Tex fabric for example, for a lot of the fowl weather gear, is breathable. Layering does seem to work and it seems to keep people warm and dry. But creature comforts, again, are something that should be thought about for the future. Only the competitors themselves can tell us if it was too tough or where changes should happen. That'll be something that will be reviewed at the end of the race.

As far as water is concerned, each boat has a water maker. One boat had theirs break for a few days, so that was probably anxious. But they got the thing going again. Fuel, you're under sail, you're not under power. You do use the engine to fire up the water maker, to fire up the pumps for the ballast, and a reserve if you need to get into it. So it's managing your assets just like on any ship. Food, fuel, and water are some things to watch very carefully. There are emergency rations, and you do have a lifeboat. So if it ever got to an extreme situation, life threatening, there are some reserves there to go and get. You'll probably get penalized a little, but I think at that point you'd be damn glad to have it, not worried about a penalty but just to survive.

Some guys go from saying, 'This is a real struggle,' to saying, 'This is the most beautiful thing I ever did.' Consider this: these boats will go around the world averaging about 12 miles per hour. On sailboats that's pretty quick. On an airplane that's kind of slow. But at 12 miles per hour as you go all the way around the world, 32,000 miles, it gives you the opportunity to actually see it, to feel it, and be a part of it. These 97 competitors on the 12 boats are really going to have a sense of what the world is all about. Seeing these different headlands, experiencing the different oceans, getting to all these different ports, understanding what different people in different parts of the world are all about. It's an experience second to none for these competitors.

As far as being out there in extreme conditions, I think one of the great things with ocean racing is that things change. You're in a storm, it's blowing hard, it's raining, you're freezing, and it's cold. What am I doing here? Four hours later the wind calms down, it stops raining, the sailing's pretty good, you have a sandwich, and you're feeling pretty good about life. So, it's these changing conditions that keep you sane. And in the ocean conditions seem to change very quickly. That's the essence of it—dealing with the change.

I was up in the Arctic in June. 24 hour daylight. Way north. We'd be sailing along at 11:30 at night in daylight, 50 degrees out, blowing 12 knots. Within a minute, snap, some cloud comes in out of nowhere and it's blowing 35 knots. The temperature goes down to 22 degrees. On the water things change fast. You've got to be able to adapt your boat to those changes. So the concept of shifting gears to maximize boat speed is what these sailors are doing all the time.

How much crew attrition? In the B.T. Challenge I think after the second leg, 27 crew had gotten off. They were scheduled to continue but they said, 'I don't want to do this any- more!' But in the Volvo Ocean Race, they don't seem to have those problems. I have this feeling that when you're going fast, the boat is stable and you're sailing safe. You're sailing safe because the pressures are low and people are paying at- tention. I think when people don't pay attention or you're go- ing slowly, that's when you have the problems."

The sleeping conditions on the Volvo Ocean Race boats can be brutal. Sleeping with the noise of heading into waves, the movement, and the space limitations can be impossible. Sailors share their berths with food supplies and sail bags. When it's time to tack, everything has to be shifted from side to side. One boat reported tacking 400 times in one night.

"Life on these boats is very tough for the crews," Gary said. "Every time you maneuver, tack or jibe you're moving your stack—your sails and spare equipment. The noise of the boat is deafening. The water against the hull, there's no insu- lation, there's no dampening effect and there is sleep depriva- tion down there. People do get tired and a lot of times these crews sleep on the deck.

One of the amazing things about this race is the huge differential in wind velocity. You can be in the lead, and you're cruising along at 17 knots. Then you get into a zone of wind that's not predicted, there's just no wind where you are, and the boats that are behind you, they're still going 15 to 18 knots. As much as you predict with the reports you get around the ocean, you're really not sure what you're going to get. It changes and we've seen boats fall into a pocket for hours at a time. Everybody else around them is moving. Those breaks tend to average out. Through 32,000 miles, everyone is going to have their share.

The skippers in the Volvo Ocean Race are all pretty good. I've interviewed all of them, I've sailed with most of them. I know everybody and they're all good leaders. The best pre- pared boats with the crews that push their boats the hardest, are most careful with the navigation, don't break down and keep a steady pace, are the boats that are going to win."

How do sailing events like the Volvo Ocean Race fit into the Chesapeake culture?

"The Volvo Ocean Race is an important event in the world, and it's very important for the State of Maryland, the Chesapeake Bay, Annapolis, and Baltimore. It's important because it connects us with Sydney and Auckland, Cape Town and LaRochelle. Annapolis calls itself America's Sailing Capital, but we have to prove that. Hence, we host some big events: the Rolex Women's Keelboat Championship, the Star World Championship, and the National One Design Offshore Regatta.

The economics are good for the area, too. I have seen some studies that something like 30 million dollars came through the economy of Baltimore and Annapolis specifically because the Whitbread (now the Volvo) came here. My TV production in Annapolis has been good. I think it's fair to say world-class Annapolis-based sailboat racing designer Bruce Farr and his company have done very well. Jim Allsop and North Sails, which made every sail for every boat, have also done very well. So it's good for the sport of sailing, it's good for the local economy, and most importantly, it's a lot of fun."

Photo courtesy of Chris Cameron

Terry Hutchinson, Volvo Ocean Race and America's Cup

Terry Hutchinson is one of the most experienced and accomplished sailors of his generation. He has won several world championship titles, including the IMS World Championship in 2000 and the Farr 40 Worlds at San Francisco in 2004. He's a Star Class sailor of note, and a former member of the U.S. Olympic Sailing Team. I talked with Terry at his Eastport home back in 2003, as he was campaigning a boat for the 2004 Olympics in Athens, Greece. As we sat down to talk Terry made an amazing revelation: his love of sailing and the whirlwind career all started at Hartge's Yacht Yard, in Galesville.

"We had a bunch of different cruising boats down there, growing up. But nobody in the family really raced. I was the only one that took it on. We would spend every weekend in the summer cruising around the bay... it was never pushed or forced on me. It was something that I always wanted to do. I did very little big-boat sailing up until the time I was 22 or 23. Everything was in 420s or Lasers (small sailboats). Anything under 17 feet I specialized in. My big focus when I was coming through those junior ranks was to be a really good college sailor."

After helping to lead his team to four national championships at Old Dominion, Terry Hutchinson was named Collegiate Sailing All-American in 1989/90 and was the college's Sailor of the Year from 1986-1989. He was also named Old Dominion's Most Valuable Athlete in 1990 and 1992, and was inducted into Old Dominion's Athletic Hall of Fame in 2002.

"After I graduated from college in 1990, I started to race J-24s and that was the next evolution of learning how to organize a program and organize a team and all the logistics that take place in order to go and do well in regattas.

After a brief period spent living in Newport, Rhode Island (the other sailing capital of the world, for sure,) I moved back to Annapolis and went to work for Larry Leonard at the Quantum Sail Design Group. Then, in 1998, I got my big break, a chance to work for Skipper Paul Cayard on the *America One* America's Cup team. Everything that I do and have done has kind of been focusing on the goal of, at some point in the next 20 years, steering an America's Cup boat and winning.

It takes a lot of hard work and a lot of dedication. You have to be willing to drop everything in an instant and go to the regatta that is going help you meet people, and improve your sailing skills. I'm a firm believer that I have to continue to keep honing my sailing skill so that when I am racing at that level, I'm as sharp and well-prepared as I can possibly be mentally and physically."

Living in Annapolis, Newport, and Michigan led Terry Hutchinson to work with some amazing professional sailors. These were the guys who could help him get to his goal, guys who had been there before.

"For sure, in this area there are influences," he said. "Gary Jobson has been a big influence on me and my sailing career, helping steer me in the right directions from a personal perspective. He's somebody I've always looked up to and admired for what he's accomplished in the sailing world. He's still one of the few Annapolitans that can say he's won the America's Cup. I'd like to join that rank with him.

The gentleman that I went to work for in Michigan, Ed Reynolds, taught me a lot about logistics and how to organize things. Locally there have been guys like Larry Leonard who have been a huge help to me personally and in my sailing career. All those people have each in their own way affected my life and taught me.

In 2000 I was on the *America One* team with Paul Cayard and John Kostecki. I got involved in *America One* through my relationship with John. He was with *Chessie Racing* (Maryland's

Entry in the 1997-1998 Whitbread Round the World Race) and he was a great influence. He's so methodical with his approach, such a really, really good sailor. The same goes for sailing with Paul Cayard. There are a lot of things that you learn just by watching and observing. Paul won the Whitbread in 1998 and John won it last time on *Illbruck*. These are pretty good teachers to be sailing with, and to be affiliated with, because right now they are the best people out there in our sport.

This last America's Cup, I sailed with Dennis Connor on the *Stars and Stripes*. I was trimming the mainsail for *America One*, I was tactician for *Stars and Stripes,* and I drove the tune-up boat, or practice boat, that we sparred against. So my evolution is there and hopefully the next time I'll steer one of those boats. That's kind of the process you have to go through."

Describe the America's Cup competition.

"The America's Cup, they call it the oldest competition in sports history. I think its 155 years old. Primarily it's a battle of technology and teamwork, and also who can come up with the fastest designed boat and put together the best team to sail it. The boats are engineering marvels. They're all carbon fiber. It's a very high technology on the hulls, the sails, the keel and the rudder, to have a boat that's just perfect in all conditions. That's what you're shooting for. Whether you actually get that is a different thing.

It's a long process to get to the regatta. *Stars and Stripes* trained for a year prior to the actual start and we were late in getting started. The team that won trained for three years and then there was the America's Cup race, so they had been together for four years in preparing for one event. It's a long commitment; it's a lot of work. It sounds like it's a lot of fun because you get to go sailing every day but the days are long. You spend 12 hours a day between workout and sailing and debriefing. It's a huge, a monumental task.

The races are 18 and a half miles. There are six legs to a race. The idea is to keep the racing close. It's a match race so there are only two boats. Your whole goal is just to beat your opponent. They are the same type of boat, the international America's Cup Class. It's all designed to a certain rule. The boats are 75 feet long, they weigh 55,000 pounds, and are exceptionally over-canvassed with their sail area. Relatively speaking they go very, very well upwind, and they're very close-angled boats. They're not very fast downwind. Generally if you were out racing a 75 foot boat on a weekend you'd sail with 20 or 22 people. In these boats you sail with 16 people. So teamwork is the other challenge. You're shorthanded at all times, so it makes it fun in a way, as well.

Annapolis is home to two of the most important sailboat design firms in the world, North Sails (which has provided full inventories of sails for both Volvo and America's Cup challenges) and Bruce Farr's design company. Bruce Farr and Associates of Annapolis is one of the leading designers of racing boats in the world. About the only thing he doesn't have on his resume is an America's Cup win. He was the lead designer for the *Oracle* team this last time. He was the lead designer in 2000 for *Young America.* He's been heavily involved and his boats are always right there and very competitive."

Gary Jobson mentioned the excitement of sailing at top speed into the night with the prospect of hitting a growler in the Southern ocean. What was that like for you?

"The leg of the Volvo Race that I did, the Cape Town to Sydney leg, was more mountains of ice instead of growlers. The Southern Ocean has a southerly breeze that goes around Antarctica and it's completely unimpeded. You have huge waves. They call them the Himalayas of the ocean. The waves are really big, about 40 to 50 feet, and really long. The previous time they'd done it they had hurricane-force winds and just ridiculously large breaking waves. We had a couple of days where we easily went over 425 to 430 miles. The record on that leg was 460 miles. Later on in the race, actually going across the Atlantic, they broke the monohull record, going over 484 miles in one day. We did, no problem, 25 to 30 knots down these waves, and the cool thing is, you get up on top of these things and you're standing up on top of the boat and you have the boat as a reference of how big the wave actually is. You get on top of this wave and the boat is 65 to 70 feet long and you look at the face of the wave in front of you and it's three times the length of the boat. When the boat starts breaking free it's an unbelievable rush of speed. It's just an incredible feeling."

Terry Hutchinson has now competed on three America's Cup campaigns including America One *in 2000 and* Stars and Stripes *in 2003. Most recently, he was in the key position of tactician with* Emirates, *Team New Zealand's America's Cup challenge in 2007. The team came up short, but for Terry Hutchinson and his dream of an America's Cup victory there is a new challenge from Emirates New Zealand, just over the horizon in 2009.*

Tom Weaver, Weaver Price

Sitting down to talk with Annapolis pro sailboat racer Tom Weaver in early 2007, the first thing I noticed was that he speaks with a warm Kiwi accent. A closer look revealed the quintessential lifelong world traveler.

"I've been living in the Annapolis area since 1991 when I first showed up here. It's home now and I'm married to a local girl. That kept me here. I grew up all over the place; my mother's from New Zealand, my father was a Civil Engineer building roads, bridges, airports, and dams. We moved all over the place: Kenya, Tanzania, Mauritius, Pakistan, Bahrain, Dubai, everywhere. I went to school on a long-wave radio once a week. My teacher was in South Africa. I had half an hour and my sister had half an hour and that was it. I met my teacher once in four years, I think. Essentially we were home-schooled, but we had a curriculum teacher that had us do tests and things like that. It worked out okay for me, I suppose. I think it was more a school of life, traveling to places we visited. Everybody says, 'Wow, that must have been an amazing childhood!' But it's the only one I know.

My family is from a small village just above Christ Church, New Zealand. Most of my family are scattered all over the north island now—Auckland and Wellington. I wasn't born there. I was born in Baghdad, Iraq. A lot of people know that and it's quite funny. It's made my life interesting for the past 10 years, traveling the way I do. But I've got a good relationship with the government authorities. They came and banged on my door about four or five years ago. I got back from an America's Cup campaign and they were waiting. They just wanted to say hi, and we all shook hands. Now I have a great time getting in and out of the country. I'm like a super VIP. The main question they always ask me is, 'Why were you born there?' I've always got the same smartass reply: 'I don't remember. I was really small.' That doesn't go over very well.

I sailed with my grandfather during the late 60's and early 70's in east Africa quite a lot, sailing down there. In the Middle East I sailed a lot with my father. He had a variety of boats. We started in 16 to 18 foot dinghies, then he got some little cruising keel boats. In the Middle East we'd sail on the Gulf. We'd do trips from Bahrain to Kuwait, then down to Dubai. These would be like four or five day trips sometimes. My mother sailed and brothers and sisters all sailed at various stages. None of them really sail any more. I was the only one who stuck with it. Dad always wanted me to get a real job, but here I am.

I did get a degree in Naval Architecture and Marine Engineering from University of Sunburn in England. I got packed off to England for about five or six years. My father pushed me kicking and screaming through university there. At that time the America's Cup thing was happening. The only real professional sailing was the America's Cup and there was a challenge that was starting to launch called the White Crusader Challenge and all my friends bailed off to do that. I felt that if I missed out on that that my career would be over, my life would be over. But I ended up sticking it out, did what dad told me to do, went to university. Afterwards came out and had a bit of catch up to do on the sailing side of things. But it was certainly a huge advantage later in my life to be able to fall back on something.

Somewhere I managed to jump on a boat and sail across the Atlantic to the Caribbean, and I let my hair grow long. I met my wife in Miami. She was at university down there. She asked me if I was a sailor and I said, 'No, not anymore. I'm a businessman.' And she said, 'Oh, you'll do.' A week later she found out that it was just that one week when I was trying not to be a sailor. I persuaded her to move up here and get a job locally and maybe move in together. So she did that and within a week I'd left, I was gone. I signed up with *PlayStation* to sail around the world. That took a year and a half. We ended up getting married about seven years ago and it's been great. We have a home here in Eastport.

I started at the front of the boat like most kids, doing bow and moving back. I was very fortunate to get involved in a couple of very good programs, particularly the one that brought me to the Chesapeake Bay. It was run by a gentleman by the name of Peter Gordon, who's Commodore of the Annapolis Yacht Club right now. He got a program going that turned out to be one of the defining programs of the mid 70's. I happened to be involved in that with Bruce Farr and Jeff Stag and all Annapolis-based people. They moved here for a reason, I ended up here too. I had the choice essentially to live wherever I wanted to live. I arrived here as a sailor, then one day I'm in Australia the next I'm in Europe. You have to be fairly central and there are quite a few Kiwis and some Australians who would try and do the pro sailing thing. But if you've got the 23 hour flight from New Zealand every other weekend to get to Europe it turns out to be pretty tough. The most central place to be is on the East Coast of the United States. Florida was a bit flat and Newport was too cold. Annapolis just turned out to be geographically the greatest place, with major airports nearby."

At 42 years old, with degrees in Naval Architecture and Mechanical Engineering in-hand Tom Weaver has a strong resume, not only as a sailor and team manager, but also as a designer in his own right. He helped Bruce Farr and his company, Farr International, develop several grand prix class sailing vessels including the Mumm 30, Corel 45 and Farr 40. Tom and fellow Annapolis sailor/designer Mick Price have started their own design firm, Weaver/Price. And, having already spent five years as team manager of the Mascalzone Latino America's Cup campaign, he continues to work as a consultant to major sailing race teams around the world.

"I'm much more involved in the management in these large campaigns now. Like anything else in sports, you wouldn't recognize it from 20 to 30 years ago; the level of professionalism, the amount of technology required to compete. It's very heavily reliant on technology and on team sports. If you compare sailing to NASCAR and pro football, NASCAR, as well as Formula One, is very technologically oriented; but in the motor sports you only need one driver. Football has not really much technology involved but requires a whole team. So sailing at the level of America's Cup or the average Grand Prix Campaign combines both. You have to have top technology and you need multi-talented, multi-skilled, team-oriented people.

It was fortunate I came through at the right age. I learned little bits of everything. I'm not particularly good at any one thing but I do know a lot about all the pieces that go together. I think that makes me quite a good manager and a good consultant.

My passion has been some of the Unlimited Catamaran-style sailing—I just like to go fast with no limits and no rules. I did a bunch of races up and down the East Coast of the States on the Beach Cats. We'd go from Miami Beach to Virginia Beach on a 21 Beach Cat, me and a very good friend of mine, Ricky Deppe. We didn't have a clue what we were doing the first time and off we went. We had a series of misadventures. We got there. We arrived. Oh man, that whole deal was two weeks.

My wife had just graduated university, so I said, 'Hey! Would you like to come on a beach holiday? We're going to stop at 12 beaches up and down the coast.' She said, 'That sounds great!' I think she got to beach 10 before she packed it in and said, 'This is crazy.' We were trudging in and out of hotels. We needed shore support for that one. We sank the boat, we broke the mast, we got lost, we ran out of food, we ran out of wind, we got flipped upside down in the middle of the Gulf Stream in 30 knots of wind.

We had little rescue EPIRBs (Emergency Position-Indicating Beacons) that we could have used if we wanted to pull them, but once we'd done that we'd have been out of the race. After 24 hours we had run out of water, and it was funny because that leg had started at night, so we hadn't put sunscreen on. By noon the next day we were just fried, we'd run out of water and food. Here we were, 30 miles offshore in 30 foot waves, upside down, with not really any chance of getting the boat upright. We were starting to think of pulling this little button and I was like, 'Man, this is gonna hurt,' because people are going to say you had to pull the button. And then, it was bizarre, a big wave came and rolled the boat upright just as we were about to pull the button. We sat and we contemplated it for about five minutes, exhausted. Then we sailed it into the beach.

The boat was all broken. All the beams had broken off. It was just north of Daytona Beach and there was a bike rally, Bike Week was going on. We pull up onto the beach with identical dry suits with these EPIRBs hanging off us. We go bang on this door and there were all these bikers lying asleep all over this porch. With swollen tongues and sunburned faces we said, 'Wee-nee-thum-watha!' They rallied and they came down with straps and hacksaws and patched our boat up. We pulled up the last 12 miles and managed to get to the finish... just in time to put some sunscreen on and sail off again for the next 100 miles! Fabulous, fabulous racing!"

12

Activists

John Flood, South River Federation

Beyond sport and entertainment, rest and relaxation, there is another Chesapeake Bay extra-curricular activity known as "activism." Activists are people who dedicate their lives to "service," creating opportunities to do something helpful for somebody other than themselves. Just like sailing, kayaking or crewing a sailboat for a weekend race, activism engages a variety of skills including team work, intuition, resourcefulness, safety, communication, and dedication. The correlation between selflessness and selfishness directly reflects the overall success or failure, not just of an individual, but for our society as a whole. A friend of mine used to say, 'You're either juice or you're a drain' meaning we have the chance to make a contribution to our society or be self-centered and only look out for number one.

Participation is the first tenet of citizenship in a working democracy. Citizenship requires that everyone plays a part and that everyone gives back. Citizenship means reaching out beyond ourselves and our immediate families to contribute to what Thomas Jefferson referred to as 'the common good.'

Just how severe are the problems we face in our society, in our environment? How imminent are threats to our safety and to our health? Are there enough resources to feed, house, and employ everyone on our planet? Is it possible to equip everyone with modern conveniences, such as microwave ovens, cell phones, and automobiles? What kind of world will that be? More simply, is there enough clean water and clean air to go around? Can we afford to squander anymore of our resources? How are our resources, our finite capital, best invested?

The environmental health issues we face are as immediate as the rising cost of war, inflation, spiritual and cultural bankruptcy. The choices we make affect generations to come, including the next one already with us. Denial and inaction have immediate consequences.

But there is good news, too. In our lifetime we have seen amazingly positive things happen. The information superhighway has made the planet a smaller place. Freedom of speech is alive and well on the internet. A larger picture of our interconnectedness has formed and now the task of recognizing and facing up to our own fears is unavoidable. But these challenges are not insurmountable. Solutions are all around us. By putting our collective heads together the answers will be found. Many of those answers will come from the grassroots, from everyday people—from activists.

The voices we hear in this chapter have all chosen to dedicate their time and resources in service of the greater good. They remind us just how fragile our environment is, and of our power to swallow resources at an alarming rate. Activists such as these have chosen to be fuel for the fire of inventiveness, and to confront the major issues and choices that we face as a society at this auspicious time in history. These highly motivated and committed people work to ensure a safe and healthy environment for their families and for the generations to come.

John Flood, a local who grew up on Harness Creek in Annapolis, is one such activist. He has dedicated thousands of hours as a volunteer, protecting and restoring the watershed in his own backyard. In 2004, John Flood was honored by CBF as a "Conservationist of the Year."

John set up the Harness Creek Project, securing a 30

acre oyster sanctuary lease on his home waterway, raising funds and donated services to help CBF build reefs on it, while encouraging waterfront property owners to grow oysters in buckets hung from their docks, for stocking the reefs. With John's assistance and experience, property owners on a near-by creek replicated the project using "Flood buckets" to grow oysters. He's been a volunteer board member for both the Severn River Association and the Severn River Commission, and a founding member of the South River Federation. John Flood is, in a way, a folk hero in the Annapolis region. And in the spring of 2000, John Flood took Voices *correspondents Claudia Donegan and Dr. Robin Jung out on his skiff, to check the progress of the Harness Creek oyster recovery project.*

"Let's get in the boat and go for a ride!" John said. "I showed you these, right? These are oyster spat that are stuck on shell. This is real habitat here. We're talking habitat here. Right now I'm trying to replace the oysters we took out of the buckets and put out on the bar that the South River Federation purchased with Chesapeake Bay Trust money. Those oysters were housed in these buckets. There are about 200 of them hung under docks on the creek. Once we had a place to put them we didn't want to keep them on the creek because outside oysters might have Dermo and MSX (diseases associated with oyster mortalities). We determined that it would be better to put them out on the river and to plant them. We're using certified stock only, on the creek.

These oysters were struck onto shell at Horn Point Lab on the Eastern Shore last year. They're about six months old now. You can see that some of these half oyster shells have as many as 10, 12, 15 oysters attached. Now these whole shells that I'm culling out and putting in this basket are going to be reused to replace the oysters that we count into the buckets. Those buckets have holes drilled in them that are an inch and a half in diameter. If we put all of the shell in those buckets a lot of it would fall out and sink into the mud, and the oysters would smother. So I'm taking the big shells and we're going to put them into the buckets. All the smaller shell scrap will be put into mesh bags and then into these Taylor floats at the dock here. Even though it looks just like a bunch of shell scrap, they're lots and lots of oysters attached to these little pieces. They'll grow into adults. Lose some, but some will grow big enough and we'll eventually add them to the stock here on the creek.

The goal is to do this every year. Under this dock is a warehouse for these bags of shell, which are produced by volunteers who actually take the dried clean shell and put it into these mesh bags. Work parties do it all through the late spring and summer over at Horn Point. They need more volunteers. We hope to get a whole lot more of this from Horn Point. So we need to provide volunteers to bag them up."

What are the names of the buckets that are hanging off the pier?

"People are calling them Flood Buckets but I didn't give them that name," John said. "There are lots of holes in these buckets, as many as we can get. In fact, there's about 150 holes in each bucket. Our buckets are more hole than bucket. If we were to drop these oysters in a bucket and hang it under a dock and didn't drill the holes, the silt and algae and oyster droppings that would accumulate in the bucket would eventually literally smother them. But with the bucket, it's self-maintaining and you can easily clean it and aid the process by just pulling the bucket up and shaking it around, plunging it in and out of the water.

Let's dump them out on the dock, so you can see what's in the bucket. You can take out your parasites like the flat worm. I'll try to find one and show it to you. Here we go—this flatworm is something that I knew nothing about, even though I grew up here and I'd thought I'd seen most of the critters. The flatworm is a very inconspicuous critter. He looks kind of like a flat tongue without a head attached, like a piece of decaying wood fungus on the side of a decaying tree that's still standing. They're like a little muscle that crawls along a flat surface. Then they get to the opening of the oyster shell, which I believe is called the mantle, and they slip in that opening and get inside the oyster.

There are lots of things that graze the oyster bar. I don't pretend to be an expert on all these forms of life. I'll bet you that Bill Goldsborough and Stu Harris at the Bay Foundation and John Page Williams could give you a lot more detail. But the reef structure of an oyster bar, particularly the vertical structure, provides habitat for all kinds of things. A good fisherman is going to know where the hard bottoms are and where the oyster piles are because that's where he's going to catch his fish.

We had 30 inch rockfish hanging around this dock last summer, literally swimming around in between the floats. I doubt if you're going to believe this, I came down one night and heard a splashing noise down here. I turned on the light on the dock and there was a rockfish trying to jump into my Taylor floats. So I ran up and got my neighbor. He came down with his buddy, who was here to fish, and I believe had come from a distance to fish. He was very excited and I'm not sure that this was such a good thing for him to see. To come down here and see that I had my own pet rockfish that within a few days would come to me when I would come to the dock. If I reached overboard and splashed my hand in the water he would swim up to me and let me pet him. That's why I said you wouldn't believe me, but it's true. He hung around for three or four days and then I would give him a little shove after I'd pet him and he would scoot out into the creek and swim around in a very frolicking fashion. He'd come back, and then after a few days he just left. But I don't think he liked the time my neighbor came down to show other people and he got his fishing net out and landed the fish onto the dock. I think that the fish got a little bit upset when that happened."

Where did this work begin, and how far back does it go for you?

"I think I was born into my epiphany for the river because I was lucky enough to be born on South River right across the river at Colonial Londontown," John said. "My family's property is there and we spent lots of time down on the Shore. My granddad was one of the earliest chairmen of the Fish and Game commission. He was an avid quail hunter and trout fisherman. He liked to fish on the river here as well as in saltwater. He took me fishing quite a bit. I learned to duck hunt when I was a kid.

The river is a great playground. It's a resource, and it used to be a wonderfully healthy one. Anybody could swim anytime in the summertime and come out clean. You couldn't swim now without taking a shower afterwards because we have so many algae in the water.

The resource is not ours. We learned in Boy Scouts some pretty basic precepts which are good guidelines for life. One of the most basic ones was that you should leave your campsite cleaner than you find it. Well, we sure are not doing that. I witnessed this campsite being trashed. We didn't really realize what we were doing. It wasn't purposely done. But when I was eight years old this river was crystal clear to the bottom in eight feet of water. We had thick seaweed beds. We had loads of crabs. We didn't bother with hard crabs. If you went crabbing it was assumed you were soft crabbing. If you caught some hard crabs, which was unavoidable, and you wanted some hard crabs later, you'd have them before you'd have a soft-crab supper. Now hard crabs are $120 a bushel at Memorial Day!

We also didn't have people. I don't mind the people so much because I'm a people person. But the impact that human beings are having on the watershed is tremendous, and in many ways irreversible. We clear forest cover to put in subdivisions. We pave 20 percent of that ground. It's permanently paved. Sure the streetscape will grow back in and the tree canopy will fill in the yards and things like that, but that watershed is not functioning properly. Permanently. All that water that's going to escape through the storm drain system should percolate into the ground. A lot of it should evaporate into the canopy as the trees and shrub layer use it. A lot of it should be stored in the ground to serve as the reservoir for the underground springs, which are basically the lifeblood of the Chesapeake Bay. Instead now all that runoff escapes in one big flush in the storm. And so we've turned what was the medicine for the bay, groundwater, recharged rainwater that soaked into the ground, we've turned that into poison—runoff. You can't take someone's medicine away and give them poison instead."

John pointed to the flatworm he had showed me earlier, still sitting on the top of a dock piling.

"There's your flatworm. This flatworm will die a painful death on this copper piling cover from heat from the sun. There's your poison.

We need to get into the watershed, not just into the water. We need to get up into the land around the watershed and clean it back up. We need to put the campsite back in shape. What I lost when the algae blooms started is something that can't be measured. In 1964, the seaweed beds had gotten so thick that we had huge mats wash up on the shorelines. The seaweed expanded so much that I believe it had maxed out its habitat. I didn't even know the names of the seaweeds then. Now I know a lot more about them. We considered them to be a kind of pain in the neck. We had to pull out the seaweed in our swimming area along the shore. We'd pull the seaweed off the beach in order to kick the sand. All native. They claimed we had the Eurasian Milfoil and it was in the bay. But the big mistake came when the state decided to do some eradication based on the fact that we had Milfoil. It shouldn't be called seaweed. The common name is submersed aquatic vegetation. Whether it's submersed depends on the tide and the depth that it's growing in. But submersed aquatic vegetation is seaweed. The state decided to take action. We had people that were paid full time to study seaweed and map it. Those maps are valuable resource maps now to locate where historic habitats were. The solution was to issue permits and to do some controlled removal with herbicide. The main choice of herbicide was the 2-4D pellet formula that had a 20 year release. Well 2-4D is not a very pleasant product. I don't know all the chemicals in it, but it takes 20 years for it to dissipate. What happened was they dumped the 2-4D... and the seaweed that they were killing with the 2-4D was the only thing balancing the excessive nutrients in the water column. Then add nitrogen and phosphorous, mostly from runoff and from septic systems that were failing. Plus farming practices in the 50's and 60's were just getting into the use of large-scale chemical fertilizer applications.

So we don't have any storm water management laws, we're paving like crazy, we're taking down forests and building houses. The river is responding. It's spreading its seaweed beds to accommodate the ever-increasing nutrient loads. The 2-4D goes in and the nutrients are still available in the water column, only more now because the seaweed is dead. It isn't there to take up the nutrients. So algae gets into the water column.

Once algae started to grow it began to cloud the water. As soon as that happened the seaweed that was left lost its sunlight. The more it died back the more nutrient release there was, not just from the dying seaweed but from the nutrients that the seaweed used to uptake. So this nutrient imbalance created this algae bloom that we've had ever since. It was like a curtain was drawn across this river and the bay.

We began to have increased shoreline erosion, as the seaweed beds weren't absorbing the wave energy on the nearshore region. We began to have more sediment deposition in deeper waters because of these sediments. Imagine that the sun disappeared for years. What do you think your lawn would look like? It'd be a dustbowl. So imagine that the air became water. All of that soil becomes exposed with nothing to hold it down. It's underwater and it begins to move about. Well, the course particles settle deep into the mud and the real fine particles, the silts which are the most harmful and grow the few-est things, they settle on the surface. So we smothered the bay by killing the grasses, and we never got it kick-started again.

Then in the early 70's we had several hurricanes, Agnes being the most prominent. Agnes kicked this river's butt pret-ty bad. Now I know that it was hard on the whole bay system but this river really suffered. It took months for the water to clear. By the time that it had cleared we had silt that covered all the oyster beds.

The bay has been trying to recover from that ever since. But with the chemical herbicides in the water in this county and then the turbidity problems that were caused by Agnes, the bottom was scoured. The wave action was severe. 2-4D that had been locked up in the bottom sediments was re-re-leased, and it was spread. That is what I believe we're still try-ing to recover from. Now I don't have any scientific evidence to prove any of this. But it just makes sense to me that dumping herbicide on seaweed beds is the worst thing you can do. We didn't know any better then."

At what point were did you start to catch on to the im-portance of the oysters?

"We need to get the algae out of the water, and the big-gest vacuum cleaner that we can find is an oyster. He never stops working. Unless he gets really cold or unless the water gets so filthy dirty with silt that he will shut down for a while, and take a break. But generally the oyster is at the ready and waiting to get to work and will do as much work as conditions allow.

Interesting enough they grew on the edge of seaweed beds when I was a kid. I remember learning later, when I was learning more about seaweed, which by then was gone, that we would have oysters struck on the stalks of the redhead grass on the outer edge of the bed. When we would go out the outer edge if we kept pulling seaweed there to make our swim area, we would slice our hands. There's nothing to a seaweed plant that could cut you. But when it's on the edge of the deeper habitat which supports an oyster bed...and then later on in the summer the stalks would get weighted down by the growing spat which had attached and they would fall over and lay with the plant on the bottom. We'd have a nice edge of oysters filtering the algae out of the water column right next to the seaweed bed. Very symbiotic relationship.

If we can get the algae knocked down, the seaweed will come back. There's seaweed right on that mudflat right there, that will expand its habitat if we can reduce the amount of algae in the water column and increase light penetration to the growing plants.

At the same time we killed our seaweed beds, we over-harvested our oysters and these storms came along and decimated our oyster population even more. When you're at one or two percent of historic oyster populations, you can't expect your oysters to be healthy. And the ones that are left are in severe stress, or the population would be expanding. So our biggest fight now will be disease and crossing the threshold to higher water quality, which will make it easier for everything."

Describe the disease problem.

"Dermo. It's a parasite. I don't know enough about it to tell you much more than that. I learned yesterday from wetland scientist Drew Koslow that Dermo won't kill an oyster until it reaches adult size, market size. I don't understand the complexities of that mechanism. It's a very complex parasite and it's a simple organism, the oyster. We've got a lot to learn. We're going to learn it in these gardens that are hanging under these docks. We're going to get the neighbors participating. My approval rate from people I've asked has been 100 percent. Nobody has said no yet. These buckets are out of the way. They're doing a good thing for the creek. They're kind of neat for kids to pull up and look into. The docks are here so let's try to make some habitat out of them.

I think that compared to when I was a kid, that there's a

lot more general awareness of our impact on the environment and the desire to preserve some of the natural world. Because we have children and they do have a right to it. And I hope that they'll be good stewards. But if we don't protect these resources from a grassroots level, then our kids aren't going to appreciate these things and it's going to just disappear. Well, that'll be up to them."

John Rodenhausen, Captain and Educator, Chesapeake Bay Foundation

John Rodenhausen seems eternally optimistic and enchanted about his life and work on the Chesapeake Bay. His work over many years with the Chesapeake Bay Foundation is reflected in a new web-based program called the Student Action Network. The program goes above and beyond simply hosting field trips to the outdoors. Through it kids learn to get active, developing intangible skills such as commitment, dedication, and a lifelong concern for their environment. John and his wife Francis recently welcomed two beautiful babies into the world. Now, more than ever, John Rodenhausen understands just what's at stake for the kids and for the environment. When we met at the Voices *studio in early spring 2007, I asked John to talk about what sparked the environmental ethic in him when he was a kid.*

"I was introduced to the Chesapeake when I was about 12. I started going to a summer camp up in the northern bay and I learned how to sail. It was a YMCA camp just outside of Chestertown, right on the main stem of the bay, that changed my life forever. Early mornings we spent time watching the herons fly. There were legends about a bald eagle that would fly. Hardly anybody ever saw that eagle. Now you go up there and you'd see 10 or 15 in just one afternoon. Being on the water you realize that there is something so very awesome about the power of it, of how we're all attracted to it. It's always just been a huge, powerful influence for me. It was during my time there that I started a small environmental lesson for 200 students. When I wanted to get information about how to set something like that up, I contacted the Chesapeake Bay Foundation.

I moved here to take a job working on boats. I had lived mostly in Pennsylvania, which is somewhat landlocked. When I came here it was kind of like someone had opened the flood-gates and it was a huge playground. I started working on the water. It's a relatively small community of people who actually work on the water. I met a lot of great folks who just happened to work for CBF. At one point they offered me a job as an edu-cator, and it seemed to marry the best of both worlds: working with kids and working on the water.

Working as a captain for CBF was a real eye-opening experience for me. I got to work with up to 4,000 kids every single year. When I started running field trips with these stu-dents my most favorite trips were working with kids who were doing restoration projects. They'd come out with their oysters or their underwater grasses that they had been growing in their classroom, and they'd really gotten attached to them. They had names for their oysters. One little girl actually cried when she was dumping her oysters overboard onto a sanctu-ary reef. She was that attached to them. I thought to myself, 'There's really something to this. This is really having an im-pact on these students.' So, I was looking for a way to be a big-ger part in that. A way to develop longer lasting relationships with the teachers who were creating this programming for the students, and also to be a resource for these students so they knew there was a place that they could go to get involved.

Students have an amazing, almost immediate love for something like the bay and the water and their backyards and the streams that run through their backyards. It's their play-ground and an amazing resource for learning. Our restoration programs offered a lot of that for these students. I worked with our partners at the Department of Natural Resources and Horn Point Lab and Virginia Institute of Marine Science.

The program that we now have at CBF is a little bit more comprehensive. It includes those restoration projects, but it also gives students the opportunity to get funding for their own projects. It gives them an opportunity to get involved with advocacy. It gives them opportunities to connect and network with other students who are doing the same thing. It's really powerful to have your peers involved.

One of the other neat things that we noticed in these programs is that it takes confidence, leadership, the ability to speak in public and the ability to be compelling with your story for these kids to do these projects. By any definition in any profession those are great leadership skills. How can these students then get better jobs, get the jobs that they want with better pay? How can they move up and get into great occupations, great professions, just by being involved with the environment? We've really taken the environment and tried to use it as a context for leadership.

CBF started working with students and teachers about 35 years ago at a little cabin just outside Annapolis on Meredith Creek. We have always thought that by getting kids out into the outdoors they're going to love it, they're going to have fun and they're going to want to take care of it. They're going to increase their passion for the environment. So our goal with the Student Leadership Program is to give these kids the training and resources that they need in order to take action in their community.

The internet has really provided an amazing tool for us. Over the last year and a half we've developed what's called the Student Action Network. This is a comprehensive listing of resources, trainings extending over the entire Chesapeake Bay region. This is available 24 hours a day so kids can go there any day of the week. They can learn how to build their skills. They can connect with their community. They can learn how to take action and get funds for taking those actions. We're also helping them to get jobs in the environmental world. They can post their resumes on the website as well. It includes blogs, and calendars of local watershed groups in their specific area.

The Education Department at CBF has, for years, promoted experiential education. Books are a fascinating, wonderful, and comprehensive way to learn a lot of information. But there is something about being outdoors, feeling the mud between your toes, feeling the wind in your hair, and having the water all around you all day, everyday, that is just going to change you. These 'immersion' courses that we offer are all about creating that passion, creating that drive, and just making you so fired up about what's going on out there, it's going to change your life! I've seen it in tens of thousands of kids. It's a powerful resource.

One of the places we take the kids is to our Fox Island study center. There's nobody around except for the animals that live and breathe there. You catch crabs, you see oysters, you see Peregrine falcons diving at 200 miles an hour, and you see arrowheads left on the Shore from thousands of years ago. That's our classroom, the Chesapeake Bay.

The education staff at CBF is amazing. They are one of the most diverse groups of people you'll ever find. We have people who have been teaching here for 10 or 15 years, and folks who are fresh out of college. Every single one of them has a unique drive to work with students and to create experiences that will change your life. You're going to find people who have a science background, who have a history background, maybe a legal background. There are people from all over the place, people who have sailed on schooners and are taking that experience and bringing it to the bay. You'll also find people who have worked in the marshes and the swamps all over the world. They're bringing that experience to the Chesapeake Bay. It's fascinating to watch these people work because knowing them is one of the single most life-changing experiences you'll ever have.

Within that diverse culture of CBF's Education Department we have been very fortunate to work with a number of traditional watermen, people who have fished the water for their entire lives. What these folks bring to our education department is something that you really can't find in a book or a classroom. These are people who have hundreds of years of tradition passed down from father to son, from mother to daughter. What these guys have learned is how to read the tides, how to watch the weather, how to recognize when the crabs are coming or if they aren't. As much as they know about crabs, they'll be the first to tell you they only know three things about crabs: they come, they go, and they bite. That's what they know.

To sit and hear these guys tell the stories about what it was like growing up at a time when you could actually make a decent living on the water is just spellbinding. It's very sad because one of the true treasures of working with these folks is that their culture is slowly dissipating, each time a wave hits the shore of our eroding islands. So for us to be connected with these folks who can touch the lives of thousands of students is invaluable. Every time I heard these folks like Charles Parks, Jesse Marsh, Eric Marshall, Dallas Bradshaw, and all the other captains in Tangier Sound... it's changed me. It's changed the way that I look at the bay and our culture. It's a culture and a heritage that I really feel is important to preserve.

No two days are the same on the water. The weather is different, the tide is different, the animals that are around you are different. We get up with a group of students at sunrise and everyone's rubbing their eyes and they're kind of grumpy. They're not happy about being up that early, it's kind of cold out and they've got to put their jackets on. We'll go out and sit in the middle of a marsh, just sit there and watch the sunrise. Something happens during that brief little time. That big ball of fire comes up over the horizon and starts your day. That magic light, that magic hour that everybody talks about when the light is golden and rose-colored. You see the reflection off the student's eyes and you can see something is changing within their brains. They are remembering this. They are feeling this. They are using all their senses to feel what's going on, to feel connected with it. You're going to find that as you go through the day, they're thinking about that. Then when the sun goes down at the end of the day they feel like they've done something. They went out, they learned, they saw, they felt, they played, they ran, they jumped, they cruised through the marsh on their bellies. Whatever it was, as odd as that may sound, it was some of the most incredible experiences that some of these students will ever have.

There have been a number of times on the bay when you can see a storm coming across the water. We've been out there with our boats, running in just before the storm, and you feel that 15 to 20 degree temperature change as the front moves through. You feel the wind and the kids are just like, 'Yeaaahhh!' It is unbelievable how quickly things can change on the water. You watch the lightening strikes, you watch the waterspouts, you watch the tide come and go. It can be a real crazy thrill ride. You're coming across the sound or the bay and you're in big waves and watching to see what's going on. You just don't know what's going to happen. But...you always get home."

Claudia Donegan, Tributary Strategies Team Coordinator, Maryland Department of Natural Resources

Voices of the Chesapeake Bay *co-founder Claudia Donegan is just crazy about the bay. Claudia has a knack for seeking out informative and entertaining opportunities, or, as Iggy Pop would say, she has a 'lust for life.' When I met Claudia and her husband Mike Coleman they were opening their Homeport farm house on a regular basis, to huge community gatherings. Being a part of that great, diverse group of welcoming friends has been an inspiration to the whole* Voices of the Chesapeake Bay *concept.*

Claudia is also a person who has a knack for making others feel important and valued. She's always interested and inquiring about what you've been up too, what you know, and what you feel about what you know. Her husband Mike is just as resourceful, inspiring and fun to be around. He's an avid sailor and a proponent for smart leadership and a healthy bay. They have two children, Eva and Fiona. If that isn't a good reason for optimism and activism, I don't know what is!

Claudia is a Tributary Strategies Team Coordinator at the Maryland Department of Natural Resources. I love it when she calls and offers to take us all out on a canoe trip, or to wade into one of the bay's tributaries. Her familiar group emails keeping the community abreast of what is going on socially and environmentally are a welcome sight. We sat down to talk about the work of the Maryland Department of Natural Resources Tributaries Strategies Teams, and about her life, one afternoon in the spring of 2007.

"I am a Tributary Team Coordinator assigned to a few basins: the Patuxent River Basin which includes seven counties, the Middle Potomac Basin which sort of starts at the Monocacy River banks and goes north to Damascus, to the edges of the Patuxent and east to the Piscataway Creek, and the Western

Shore Basin which starts south of the Patapsco and runs down to the tip of Calvert County and west to the Patuxent. Every tributary team in Maryland meets monthly. We have a Website and on it there's a map of each basin, to give you an idea of where you might find a tributary team. We also list the next meeting.

We do outreach to local governments, citizens, farmers, and businesses, regarding nutrient pollution in our tributaries. We invite the public to our meetings, and people appointed by the Governor, and they help us work on environmental policy that strengthens the restoration efforts. We also do environmental best-management pilot projects, such as rain gardens or techniques for low-impact development. We'll try to get grants and help a community put a pilot project in to demonstrate ways people can go about their business without polluting in the ways they have in the past. We also put on a lot of educational forums, summit meetings about different topics that are directed towards water pollution.

These meetings are open to the public, but if somebody wants to take it another step they can actually apply to be a tributary team member. They send us their resume and we forward it up the chain. These meetings are staffed by government employees like myself, and they're sanctioned by the Governor. They're part of Maryland's efforts to restore the bay. So you can actually be appointed to the tributary team.

Some of our most recent accomplishments: the Lower Western Shore Tributary Team initiated a proposal that they ran through the Capital newspaper, and now we have a venue to talk about the bay every two weeks. It's a section of the newspaper that's in color and it's supposed to inspire, inform, and direct people toward activities with regard to the Chesapeake; it's called Our Bay."

How did you catch the 'bay bug.'

"I'm from Baltimore originally. I moved Annapolis when I was six, grew up on the bay in Bay Ridge. My father was a

Chesapeake Bay pilot. His name was Captain Roger Donegan. He went in as a teenager, used to row out to the ships as an apprentice. If you were an apprentice for, I think, six or nine years, you worked your way up to being certified as a captain of a ship. He moved the ships up and down the bay from Lynnhaven inlet, which is down in Virginia, up to Baltimore Harbor. Pilots are the official shipping navigators for the Chesapeake Bay. When a foreign vessel enters the bay, they aren't allowed to drive their ship around willy-nilly. The bay is very shallow, has a lot of shoals, and very uncertain topography. Pilots know that topography. They know how to navigate through the bay with these 1,000 foot ships, through the spans of the Bay Bridge and the Chesapeake Bay Bridge Tunnel.

They used to get on a ship for 13 hours, right up on the bridge for that length of time. But now they split that and they have eight hour shifts. Pilots come up on a launch and they get on a ladder and they climb up to the ship. That's dangerous—in the course of my father's career they lost a couple of pilots in bad weather, who had fallen off the ladder between the ship and the launch. You know, you've still got to get on the ship whether it's good or bad weather.

They met people from all over the world. I was just telling someone the other day about an invasive species, and I said I remember growing up and having a tarantula in my parents' bedroom—it crawled out of my father's pilot bag off a banana ship. And I'm sure there were other bugs he brought home off those ships.

I did tell him I wanted to be a pilot at one point, and he had a fit. He said, 'I don't want you to be the only woman on a Greek freighter.' Well, ha-ha! Now there are plenty of women pilots.

I grew up in downtown Annapolis and went to St. Mary's High School. That's where I really started getting sensitized to the environment, living around all the boats and boatyards. I worked in boatyards most of my teen years, then went to college in Ohio. I studied geology and was planning on a career in petroleum or mining. I ended up working for a big bridge-building company when I first came out of school. I did concrete testing on the concrete that was being poured for the Metro in DC. That was so not my personality. I had very little interaction with people and the environment...and so I didn't pursue that career.

When I was in school I had interned at the Chesapeake Bay Foundation, and that's really where I got my bay bug. I liked the idea of environmental advocacy, education and outreach. I liked the people. At the time we really spent a lot of time interacting with the bay and every aspect of it. So you really just couldn't ever turn your back on it again after what you learned about the bay and all the little idiosyncrasies and little facets about it. I was volunteering with CBF when a position opened in the public communications office, and I jumped on it. I did press releases and festivals and fairs. I did activities for kids.

At CBF I started an outreach program that went into communities and focused on streams. Nobody was really getting people riled up about the little tiny streams that run behind grocery stores and things like that. So we started an outreach and education program that went in and worked with a school in their own community for two days. They spent the whole two days on their local stream, something they could walk to. One day it was stream ecology and learning about the dynamics of streams and how they work themselves down into the watershed. Another day was a conservation project that would enhance the stream. Usually it was storm drain painting, stenciling storm drains or picking up trash or planting trees. We were the first people to get these stencils made that said, 'Don't dump. Chesapeake Bay drainage.' We learned about it at a conference, me and a co-worker. So we had them made for the bay and we did them all over the place.

I've noticed that streams are much more sensitive to land use than we thought originally. Just a little housing development on the east bank of a stream, maybe if it's just 20 or 30 houses, can totally degrade a stream. I don't want to say overnight, but pretty much between the process of building something and then the impact of the people that own the land after that. Washing their cars, pouring off cleaning fluids or oil... a stream gets degraded very easily. If five to 10 percent of the land around the watershed becomes impervious, it really starts affecting it. When I say impervious, I mean that 10 percent of the land is covered with some substrate like concrete or asphalt, or some turf or rooftops.

These streams are a linear ecosystem and what starts at the top, like the little May flies and the fish, all spirals downstream in the ecosystem. If you take some species out of the food chain, out of the stream, you're going to eliminate some downstream, until you work yourself right out into your rivers. If there aren't any stone flies or May flies, eventually there will be no rockfish in the bay. Those streams influence those rivers that influence the bay. It's a food chain reaction."

What other strategies do the Tributary Teams use to protect and improve these small local waterways?

"My Middle Potomac Tributary Team initiated a project that focused on outreach to the urban public about lawn care and fertilizer. They worked with the Scotts Company and some other fertilizer companies and the Chesapeake Bay Program, and have come up with a memorandum of understanding. When we got the attention of Scotts they actually came to us and asked what we wanted, what would make us happy regarding their products and the bay. We talked about how we have high-phosphorus soils here, and we don't need fertilizer that has phosphorus to get our grass to grow. In fact, the soils here are so packed with phosphorus that it moves out of the soil, enters the tributaries, and ends up in the bay.

Scotts is going to cut their phosphorus in the fertilizer—not just in the bay states but nationally—by 50 percent. They'll be able to measure the pound-reduction of phosphorus going into the bay because they know exactly how many bags they sell in this region. The most interesting part of this is that they have agreed to do a point-of-sale education campaign for homeowners, about how their lawns impact water quality in their area. They're going to have a 'Top Five' or 'Top 10' list that people need to consider to help local water quality. That'll be like a tear-off, right where you grab your bag of fertilizer. Their merchandisers will actually maintain and supply the educational material.

It was the Tributary team that generated the forum and started this ball rolling. We got a grant, we brought in people who had already banned phosphorus containing fertilizers, people from Minnesota and Wisconsin. We got them to come and tell us why they did it, how they did it, and what results they're seeing. We invited the industry. Just bringing all those people to the table was effective in getting action.

The Tributary Teams do a lot of fun stuff, too. We have wade-ins that we sponsor throughout the state. A wade-in is like an old-fashioned Southern baptism, except that the focus is water clarity. You get a group of people together, you have some lunch. All of a sudden everybody gets in a line and they walk out slowly in the water, together. Hopefully, everyone has white shoes on. What were doing is we're walking out until we can no longer see our toes.

This ritual was initiated by Bernie Fowler, the famous Senator from Calvert County who got very upset with the degradation of the water quality in the Patuxent River. He said he didn't need any scientists, he didn't need fancy probes. Once a year he was going to walk out with his white shoes on. When he couldn't see his shoes anymore, he would take a measurement. That would tell him whether the water was getting better. So we do that with groups of people throughout Maryland. We probably had 15 or 16 wade-ins this year, with groups of 8 to over 100.

A wade-in isn't a true scientific measurement, but we also compile Secchi disk data. Scientists at the Maryland Department of Natural Resources go out and use this instrument, a black and white disc. They lower it in the water and when they can't see the white part of the disc any longer they measure the length of the rope. We correlated the Secchi disc depths with the wade-in depths, and they were pretty similar. Both measurements pretty much follow the amount of rain we've had. Because when it rains we get a lot of runoff and lot of dirt coming off of the land. So we have rainy years and we have not so rainy years. The non-rainy years just happen to be better for the bay. They're better for the bay because we get a lot less runoff which carries oils and toxics and nutrients and all kinds of unwanted things into the water. In dry years we don't have that. We have a big rebound in the bay.

Lately with my Middle Potomac Team, we've been putting more emphasis on the individual home owner and their lawn care practices. The most important thing to the homeowners is to understand their individual impact—automobile exhaust is one of the biggest impacts they have on the Chesapeake Bay. Car exhaust has a lot of nitrogen in it that ends up in the bay. We also have a lot of people who apply way too much fertilizer to their lawn. They don't read the package and they do it before the rain, or they do it in the spring when it's better to do it in the fall. There are different things that homeowners do and it's amazing how they can affect local waterways.

We call a waterway 'local' when it's within a 10 to 15 minute walk from your house. I would pretty much guarantee that there isn't one person in Maryland who can't walk 15 minutes to some type of waterway, be it a culvert or a stream or a creek or a river. And it all ends up in the tributaries, then goes into the bay."

David O'Neill, Former Executive Director, Chesapeake Bay Trust

Project funding is needed to equip people embarking upon Chesapeake Bay restoration programs. David O'Neill, Executive Director of the Chesapeake Bay Trust, is an inspiration to citizen-activists throughout Maryland. The openness and camaraderie with which he welcomes and encourages community members eager to get involved is a major reason for the overall success of the Chesapeake Bay restoration effort. The Trust has given financial assistance to neighborhoods, schools, watershed groups, and conservation-minded organizations for over two decades. Since 1985 it has awarded grants supporting thousands of hands-on restoration programs, encouraging citizens to get their hands muddy and their feet wet. Through the tireless work and teambuilding skills of O'Neill and the rest of the staff, the Trust has grown into a wonderful success story. If you are a citizen-activist with a restoration project in mind for your neighborhood, organization or school, it's the folks at the Chesapeake Bay Trust whom you should call first.

In April of 2006, I met with David O'Neill at the Chesapeake Bay Trust offices in Annapolis to get a better understanding about the organization and the programs they offer.

"The Chesapeake Bay Trust is a private non-profit organization that collects private donations and then puts those donations out in grants," David explained. "We collect dollars and use those dollars to engage the public in activities that directly help the Chesapeake Bay and raise awareness about what can be done to help the bay. The Trust was created in 1985 by the Maryland General Assembly. Over the 21 year history of the organization we have been able to grant over 20 million dollars.

An important part of our fundraising each year is the

tax check-off program, Line 37 on the Maryland State income tax form. Donate $1, or $1,000, whatever amount you'd like. Those dollars are instantly deducted from your refund and are tax deductible. We receive roughly $600,000 a year because of the generosity of Marylanders who contribute, on average, around $25 per donation. $600,000 means literally 50 grants involving tens of thousands of kids and adults in projects that can make a difference in the Chesapeake Bay.

Marylanders have also shown an unwavering commitment to the Chesapeake Bay by buying bay license plates. The license plate program became the most popular license plate program of its kind in the nation, and now one in 10 Marylanders drive around with it on their car. As a result of the bay plate, we've been able to increase our grant making from a million and a half to close to four million dollars this year. Ninety cents of every dollar goes right out the door to our grant programs, our restoration programs, and our education programs. We work very hard to be efficient and effective with those contributions from the Chesapeake Bay license plates.

Back in the early 80's public officials did a significant analysis on what was causing the pollution in the Chesapeake Bay. They saw it degrade over time. One of the things they realized from that analysis was that we all contribute to the degradation of the bay. So what these forward-thinking leaders in the State House and the Legislature wanted to do was create an organization that would engage the public, make them more aware of the impact they were having and aware of what they could actually do to help the bay. The philosophy of the Chesapeake Bay Trust is to get as many people involved as we possibly can. So we will literally award grants as small as $25 all the way up to $200,000. Our theory has been to make it easy for folks to apply, and easy to get out in the field and experience these activities. Hopefully, people walk away from Trust-funded projects as real bay stewards, people that are going to focus they're own behavior in a way that's beneficial to the Chesapeake.

A couple of years ago we aligned all our grant programs

up with the key goals of the Chesapeake Bay 2000 Agreement. Our grant programs are designed to help advance those specific goals which were defined by the state governors, the Secretary of the EPA and the Mayor of the District of Columbia. That was our first step. The next step was to actually define the grant programs that help move those goals forward, and then to measure the impact those grants are having on the bottom line: are we improving the bay, or aren't we?

We now have eight grant programs, all designed to get the public involved in practices that can help the Chesapeake Bay and raise public awareness. Our smallest one encourages individuals, organizations, and groups to come to the Trust and apply for mini grants. For instance, there might be an educational field trip to get students out on the Bay. There might be a habitat project on the grounds of a school to get students involved in hands-on activities that strengthen what they're learning in the classroom, so that they have a better appreciation for what can be done in their own backyards to help it. Or there might be a small rain-garden project in a community that wants to do something beneficial for the Chesapeake. That small project might serve as a demonstration to citizens within that community who will want to do something on their own land to help the Chesapeake Bay. Mini grants might also include funding for conferences and workshops and other things that spread the word about what can be done, events that share best practices and lessons learned so that we continue to learn from our experiences and improve.

The Stewardship Grant program is a very similar program, funding projects that are designed to engage the public, raise awareness and get people more involved. But they're typically larger. We have a number of other grant programs, and I'll just touch on two of them. One is the Targeted Watershed Grant Program, which essentially helps us achieve that number one priority, to restore local watersheds. The Targeted Watershed Grants Program provides up to $200,000 for activities that help restore a specific creek or stream which enters into a river system. The program is designed to concentrate money, build partnerships, leverage resources and expertise at the local level, and demonstrate that you can make a difference in restoring water quality and habitat.

The other I want to tell you about is the Pioneer Grants Program, which is a relatively new initiative. It focuses on new ideas and technologies that can accelerate bay restoration efforts. Right now we're focused on two challenging issues: managing agricultural manure and dealing with rapid land development. How can we deal with those two issues so that they have less impact on water quality in streams, rivers and ultimately the Chesapeake Bay? One example is a grant that we awarded to the town of Denton, on the Eastern Shore. In that project, the partners include a development company, the Low Impact Development Center (which is focused on trying to reduce the impacts of development on water quality), Atkins Arboretum (which focuses on native plant material and planting in a way that's beneficial to wildlife and water quality), and, of course, the town. That partnership is attempting to apply low-impact development techniques. This includes landscape improvements that better filter pollutants running off of roofs and driveways and so on. The program demonstrates how low-impact development can be successful on a development in the town of Denton. The town will use this example and potentially codify it in their ordinances and codes. We hope this will be a model for growth on the Eastern Shore.

As the Chesapeake Bay region grows—and we are expected to grow by millions over the next 20 years—we're going to have to find the best ways to do it. We have to acknowledge that growth is going to occur, and take every possible step to reduce its impact. In the last round for the Pioneer Grant Program we received four million dollars in requests. We only had $600,000 to award, so obviously demand far outreached what we could offer in resources. But what that said to us was that there are a lot of great ideas out there, and a lot of people that are trying to figure out how to deal with the most pressing challenges facing the Chesapeake Bay today. We're going to do our part and we're going to partner with others who can also provide funding towards this effort.

Partnerships are a key to cleaning up the Chesapeake Bay. We help run a program called the Living Shoreline Grants Program, a partnership among various funders including the Keith Campbell Foundation for the Environment, Noah Restoration Center, National Fish and Wildlife Foundation, and the Trust. Together we pool resources and then make grants to projects that help restore shorelines in a way that mimics the natural environment. The living shoreline restoration at St. John's College, on College Creek, was funded by this program. Driving down Rowe Boulevard into Annapolis as you'll cross the new College Creek Bridge, take a peek on your left-hand side and you'll see this beautiful marsh that's been developed through the living shoreline's program. While this grant program is a partnership, the groups that receive these funds tend to be partnerships as well. The St. John's College restoration project includes CBF, St. John's College, and a number of other groups working hand-in-hand to advance the concept of the living shoreline. For this project, the partners were able to remove 700 feet of bulkhead, replacing it with a shallow marsh. It will serve as a natural filter for pollutants that would run into the creek.

We also support individual schools that come to the Trust with specific projects. There is a learning-by-doing philosophy that has been proven in evaluations to be effective for teaching. One of the exciting projects we've been funding for many years now is called the Schools and Streams Program, in Howard County. The program is led by the Howard County Master Gardeners in partnership with the public schools. They take fifth graders, their parents, and master gardeners, to parks where they plant trees. This year they planted 1,300 trees! Over the last 10 years or so they've planted literally miles of streamside forest buffers. These buffers are 300 feet wide, and that has a real ecological impact. So these kids are learning about the Chesapeake Bay by understanding their local environment and then actually participating in a project that helps it. I think that's really important for kids today, particularly when we're facing not only issues about the Chesapeake Bay, but also global environmental issues that need to be understood at the earliest levels."

Mike Tidwell, Founder/Executive Director, Chesapeake Climate Action Network

Mike Tidwell says he's a reluctant activist, inspired by the world situation and his immediate surroundings. Mike is compelled to defend that which belongs to all of us, the water we drink, and the air that we breathe. He's a guy who practices what he preaches, an all-too-rare quality, even sometimes in the most dedicated of conversationists. Mike is well-spoken and driven to get his message across. As Director of the Chesapeake Climate Action Network, Mike speaks passionately about the effects of global warming and what we can do to slow the process down in our home states of Maryland, Virginia and the District of Columbia. A longtime professional journalist, Mike Tidwell has worked as a freelance writer for the Washington Post. His 2003 book Bayou Farewell *predicted the effects of a major hurricane on the State of Louisiana and the City of New Orleans two years before Katrina's deadly strike flooded the Crescent city.*

I spoke with Mike in late February 2006 at his Takoma Park home. As we pulled up our chairs close to the potbelly stove I asked about the unfamiliar odor which came from it.

"We're sitting in my house which is almost 100 years old, in one of the original trolley car suburbs of Washington, DC," said Mike. "Despite being as old as it is, I have successfully retrofitted it with almost entirely renewable energy systems in the last few years. For example, it's a fairly cold February day today, yet it's nice and warm inside. My gas radiators, which are also about 100 years old, are cold to the touch. They're not on. I haven't used gas or oil or anything like that to heat my home in five years. I haven't used any fossil fuels to heat my home. Instead I heat my home with corn. Off to the side here there's a stand-alone corn-burning stove with a nice gentle flame. It's actually burning shelled corn kernels raised by a Mennonite Maryland farmer, who lives about 40 miles from here in Mt. Airy. He uses sustainable practices to raise his corn. It's organically fertilized with turkey manure from his turkey farm. He doesn't till the soil and it's not genetically modified corn. It's truly sustainable-raised corn. It's also full of energy and if you burn it in these ingenious corn-burning stoves, it creates a lot of heat. This one stove heats almost my entire house, all the downstairs and most of the upstairs, while at the same time saving me a lot of money.

I have in the last five years of burning corn instead of fossil fuels, saved at least $200 a season, probably a lot more than that. The reason is, corn is much less expensive than either home heating oil or natural gas. We all know what's happening to natural gas prices. Everybody I know who's still heating with gas goes through sticker shock at the beginning of every month, even as they try to conserve heat. In my house, however, we don't try to conserve heat. We keep the heat cranked up. We stay nice and warm. That's because we buy our corn for about $3.30 a bushel. Over a whole heating season that comes out to about $600. In the meantime, I don't have to keep turning the heat down. The stove does use a little bit of electricity to operate. It uses the electricity equivalent to a 100-watt incandescent light bulb, to power a couple of fans that blow the hot air away from the stove. There is an electric fuel stirrer that stirs the corn, and an auger that connects the hopper that holds the corn with the fire pit. So we save money. But the main reason I did it was not to save money. It was because I'm extremely concerned about global warming.

We all know that the planet is warming very rapidly now. We see the impacts even right here where we live in the Chesapeake region. A lot of us are beginning to realize that the weather is changing; something strange is happening with the weather. Of course we've had the major hurricanes on the Gulf Coast that have served as a wakeup call. But even right here where we live in the Chesapeake Bay region, sea level rise in the bay was about 7 or 8 inches in the last 100 years, brought on by global warming. Glaciers melt worldwide and that water flows into the oceans. Also, warmer water takes up more space. It's called thermal expansion. The oceans are getting bigger because they're getting warmer. The bay is connected with the Atlantic, which means we get the same sea level rise in the Chesapeake Bay. And, that sea level rise is accelerating dramatically. It's expected that we could see three feet of sea level rise by 2100, right here in this region.

That means major, major impacts on Baltimore, Washington, DC and the entire 31,000 miles of tidal shoreline that compose Maryland's portion of the Chesapeake Bay, which is equal to about a third of the entire West Coast. We are a water state. If you think of all the photographs that are used in tourism to promote the state, it's always waterfowl, sailboats, watermen, and lighthouses. And as a water state, we are exceptionally vulnerable to global warming just because of sea level rise. You see enormous erosion all along the Chesapeake Bay. You see that in the 20th century, 13 inhabited islands in the Chesapeake Bay were abandoned because of sea level rise. There's only one inhabited island left in Maryland's portion of the Chesapeake Bay, and that's Smith Island. Now, by island I mean a true island, one that's not connected to the mainland by a causeway, but one you can only get to by boat. And Smith Island is rapidly eroding, too. There are some portions of the island where the shore is receding 30 feet a year because of sea level rise.

I wrote a book called *Bayou Farewell: The Rich Life and Tragic Death of Louisiana's Cajun Coast,* which came out in 2003. It basically predicted that a storm like Katrina would wipe out New Orleans and much of coastal Louisiana a full two years before it actually happened. I stumbled on the story as a freelance writer for the *Washington Post.* Although I do environmental activism full time right now, I'm not a career environmentalist. I'm a career print journalist. I spent years and years writing as a freelancer for magazines and newspapers, including the *Washington Post.* But it was my writing about global warming for the *Washington Post* and other organizations, as I immersed myself in the science and interviews some of the world's leading climatologists, that I became very alarmed by the enormous gulf between what we know about global warming and what we're actually doing about it. The gulf between those two poles is intergalactic in distance. We need to do more. So I took off my journalism hat and put on an activist hat, and I'm more or less a citizen activist. I got into this not because it's something I always wanted to do, or because I want to be the head of a big environmental group. Actually, no, I'd rather just be a journalist. But I feel compelled to fight global warming because I have an eight year-old son and I love the Chesapeake Bay and this entire region. Major, major pain is coming, unless we take rapid action."

Drew Koslow, South River Riverkeeper

When I met Drew Koslow in 1999 he was working part-time as a fisheries biologist on contract with the Maryland Department of Natural Resources, while also cutting fish at the Annapolis Whole Foods Market. Shortly thereafter, Drew was elected President of his local watershed organization, the South River Federation (SRF,) and a few years later became the first South River Riverkeeper. A riverkeeper is a person hired by the public, in this case the SRF, to be the eyes and ears of a particular natural resource, in Drew's case, the South River. These activists look after our rivers, bays, and harbors without influence from government or corporate interests. We'll learn more about the evolution and work of the national umbrella organization, the Waterkeeper Alliance, in a little bit. For now, join us for a late winter journey up the South River with riverkeeper Drew Koslow.

"I try to get out once a week or every couple of weeks during the wintertime," Drew said. "Usually you only see hunters and commercial oysterman and fisherman out here in the winter months. Hunting season starts around late October and runs through January. Sometimes you have quite good duck hunting out here on the river. This year it was very slow because of the mild weather.

Duck hunters use shotgun pellets, which are effective at very close range inside about 50 yards or so. If you're more than 50 yards away from a hunter and you accidentally get hit you're not going to be mortally wounded. If you're more than 100 yards away, the pellets will just be dropping out of the sky, and they won't really have any velocity to them. Generally, you'll see a blind or a boat that's camouflaged and you'll see a spread of decoys. Duck hunters use anywhere from a dozen to 100 decoys to attract ducks.

Everything else slows down when the water gets cold.

With spring kind of busting, the osprey just came back to South River over the weekend. I saw one on Saturday and I've seen a dozen today. When water temperature reaches about 50 degrees, yellow perch start running up freshwater streams and they start spawning. Last year I got to witness it and it was really amazing. There were hundreds and hundreds of fish right up on the North River, which is one of the tributaries to the South River. You would see a big female—the females are generally larger than the males—set up to spawn on a gravel bed. The males would come right to her and get into position to fertilize the eggs as soon as she released them. It was amazing to watch. There were yellow perch that were up to 15 inches long. They just kept working to get right where they wanted to be. When the males came in the water would turn all milky white with their sperm.

In this river, the yellow perch are struggling. I think in the South River we suffer from poor quality water in the headwaters, and that really impacts the survivability of young yellow perch. There's not a lot of habitat for them. And also storm water plays a big role in knocking out their young. The yellow perch want their egg strands to be attached to woody vegetation in the water column. That way, freshwater is running over them the whole time and it keeps the eggs clean and oxygenated. What happens is, we get a big rain event and because of all the impervious surfaces like roads and roof tops and parking lots, water rushes through these streams and instead of your normal flows, you get this incredible rush of water. And that powerful rush actually pulls these egg strands off of the debris in the water and brings them downstream where they are no longer viable. When they hit salty water or muddy water or they're no longer suspended in the water column but fall down on the bottom, and the eggs die.

Yellow perch eggs are actually a strand which is about 18 inches to two feet long. They're kind of orange colored, and if you look at them closely you can see the embryo inside and you can see a little eye. As soon as they hatch they become food for other fish. That's the thing about fish; they all eat each other, so the smaller you are the more vulnerable you are. Only a very small percentage of the eggs that hatch will actually survive to become adult yellow perch. That's why it's important to have high fish populations for successful spawning. You know, for instance, an adult female striped bass will hold a million eggs per pound of body weight. Think about that. If you can get a spawning female fish that's 60 pounds, she's carrying somewhere in the neighborhood of 60 million eggs. That's really astonishing to me. It just blows me away.

The yellow perch spawn first and then the white perch move up our streams. The herring start to run and then the American shad start. All these fish make that journey from the ocean back up into the freshwater streams. The shad run to their natal stream; they go to the same streams that they were hatched in. It's pretty amazing. Most spend up to four or five years in the ocean and then come back and are able to find the very place they originated in. They have an internal clock which relies on signals like the length of the days, and the water temperature, to tell them when it's time to spawn.

Once you get eggs and sperm in the water, that attracts other fish and then they really start going. I've been out there electro-shocking striped bass on days when they're doing their thing—you just touch a male and the milk just comes pouring out of it's body. It's hilarious. Talk about a hair trigger! Electro-fishing is a method we use to look at fish stocks, to see how healthy the populations are. In freshwater streams we use a backpack shocker. You put your probe in the river or stream, it sends an electric current into the water, and it knocks the fish out without killing them. They float to the surface and you dip them in a net and put them into a holding tank. With the striped bass it's wild because you're shocking out of a boat. You have a generator on the boat and two probes at the bow. Each person has their foot on a button and as long as their feet are on those buttons the juice is going into the water... you don't want to touch the water as long as that is happening.

Sometimes the rockfish will come out of the water. They're still swimming but they don't really have control of where they're going. They're vibrating and they surface out of the water like torpedoes. It's really wild. We've had them jump into the boat before. They're hit with that current and really can't escape it. If they hit the probe it will generally kill them. You have to be really aware of what you're doing and take your foot off the juice when you see fish approaching.

In the South River, our salinity ranges from somewhere around six parts per thousand to 15 parts per thousand, depending on the season and where on the river we are. Brackish is a mix of salty and freshwater and that's kind of what the whole Chesapeake is. But up here in the South River we're at the lower end of the salinity ranges.

Oysters grow very well in the South River but they tend not to reproduce well because they like saltier water for reproducing. In the saltier water, they're more vulnerable to disease. So we grow good oysters in the South River but we don't have very good reproduction. This used to be a very popular river for the hand-tongers. Five or six years ago you would see a dozen guys out here tonging. The last two winters I think there has been one person hand-tonging on the South River. It's still legal but there just aren't a lot of harvestable oysters. For these guys to really make it worth their while they've got to catch half a dozen bushels of oysters. These days, I think you'd be hard pressed to do that."

We see about a half dozen mallards fly in front of us.

"Earlier when I was coming in to pick you up I saw about two dozen canvasbacks. You'll also see a lot of black heads or lesser scaup, the occasional wood duck, the occasional black duck, lots of mallards, the occasional redhead. I think there are a fewer and fewer duck hunters every year. Duck populations are kind of in decline. Some ducks have adapted and are able to feed on grain fields rather than in wetlands or submerged aquatic vegetation. Other ducks, like the canvasback, haven't adapted to feeding on fields. They're a diving duck and their population has been in decline for some time. The scaup population is also in pretty drastic decline right now. And the main reason for that is because in the Great Lakes they have adapted to eating zebra mussels. Over the last 15 years huge populations of zebra mussels have grown in the Great Lakes. The water is crystal clear there now, because those mussels are filter feeders. Sadly, they also concentrate metals. One metal in particular, selenium. It's caused the scaup's eggshells to get really thin, so that the weight of the hen causes the eggs to break. It's very similar to the way DDT acted on raptor eggshells. The raptors have come back because DDT was banned back in the early 1970's, but selenium is having the same effect on the scaup.

Another interesting thing happened up here in the headwaters of the South River: we found that our brown bullhead catfish have very high rates of cancer. I guess the story of these bullhead catfish started for us a couple of springs ago at almost exactly this time of year. Because of all the stocking efforts that have gone on the U.S. Fish and Wildlife Service was out here trying to net yellow perch, to see how those populations were doing. They started catching a bunch of these brown bullhead catfish and they noticed that a lot of them had these reddish-pink lesions on them.

PAH, (polynuclear aromatic hydrocarbons) have been shown to cause this sort of cancer in other populations of catfish. It comes from un-burnt or partially burnt fossil fuels, combustion burning gasoline from an automobile engine, and run off of highways where you get lots of cars. It's the crankcase drippings and the stuff that comes out of the tailpipe. It's the particles off of tires and it's un-burnt fuel. All of that gets washed into the river as part of the runoff. In the South River I think it was 50 percent of the catfish they caught in a random sample had skin cancer around their mouths, and more than 20 percent had liver cancer.

We don't have any industry on the rivers... but we also haven't been able to demonstrate that the PAHs are a factor here. So essentially we are trying to figure out what's causing the cancer in the catfish, where it's coming from, where it accumulates in the river. We want to stop that cancer-causing agent from getting into the water, and clean up the stuff that's in here now. We've had some local foundations come to us and say they want to help us with this, and individual members of the South River Federation have been calling because it's something people understand. They understand it in a way that they might not be able to understand nutrient loading and algae blooms affecting water quality—I think everybody out there understands cancer in a very real way.

I've been here about 13 years and the traffic and congestion have increased exponentially. The amount of development has been really extraordinary and it seems to me that our quality of life is threatened by what's happening around us. We really need to think hard about how we're growing and what our legacy is going to be. I think in the past our concentration has been on growth at any cost. It just means more people, more traffic, the need for more services, and more runoff. The more impervious surfaces we have, the more pollution entering our rivers and our bays. In the summertime we have a particular problem with thermal pollution. You get a big thunder storm on 100 degree day when the pavement's about 150 degrees, and then the water hits all that asphalt and runs off into our creeks. The water temperature in the creek is usually 70 to 75 degrees, but all of a sudden this hot water comes rushing into the creeks and it kills everything.

Last year the dead zone in the bay was the second highest on record. The dead zone is the area of the bay that doesn't hold enough dissolved oxygen to support life. It's a very literal translation. We have high mercury levels in our rockfish. We have algae blooms that go off kind of like clock work through mid to late summer. You can come out here on any given day and the water is going to look like pea soup, just totally cloudy and murky.

One of the things we've been working on over the past year is trying to get Anne Arundel County to incorporate a storm-water utility. It would essentially be a fee that every taxpayer would pay, roughly $60 per household per year. This would be a dedicated fee like our trash collection and our water and sewer service fees. Those funds can't be pirated off to appropriate for other uses, like the states open space funds were a couple of years ago. The fee would be administered by the Department of Public Works, and they would be able to use that money to start putting filters in place in subdivisions and where highways were built. You know that as most of this county developed, we thought storm water management was just getting water off the site and into our waterways as quickly as possible? Now we're trying to build filters out of gravel, sand, mulch, and plants.

Is it safe to eat the crabs, is it safe to swim in the river, is it safe to muck around? I love nothing more than playing around in the mud, you know, looking for frogs in the springtime, and walking around in these headwater streams. But I can't answer those questions right now.

The South River is one of the busiest rivers in the nation because of the concentration of people that live here, how close we are to DC, the number of marinas here, and the fact that people love the bay. I think that what brings most people to the Annapolis area is that everybody is connected to the rivers, and to the bay. I guess we're loving this bay to death."

Robert F. Kennedy, Jr., Founder/President, Waterkeeper Alliance

The name Robert F. Kennedy is etched in the minds of the 60's generation, be they children or adults of the time. Bobby Kennedy, Jr., a boy of 14 when his father was taken from his life, is left with recollections understandably difficult to revisit. This interview was recorded during a visit to Chestertown in the fall of 2002 to celebrate the first riverkeeper on the Chester River. Here Bobby (as he prefers to be called) recalled his early childhood growing up in McLean, Virginia, and how those years shaped his lifelong commitment to protecting the natural environment. He also explains the evolution and impetus of the international Waterkeeper Alliance, of which he is a founder and President.

The Waterkeeper Alliance is a grassroots organization that provides a voice for waterways and the communities that surround them. It was formed as the Riverkeeper organization by a group of concerned and vigilant Hudson River fishermen, back in the mid-1980's.

Robert F. Kennedy, Jr. is the guy you would want to head your legal team if you were in trouble. His legacy as a formidable defender of the environment proceeds him. Mr. Kennedy was named one of Time Magazine's *"Heroes for the Planet" for leading the successful fight by the Riverkeeper organization to restore the Hudson River. He serves as Senior Attorney for the Natural Resources Defense Council, and the Chief Prosecuting Attorney and President of the Waterkeeper Alliance. He is also a Clinical Professor and Supervising Attorney at Pace University School of Law's Environmental Litigation Clinic and co-host of Ring of Fire on Air America Radio. Earlier in his career Robert F. Kennedy, Jr. served as Assistant District Attorney in New York City, and he also worked on several political campaigns, including the presidential campaigns of Edward M. Kennedy in 1980, Al Gore in 2000, and John Kerry in 2004.*

"When I grew up in McLean, Virginia, it looked very much like the area around the Chester River that I see today," Kennedy said. "People were not growing soybeans back then but there was a lot of corn, there were barns, there were woodlands, it was farm country. Today those landscapes are covered up with pavement. The creeks that I used to play in when I was a little boy have been channelized, forests are covered with stores and McMansions, and it looks like every other strip mall in America. There really is no sense of place left.

I remember when they put the Dolly Madison highway there at Route 123 when I was a little kid, and the feeling of anger that I had that these landscapes, which were so important to my identity, were going to disappear. I had no idea how much they were going to disappear. But now they're gone. So I come to a place like this where there's still a lot of that magic. You know this is a maritime community, and a farm community. Yet there is encroachment here now, the rapid encroachment of sprawl development.

My brother and I rolled some cement pipes down an embankment one day because we were trying to stop the highway from being built. We got caught and punished by my father. In the long run I was not right to be breaking the law, but I was right about what was going on. When I was growing up, my father was a very good military historian and every night at dinner we had to recite poetry. We had to memorize poems every week, or biographies of historic figures. He would tell us stories, usually about the great battles in history. About Bunker Hill, about Marathon. He loved the Greeks and was very familiar with the battles of the Romans. That sense of history was important to him. He had a very, very strong sense of history about the place that we lived and about how important it had been in American history.

McLean was one of the major battlefields of the Civil War. It was the home of General George McClellan, who was general during the first years of the Civil War. We had Union troops stationed all over there, at virtually every creek. Every hillside has a story that's important to American history. And it's all gone now. We were very conscious as kids that wherever we dug in the ground, we would find bullets from the Civil War and other artifacts of American history, arrowheads and those kinds of things. You know so we felt a connection to our history and to our culture and to the common experience that really unites our country—the experience of the land. A child growing up in that environment today will have none of those feelings, no sense of place. And I think ultimately our values come from that sense of place. We are divorcing ourselves from those values.

I was interested in wildlife, too, when I was a little kid. My uncles on my mother's side were all hunters and fishermen. I grew up in that milieu. I was hunting and fishing from when I was five or six years old, and I began breeding and raising homing pigeons when I was about seven. And then when I was nine or 10 I read T.H. White's *The Sword in the Stone,* which was about Camelot. While my uncle was present I read that book, and there was a chapter on falconry. As it happened there was a falconer who lived down the street from me. He is one of the people who discovered the peregrine migration on Assateague Island, and he taught me falconry. I started training hawks when I was 11 and I've been doing it ever since. I just recently stepped down as president of the New York State Falconer's Association and I've written a book on falconry. I've been involved with it all my life.

Bob Boyle was the inspiration behind the riverkeeping movement, which was started on the Hudson River back in the early 60's by this blue collar coalition of commercial and recreational fishermen. Almost all of them were former marines, and they got together in the American Legion Hall in 1966 to talk about blowing up pipes on the Hudson River. There were 300 men and women at that first meeting and it went almost all through the night. The fishermen were angry because they had made their livelihood on the river. For the most part they came from a village called Crotonville, New York, which was an enclave of commercial fisherman on the Hudson. Some of these people came from families that had been working the river since Dutch colonial times. They got together because the pollution was killing their fishery, killing their livelihood, destroying their industry, destroying the value of their properties and homes and the recreational values and quality of life in their community. These weren't people who were radicals or militants. They were mainly Korean and Vietnam War vets. They had gone to the government agencies that are suppose to protect Americans from pollution and hit a stone wall. They were told by government officials, 'We can't go after these people. They're very powerful.' The fishermen were looking at this and they were saying, 'This is criminal behavior! They're not allowed to dump oil or PCBs into the Hudson River!' And they decided to take direct action.

At that first meeting in March 1966, the fishermen were talking about floating dynamite into pipes and plugging pipes with mattresses, or setting oil slicks on fire. A guy named Bob Boyle stood up. He was another former marine, and he was the outdoor editor of *Sports Illustrated* magazine, where he is still today. He's been there for 50 years. Boyle had discovered an ancient navigational statute while researching an article about angling in the Hudson. That statute, which was called the 1888 Rivers and Harbors Act, said that it was illegal to pollute any waterway in the United States, and, that you had to pay a high penalty if you got caught. There was also a 'bounty provision' that said that anybody who turned in a polluter got to keep half the fine. Bob Boyle came to this meeting in 1966 when all these men were talking about violence and he stood up and he said, 'You know, we should be talking about enforcing the law, not about breaking it.' And they all agreed to start a group called the Hudson River Fishermen's Association. They were going to go out and track down every polluter on the Hudson. Eighteen months later they shut down the Penn Central Pipe, which was one of the big offenders on the river. They got to keep $2,000 in bounty. It was the first bounty ever awarded under this old statute, and they used that money to go after every other big polluter on the Hudson River.

In 1973 HRFA collected the highest penalty in United States history from a corporate polluter. They got $200,000 from Anaconda Wire and Cable, and used that money to construct a boat which they called the *Riverkeeper.* They also used bounty money to hire their first full-time riverkeeper, a former commercial fishermen named John Cronin. He hired me in 1984, using bounty money. At that time I was working for the District Attorney's office in Manhattan, doing criminal prosecutions, which I loved. But I had always wanted to work on the environment. I kind of fell in with these fishermen and started doing some pro bono work for them. Then they hired me as their first full-time attorney.

About a year after that we started a clinic at Pace Law School in White Plains, New York, which I helped supervise. We have 10 third-year students, in conjunction with my work for the Waterkeeper Alliance. All of our cases are keeper cases. The patrol boats that patrol the rivers bring us polluters. We give each of the students four polluters to sue at the beginning of the semester. They file complaints, do discovery and depositions. And they go to court and argue their cases. I'll be trying a case in Syracuse next week with about five of my students, against the City of New York for polluting one of the major trout fisheries in the Catskills, Esopus Creek.

We've won about 300 cases since we started doing this work, since we started the clinic. We forced polluters on the river to spend about three billion dollars on remediation. Today the Hudson is an international model for ecosystem protection. This is a river that was a national joke back in the 60's. Today it's the richest water body in the North Atlantic; it's not richer than the Chesapeake in terms of the total biomass produced, but in terms of the biomass produced per acre per gallon, and the pounds of fish per acre, there is no river system that is more productive. And the resurrection of the Hudson has inspired the creation of riverkeepers all over the country.

I'm really happy to be down here to launch the Chester River Riverkeeper. There is no system that is more important to this country than the Chesapeake. In terms of biological productivity, 80 percent of the migratory fish on the East Coast come out of the Chesapeake. You know the fish that we catch up in Massachusetts, the striped bass, which you call rockfish down here? The likelihood is about eight out of 10 that when we catch one of those fish it's come out of the Chesapeake Bay, and that it spawned in one of the Chesapeake tributaries, like the Pocomoke, like the Chester. So when you injure these water bodies you're not just impacting what happens in your backyard. You're having ripple effects that go all the way up to Maine and Canada and all the way out past the end of the Continental Shelf. The big pelagic species like tuna and bill-fish, who never have to come near the shore during their life cycles, nevertheless rely on the abundance and health of these estuaries like the Chester and the Chesapeake.

We just licensed our 99th riverkeeper. We have over 300 applications for new riverkeepers. In this area two weeks ago we launched an Assateague coastkeeper. We have riverkeepers now on the South River, the Severn River, and the Patapsco River. The Chesapeake is the holy grail of American river systems. I mean, we have a lot of really important rivers in this country—the Mississippi, obviously, the Columbia, and the Missouri. But in terms of biological productivity, I don't think you could find a river system that's more important than the Chesapeake in terms of its impact on American culture or on our literature, on defining who we are as a people.

The message that is essential to the riverkeeper movement is what the eastern fishermen understood from the beginning, that we're not out there protecting the river so that it's safe for the fishes and the birds, but for our own sake. We want to create communities for our children that offer the same opportunities for dignity and enrichment as the communities that our parents gave us. And if we want to accomplish that mission we've got to start by protecting the infrastructure, the things that we hold in common, the public trust assets that all of us own—the air that we breathe, the flowing waters, the river systems, the wandering animals and the fisheries. We're not protecting them for their own sake, but because when we destroy them we diminish ourselves and we impoverish our children. If our children have to grow up on landscapes that all look like McLean, Virginia, they are never going to enjoy the quality of life and the richness of life that I enjoyed.

If the Chester River, the 400 mile Chester River watershed, ends up covered with McMansions and McDonalds and Walmarts, the Chestertown main street will be empty because of the mall on the edge of town. That's not a good thing. That is not a result that we're going to proud of. If there are no commercial fishermen and no recreational fishermen left on the river, if it's choked with agricultural waste and storm water, then our children can't wade in their bare feet and catch striped bass or catfish and feed it to their family with pride, with the security that they're not being poisoned. Every child has that right to that security.

The Constitution of the State of Maryland says that the people own this waterway. The people own all the rivers in the state, and they own all the fisheries in the state. They're not owned by the government or by corporations or by agriculture or industry. They are owned by the people. Everybody has a right to use them. Nobody can use them in a way that will diminish or injure their use and enjoyment by others.

You know, today there's an advisory on eating any catfish from the Chester River. Children in this area are deprived of the primal seminal experience of being able to have their dad or their mom take them catfishing on the river, pulling up a fish, and cooking it over a campfire. They can't do that anymore because the fish is too dangerous to eat. And if you think about that, you should be indignant. It's like a science-fiction nightmare—somebody has been able to steal those fish from the people of Kent County and Queen Anne's County. Those fish belong to the people and yet the people can't use them anymore. They've been stolen and liquidated into cash by somebody who then took the profit and then left. It's legally wrong, it's morally wrong, and it's irresponsible.

One of the things that we would like to do is to see a lot of coordination between all the keeper groups in the Chesapeake region working on issues of common interest. One of the issues is the fish advisories. These are advisories that come from local polluters, but there are also fish advisories that are caused by polluters from out of the state. For example, most of the fish on the east coast now have advisories because of mercury. Mercury is absolutely deadly. It causes neural damage in children and in fetuses. It causes renal damage, tissue damage, in adults. In fetuses it can cause permanent IQ loss, problems with sexual development, neural development, the spinal cord...a teaspoon of mercury will contaminate all of the fish in a 2,500 acre lake, to the extent that none of them can be safely eaten. In Connecticut there's an advisory on every single freshwater fish in the state. And we are working towards that in the State of Maryland. In fact, that would probably be true in Maryland now if the fish were adequately measured, if they were actually out testing the fish, which is not done because they don't want to. The government officials want to keep their head in the sand.

There is no geological source for that mercury in the State of Connecticut or the State of Maryland. About 90 percent of the mercury is coming from a handful of coal-burning power plants in the Ohio Valley, which were supposed to be closed down due to the Clean Air Act. The current administration is now giving these plants a waiver to operate for another 50 years. Many of them are burning high-sulfur coal with technologies that are completely outmoded. They were supposed to be closed down, but they're not. They are imposing costs on everybody in the Chesapeake Bay watershed, because the fish are now contaminated. What we'd like to do is to coordinate litigation against those industries who are out of the state but are affecting everybody in this state, including all of the keeper programs.

The best measure of how a democracy is working is how a democracy provides access to the benefits of government including the halls of justice, and how it provides access for all the people to the goods of the land, the things that we all own in common. The air, the water, the wandering animals, the fisheries, the aquifers, the wetlands, those things that are not susceptible to private ownership.

Government's primary obligation is to protect the public rights and those assets in the commons, and not let individuals who are politically powerful come and steal the commons from the public. That's exactly what has happened here in the case of the Chester River. The catfish belong to every kid in this county. Everybody can use them. You just can't take more than your share, that's the rule. But now nobody owns them anymore because somebody stole them. And the person who stole them, who contaminated the waterway, was breaking the law when they did it. We say that's real law, it's important law, and it needs to be enforced. One of the reasons we're going to put a boat out on the river is to remind the public that they own that waterway—but they will lose it if they're not vigilant and aggressive about enforcing the existing laws."

13

Leaders

Ann Pesiri Swanson, Executive Director, Chesapeake Bay Commission

In John Rodenhausen's work with students through the educational programs of the Chesapeake Bay Foundation there is an important connection made between teaching students about the environment and equipping them with the skills to become leaders. Leadership is a quality that is in some ways unique among a chosen few, but leadership qualities reside in all of us. A successful movement to restore the Chesapeake Bay requires a less top-down approach. We need an army of concerned citizens who believe that they can effect change. The turning point has been reached. After years of procrastination, questions such as, 'Should we develop alternative forms of energy?' and 'Should we recycle everything we can?' have been answered.

We have the means and the know-how to successfully solve big problems. The die has been cast. If we don't act quickly to restore and protect our natural environment we will have squandered an historic opportunity. We need strong and well-informed leadership. With leadership comes the willingness and ability to acknowledge the problems that we face; the skills to communicate the need for nationwide cooperation; and the will to change the status quo in order to effect change for the common good—for the health of our nation.

The original vision of our nation was for a democracy in which all citizens play a part. Throughout our history when the going has gotten tough we have banded together to meet our challenges, both in times of war and in times of peace. Sadly though, at other times we as citizens have wandered down the road of laziness and inactivity. We've all been there before. We all need leaders at every level of society–in government, in business, in churches—who use their power to set the pace, to lead by example; leaders who understand that a healthy environment is our greatest asset. We also need dedication to the challenge at hand, the same type of dedication that we apply to our love for family, to our work, to sports, recreation and entertainment.

The leaders we've spoken with in the Voices *project are not people veiled in secrecy or locked in ivory towers. Their doors are open. They are well-informed and fully invested in restoring our Chesapeake Bay. These leaders are interested in preserving and understanding our history, in doing scientific research, and in mobilizing citizens to participate in the restoration effort. They are doing their part to lead us into making a fresh new commitment, one of environmental sensibility and sustainability. Ann Pesiri Swanson, Executive Director of the Chesapeake Bay Commission, the tri-state legislative authority made up of House and Senate members and the governors from Maryland, Pennsylvania, and Virginia, is one such leader. In January 2007, Ann and I discussed the work of the Chesapeake Bay Commission and how our leaders must come together to solve multi-state environmental challenges.*

"It's a very, very interesting group," Ann begins, when asked about the commission. "They come from all walks of life. They come from the rural corners of the Eastern Shore to high-rises in Bethesda. They represent the Republicans; they represent the Democrats. They represent liberal thinking; they represent conservative thinking, and moderate thinking. So it's a very broad spectrum, which means if they come up with a policy recommendation it's got a good chance of moving through the general assemblies because it's already moderated by the diversity of their thought. The water and the fish don't respect political boundaries so you need lawmakers to work on laws that cross the bay watershed.

When you work as an individual legislator, of course, you're representing your own district. When you come together as the Commission, you must rise to a different place because your job is to look across political boundaries at what the bay needs. We never really end up with the lowest common dominator, which is what you would worry about, but instead the group tends to really ask, 'What does the bay need in terms of nitrogen and phosphorus reductions, in terms of fish passage, in terms of crab management?' If it has anything to do with the Chesapeake Bay—land, air, or water—then it's in our court, and we work on it."

Ann Pesiri Swanson was raised on Long Island, New York. Her parents were a doctor and nurse. "...they had a reverence for life, no doubt," *she remembers. At 17 the Swanson family moved to Vermont.* "I spent about four months living in a cabin that was 12 miles from the nearest paved road, so I've had suburban experiences and rural experiences. I've lived in the forest and I've lived in an apartment building. Now, on the Chesapeake Bay, I realize how critically important those forests are to the waters." *When she got out of graduate school at Yale, Ann came to work for the Chesapeake Bay Foundation.*

"It was two months prior to the signing of the first Chesapeake Bay Agreement in 1983 and there was no organized grassroots effort at that time. I offered to come down and try to develop the first political action, grassroots involvement in the watershed. It seemed like an incredible challenge because it was starting from a clean slate. The signing of the Bay Agreement was, as environmental policy making goes, world news. I worked for CBF for about four and a half years, and then I came over to direct the Commission. I've been here ever since.

The Commission started in 1980. Some Senators in Washington were very concerned about the Chesapeake Bay. They saw its decline, but there wasn't the science base to prove it, and they didn't know why. So they convinced the congress to fund a $27 million, seven-year-long study on the bay. There'd been ecosystem studies before, but the thing that made this so different was the scale. It was addressing a 64,000 square mile watershed. The study was going to develop information about what was wrong, and provide recommendations for how to make it right. The federal Environmental Protection Agency had never done something of this scale before. They realized there was no interstate government mechanism to receive the recommendations. The Chesapeake Bay Program didn't exist yet. The governors with the EPA and the partnership didn't exist yet. So a Senator from Maryland and one from Virginia joined forces to study a good way to look at the bay across state lines. They studied a lot of different forms of government, and ultimately they decided we needed a legislative commission. It's the laws and budgets that control what we do, and the laws and the budgets are passed by the general assemblies. So, we need to coordinate the general assemblies across state lines to protect the fish, the water, and the waterfowl, which are moving up and down across political boundaries every day. So that's what happened and the Chesapeake Bay Commission was created in 1990.

Interestingly, the very first thing it ever did was to develop the Reciprocity Laws. These laws allow watermen from Maryland to fish in Virginia waters, and vice versa. Prior to that, if they crossed a line, they were stealing resources from the other state. If you go to Tangier Sound, you realize it's not about Virginia or Maryland; it's about one big productive sound. As recently as 1957, watermen died over these issues.

The second thing they did was sponsor a conference, which brought the governors, the EPA, the mayor of the District of Columbia, the entire Commission together, to sign the first Bay Agreement. There have been two more agreements signed since then.

You have to remember that our region straddles the Mason-Dixon line, and it's alive and well. And what I mean by that is not about feuding between North and South, but the structure of government. Northern government is about towns. If you've ever lived in New England, you've gone to your town meeting. You even get the day off, because that's what government is. In the South it's big counties, and they're not all empowered by the state. They have very, very limited things they can and can not do. Virginia is very much a Southern state in that regard. Maryland, just like in the Civil War, is stuck in the middle. Maryland has 44 ruling municipalities. That's a lot, compared to Virginia. But compare that to Pennsylvania; the watershed alone has 1,350 ruling local governments. That means 1,350 different decisions being made. So if you want something to occur with land use in Pennsylvania, you need to coordinate with an extraordinary number of separate decision-making governments.

That's one of the big challenges in the Chesapeake Bay region. The other challenge is... take something like a crab. You think of crab, and you think Chesapeake Bay. Yet if you look at the natural history of the crab, in the southern bay it's mostly females. The northern bay is mostly males. It's not because we want to protect the female crabs in Maryland; it's because we don't fish them. We don't have them in the same way as Virginia. Well, in the end you need a male and a female, and we should never forget that. It's not just about protecting females. It's about protecting enough of the large, mature crabs so they can replace each other. So what you end up having is one fishery: crabs. But you have very different things going on in the two states.

Trotlining? It doesn't exist in Virginia. Therefore, if Virginia was to ban trotlining they're not doing anything because they don't have trotlines. Whereas, in Maryland, if you were to ban trotlining—and I'm not suggesting it—that's major! It's a huge cultural part of our fishery. So the region is united by the Chesapeake, but to really understand how to protect it, you have to understand the subtleties.

It was about 10 years ago now that the Commission started what's called the Bi-state Blue Crab Advisory Committee. We realized that the management of the blue crab is an extremely political thing, but it must be based on science. It's political because everyone believes they have a stake in the Chesapeake Bay blue crab. You own it, I own it, the watermen own it, the recreational fishermen own it, and the restaurateurs own it. We all love the blue crab. For most of us, it's been a part of our life. We either grew up here with crabs or we moved here to eat them. We all love them for being so iconic in our region. Well, the blue crab was declining in its population and, more importantly, they were very worried about the spawning stock. So we created the Bi-state Blue Crab Committee. It was made up of representatives from Maryland, Virginia, and the Potomac River Fisheries Commission, because the Potomac is a separate fishery, not governed by Maryland or Virginia. We tried to work with the scientists to determine the tipping-point for the blue crab. How many mature blue crabs do you need in the water to regenerate themselves? That is very fundamental to fisheries management, but fisheries are too rarely managed that way.

We developed two things: a threshold and a target. A fishery's threshold is the guardrail on the highway. It's the point beyond which you don't know if you can recover. You don't go past the guardrail because you don't know what's going to happen on the other side. But the guardrail isn't where you steer your car. You steer your car in the main lane. That's the target. It's not exact. It has some wiggle room, and there's a precautionary zone in-between. The same is true with a target for a fishery. You want to stay on the roadway. You want a little bit of a safety zone, so you're not fishing too close to that species' threshold.

And that's what we did. We negotiated the target and the threshold. And since then, we know that we are not at the threshold but we are fishing very, very close to it. We have yet to get ourselves back fully into the target zone.

When we're in the target zone, we will have doubled the spawning stock. Now, we will watch for about three years to see the impact of the regulations that we put in place. What we know already is that those regulations stopped the downward decline of the crab population. But we're still below the historic average, so there's still a long way to go.

Nature is going have natural impacts; there are going to be storms. The young crabs could be blown off the coast and we could have a bad year, so we need to be sure we're not fishing away their ability to bounce back. Nature can take a lot of pulling and tugging. It's like with a rubber band, you can pull it and pull it and pull it, and it bounces right back. But after a point you can pull that rubber band in and out so much that it loses its elasticity. We need to make sure that we're not fishing the crabs so hard that when nature hammers them, they can't come back. And that's what crab management is all about, finding that edge.

The Bistate Blue Crab Committee was an amazing bargain. It cost the two states very little money. But times got very tough, and so they were unable to continue funding it. The Commission keeps the scientists as our advisors, but the Bi-state Blue Crab Committee doesn't exist anymore.

There is heated concern right now that we are over-fishing menhaden. The menhaden is a filter-feeder and the bay's biggest problems in terms of water quality are nutrients—nitrogen and phosphorus—and sediment. Too many nutrients fuel algae blooms, which suck out the oxygen when they decompose. So the fact that menhaden filter out that nitrogen and phosphorus by filter-feeding the algae is a great thing. The question is, are we over-fishing them? There's mixed reports right now. Some feel we are, and some feel we aren't. Regardless, we know that there's a declining population of menhaden in the Chesapeake Bay. What we don't know is if they're shifting to another place the way the Baltimore oriole moved its niche north. Or, are we over-fishing them? Scientists are looking at that right now. The Commission's role is to watch the science and watch the politics, so that we know when a move needs to be made. We're still studying it.

The Susquehanna, the lifeblood of the Chesapeake, presents a completely different situation. It delivers half the fresh water in the bay, and is largely dominated by agriculture. Agriculture is a major industry in Pennsylvania, and therefore, contributes to a lot of the pollutant load that comes down river. Pennsylvania focuses its programs on agriculture, but capturing runoff from a field is way more elusive than out of a pipe, like a sewage treatment plant. You're never sure if you've captured it. You're never sure if the weather is confounding your efforts.

Pennsylvania has often been criticized, but the other side of the equation is they have no bay frontage yet they do have a Chesapeake Bay program with staff employed to work on it. Their constituents don't write them daily letters talking about the Chesapeake Bay. Now, I don't know if anyone loves crabs more than Pennsylvanians. It's amazing. They boat down here and, therefore, they're trying to work on bay issues. But if we don't get more dollars going to the Susquehanna farmers, we can't win. The loads are too great. So we need to really focus on agricultural funding in this region. And we need to get it at both the state level and the federal levels.

People don't realize it, but there are three really enormous bills in this country: the Transportation Bill (which you would imagine); the Defense Bill (which is on everybody's mind), and the Farm Bill. The Farm Bill is something that is renegotiated about every five years. They started it in the 1930's, really in response to the dust bowl and everything, but it's a way to support agriculture and food. Over the years it's morphed a bit to not only be about food, but also trade and conservation. The Farm Bill funds things like agricultural preservation, forested buffers along the waterways, or grassed waterways (which is where there's a lot of runoff from farmer's fields that can be channeled to a grassed buffers), and manure storage facilities.

The Farm Bill is up for reauthorization in 2007. This past year, to give you a sense of budget, the Farm Bill is 95.5 billion dollars. Now, about 65 billion of that goes into nutrition—food stamps, milk programs–and about 25 billion goes to farmers. That's your commodity payments, conservation, and flood insurance. Our interest is to get a lot more conservation dollars targeted to this region, since agriculture contributes more nitrogen and phosphorus than any other pollutant in the Chesapeake Bay.

We have to keep pace with the destructive activities going on, that's for sure. We lose about 100,000 acres of forest and enormous amounts of agricultural land to development each year. If development is going to play its role it has to do a couple of things. One is to make sure that when it's paving or creating impervious surfaces, that it's minimized. Every rooftop, every road, is denying the water access to the soil. If you don't get that water infiltrating slowly into the soil then you get it running off, picking up speed. The faster the water moves, the more it can erode, and the more it can carry pollutants.

The second thing is, we need to completely realign how we grow so that we're maximizing tree cover. I'm not sure we really take that seriously. Trees are part of our answer in life. They're creating our oxygen, they're cleaning our water, and they're protecting us from pollutants. Development really needs to take a good, careful look at that. I tell everybody, if you want to do something, plant a tree. Imagine if 16 million of us planted a tree. That would be a contribution.

The third thing is, people think the septic systems are failing if they're not controlling nitrogen. But septic systems are not designed to take out nitrogen. So, they're not failing, they're just not designed to do it. There are new systems that take nitrogen out. We need to somehow provide the incentives to incorporates nitrogen-removing systems in new development.

I will always be convinced that a mix of both regulatory programs and incentive-based voluntary programs that encourage you to contribute are appropriate. I think that laws that help protect the water are a very good thing, but I also think that incentive programs to help those valued land uses are also important, like for farmers. I think it's really good to have programs to help them, because I want cheap food and I want clean water. If those are my priorities, then as a taxpayer, I'd like to help them out.

I'd say I'm more than a mediator; I'm a negotiator. I help to bring together different parties to figure out a common so-lution. Remember, I work for House and Senate members and they have job interviews at least every four years when they run for re-election. They need to know that their constituents care, and that their constituents want them to do more than what they've done to date. If the constituents only want them to do what they've done so far then the bay is not saved.

If enough change happens at the local level, then that cumulative sum means we will have a healthy bay. I see a movement in that direction, but I also see complacency. I think everybody is just overwhelmed with life right now, and I think we need to have another surge and really make government leaders realize how important the bay is to us."

Don Boesch, President, University of Maryland Center for Environmental Science

Don Boesch is President of the University of Maryland Center for Environmental Science (UMCES), headquartered at Horn Point Laboratory near Cambridge, Maryland. UMCES extends to three laboratories located across the state: Horn Point Laboratory, Chesapeake Biological Laboratory at Solomons Island, and the Appalachian Laboratory in Western Maryland. The three labs give the Center access to all the environments in the state: Eastern Shore to ocean front, the Chesapeake Bay, and all the rivers and mountains of Western Maryland up to the Continental Divide. From Don's office in what was formerly an estate house of Alfred E. Dupont, we talked in 2006 about Don's career as an ecologist and biological oceanographer. After a description of the UMCES studies, he explained the reality of global warming and how scientists have used models to try to predict the future of the Chesapeake Bay.

"All of Maryland except a small part in Garrett County is in the Chesapeake Bay watershed," said Don. "Garrett County drains the other direction into the Ohio River and then down into the Mississippi River. But well in excess of 90% of the state is in the Chesapeake Bay watershed or drains into the coastal bays between Assateague Island and Ocean City.

Our Chesapeake Biological Laboratory was founded in 1925. It is the oldest state university-supported marine laboratory on the east coast of the United States. Only Scripps Institute of Oceanography in California is older. Our Chesapeake Biological Laboratory became the model for other states to create other similar laboratories. Down in Virginia, for example, there's the Virginia Institute of Marine Science. That didn't come along until the 40's. This effort, sustained for over 80 years now, has been to provide excellent research and education programs dealing with the bay and with our whole physical environment in Maryland.

We're well known for our research on many of the well-known problems such as nitrogen and phosphorus and so on, which came from the discoveries of our scientists. That was not necessarily widely understood or appreciated back even in the 1970's. So many of the issues we all deal with—the life history of crabs, the rockfish, and all those sort of things—are as a result of our work. In addition to that we've always had an educational mission and our educational mission is multi-fold. We have in our three laboratories probably 110 to 120 graduate students who are enrolled in one or more of our universities: at the University of Maryland at College Park, or Frostburg State University for example, getting Masters Degrees or PhD degrees in environmental science or in marine science. Many of those graduates go on to work in the state and federal agencies throughout the region, or they go elsewhere and become distinguished scientists in their own right."

What about the relationship between the university and state government. What is the role of each in relationship to the other? If the university is wed to the state government for funding how do they walk the line as an independent research body, when there could be a conflict of interests?

"We've always had a requirement in our mission and in the legislative mandate that created the center to provide advice to the government, to the state government in particular, on the management of our environment and its resources. So a very important part of our job is to provide independent, state of the art information and advice to state government, both to the agencies and to the political leadership in the General Assembly and the governors alike. As a result of that, I represent the university system on the Governor's Bay Cabinet. I've been serving three governors in that roll and I sit with the Secretaries of Environment, Natural Resources, Planning and Agriculture, and other state agencies, and provide advice to the Governor and his administration on the restoration of the bay as we progress.

The University of Maryland is well suited to do independent, objective research because we are not working directly for government or for appointed officials. There's always a question, if not the reality, of whether the research results have been slanted to serve some preordained director or conclusion. A good part of my job as the President is to protect our faculty members so that we can do independent research that isn't subject to political influence. We do that, among other reasons, because our faculty members do have academic freedom, and are protected by tenure and the like. We guard that very carefully so that there isn't undue pressure on our scientists to produce results which favor one side or another. Often that puts us in a situation which is unpopular, or goes against the grain of conventional wisdom or a certain direction of policy. We've had many notable examples of that in the past. One which is particularly important in our legend, if you will, is back in the days when Senator Bernie Fowler was advocating for control of nitrogen in sewage treatment plants up in the Patuxent River. At that time the EPA and the state agencies felt that was not necessary and that we were causing mischief by advising this. Senator Fowler then went to court and the case was settled through a process where we had to lay all the evidence on the table, to determine as fact that we needed to control nitrogen. Now we're very much focused on that process. When that took place, my predecessor was advised by government officials that, 'we ought to get rid of those guys. Those guys are causing mischief.' That wasn't appropriate and we've protected our scientists and protected that real tradition of independence of our research no matter how controversial it is and what the impact is. We're here to tell the truth as we know it."

Don Boesch grew up in the Crescent City of New Orleans, Louisiana, and has been actively engaged in post-Katrina restoration projects. As a child in Louisiana, Don developed a love for the outdoors life while fishing with his father.

"My father was an active sport fisherman," he recalled. "From the time I was a very little kid he used to take me out with him into the marshes to go fishing. It developed in me a real fascination for that environment. By the time high school came along I actually put that in the context of science. I had a biology teacher who was very good, and he encouraged me to think of that as a career. So I decided when I was in 10th grade that I was going to be a marine biologist. I'm one of the lucky few who had their dream at an early age and actually had the chance to live out their fantasies."

In 1967, Don Boesch moved to the Chesapeake Bay region to attend graduate school at the venerated Virginia Institute of Marine Science. But it was a subsequent trip that helped him to develop an environmental world view. "I went to Australia for a post doc year that really kind of broadened my view and horizons," *Don said. He then spent eight years on the faculty of VIMS before heading back down to Louisiana for the next decade, to head up the first marine laboratory down there.*

"The folks here in Maryland coaxed me to come back in 1990 and I did so because of my love and interest in the Chesapeake Bay during the years I worked down in the lower bay early on. But also because I firmly believe that the Chesapeake Bay is really important for the world. It's an area where we have some of the best science, we have a really good public commitment to do the right things to restore the bay, and good political leadership. If we can't do it here we really can't do it anywhere, so I think that this is a big test for us."

Dr. Boesch is an ecologist by trade. I asked him to expound on the term "ecology" and on just what an "ecosystem" is.

"We in science, in environmental science and ecology,

often use a word that's now becoming public parlance," he explained. "Even politicians use it. The word is 'ecosystem.' By that we mean the environment, both the living and nonliving environment, viewed in a way so that it all works together in a system. I'm an ecologist and a marine scientist. Rather than just thinking about the biology and about a community of organisms, a population or community of organisms, or just the physical environment, we think of it in totality. Because what we're seeing is that the physical environment— you know, the rainfall, the river flows, temperature variation, that sort of thing—obviously affect organisms, but we're also seeing that organisms can affect those physical things. The organisms regulate the composition of the atmosphere; the carbon dioxide and oxygen balances and that sort of thing. The forests regulate the amount of water that flows down the rivers and the like. So it really is interactive. The physical and chemical world influences the biological world, the biological world influences the physical and chemical world, and that's what we call an ecosystem.

Human beings are a very important part of the ecosystem. First, we're just another organism and so we've always been part of the ecosystem from the early days of the evolution of man. But nowadays it's even more important because, just as I said, organisms influence the physical world. Now we see humans able to do that on a very large scale, in the Chesapeake watershed or even the globe, the whole biosphere. Global warming is one obvious example. We're able, because of our activities, to actually change the composition of the earth's atmosphere and then have those feedbacks affect temperature, rainfalls, storms, all of those other things. We're in this as human beings, big time. We have a large roll to play in determining the outcomes in terms of how the ecosystem responds and develops and how it continues to produce the things that we depend on."

Is global warming a reality we need to be really worried about?

"I'm not a climate scientist myself. But I have been involved in a number of activities to help access the consequences of climate change. Most notably I was co-chair of the U.S. National Assessment of the Consequences of Climate Variability. I led the group that did the assessment of what it means for coastal and marine environments in this nation. As a consequence of that I have to keep abreast of the literature written by real experts, people who understand the climate system, the physical system of the world. It's really remarkable how that science has developed so dramatically over the years, by the nature of so many observations coming together to make a coherent picture. In addition, we have remarkable tools that help us understand that picture.

We have these computer models that people are able to run and actually understand how the climate will change given certain drivers or conditions. We also have a remarkable series of technologies that allow us to take measurements that we never had before, particularly satellite measurements, measurements from space. Just as an example, scientists have recently come together to understand the latest data, because there's debate about, for example, whether we are seeing a sea level rise over all the oceans of the world that's related to global warming. It's certainly projected that we will have sea level rise due to a warmer world. There are lots of reasons for that; expansion of the ocean volume as it heats, melting of glaciers, and the like. But are we actually seeing sea level rise?

A new consensus has been developed using measurements that have been in place since 1990, coming from satellites which are able to very precisely measure the distance between the satellite and the surface of the ocean. Imagine being able to measure that with the precision and accuracy of millimeters! Over the decade 1990-2000 the consensus is that there's a clear signal that we've had sea level rise that's increased from a rate of 1.8 millimeters a year to a little over 3 millimeters a year. So there's a real significant increase over the last part of the 20th century that's consistent with the theory of why sea levels should rise. There is an emerging consensus among the scientists who work on this.

There's lots of speculation, arguments and debates about exactly how fast things will change, but there's no real debate that increasing greenhouse gases, particularly carbon dioxide, and other gases as well, have already started a change in climate that's outside of the range of the natural variation and into a new territory. Furthermore, there's compelling evidence of a strong scientific consensus about the kinds of changes we will see over the next century or so.

Beyond that, of course, it becomes more difficult to predict, and also dependent on if we take action to reduce greenhouse gas emissions. Arnold Schwarzenegger signed a bill in California to reduce carbon dioxide emissions by 25 percent. If we begin to take actions like that, or even more drastic actions that some folks think that are going to be required, we can have some influence on climate change, although probably not right now, because the climate change has sort of a momentum. What's going to happen over the next 20 to 30 years is pretty much determined by what we've already done. But we do have choices to make about what happens in the rest of the century and beyond, things that effect my child and grandchild."

Don Boesch was also involved with a number of other great minds in formulating a broad spectrum study called Chesapeake Futures. The study employs various techniques for projecting the future by revisiting the past. Don's explanation of how these scientists work to predict the future reads like sort of a Batesonesque metalogue. Perhaps we're left with more questions than answers, but, as with the weather, it seems we are getting better all the time at forecasting future growth and development patterns.

"The Scientific and Technical Advisory Committee (STAC) undertook a project we called Chesapeake Futures: Choices for the 21st Century. Back around 2000 we were considering putting together the Chesapeake 2000 Agreement that all the states of the Chesapeake Bay region and the federal government signed. There were a lot of unknowns in that agreement, like by how much did you have to reduce the nitrogen and phosphorus, and sediment inputs into the bay. We undertook this project to try to get people to think about what reductions were going to be needed to restore the bay. By 'restore' we mean, not back to John Smith's bay (1708,) but maybe back to Bernie Fowler's bay where he could wade in the water up to his chest and see his feet, back in the 50's. We came to some conclusions just based on empirical evidence that actually were pretty close to the models that the EPA's Chesapeake Bay Program ran to set the new targets. So we developed a real-world appraisal of what would need to be done.

Empirical means tested by observation in the real world, rather than just developed from a projection by a theoretical model—real evidence. And the evidence was basically gathered from just going backwards in time and saying, 'ok, we want to see conditions that were like the 50's. What were the inputs that took place then?' We simply went back and used the past as a forecaster for the future.

The other thing we wanted to do was to say, 'how would you achieve these results? Are they achievable? What can we tell you on the basis of our understanding? And, what kinds of new capabilities might we have, technological breakthroughs or uses of existing technology that would help us get there?' That was also an important part of it. What we concluded was that, yeah, you could actually achieve those objectives. It's not going to be easy but it is technically achievable. It's going to take the alignment of what we want to do, and all the other things we're trying to do a little bit more effectively.

In agriculture for example: Let's try and use the subsidy programs that we have in this nation to support agriculture, which orients largely to increased production. How can we use those subsidies to increase environmental benefits so that the farmer is actually getting helped in increasing production?

What are the consequences if we look, not in the next two or three years but 10, 20 years out? What kinds of automobiles will we be driving? Will we have more hybrid vehicles, and can we find ways to lower the emissions from vehicles given the merging technology? Increased gas mileage is an important aspect as well.

The other thing that we tried to do with this is that we as human beings, particularly in political cycles, have a hard time seeing next year. Maybe we can think of four years and the next election and the like, but it's hard to see beyond that. All of the goals that the restoration effort has set heretofore have been goals like 'in the next 10 years at the most' we will do this. We tried to get people to think beyond that. Some of the challenges that we have, frankly, aren't going to be met in 10 years.

In 2000 we set these goals for the period of 2010. Some of those goals we're going to miss. Does that mean that we should give up? No. That means that they're going to take a longer time to achieve. Also, if you began thinking 20, 30 and 50 years out, you have to start thinking about things like climate change. How will that change the objectives of what we want? Is it going to make it harder or easier? We have to think of real technological innovation that might take place. Think back 50 years ago. No one thought we would be linked to the internet, that sort of thing, back then. So although it's hard to predict now, let's open our minds to the kinds of changes that might take place.

We're also going to have a lot more people and a lot more growth and development. Let's think about what that means. Let's think about what the options are for how we handle that growth and development. In Chesapeake Futures a very important part of the report was to look at population growth. We said we don't necessarily want to compare a growing population to one that's not going to grow, or at various rates, because we can't control that. Let's just use the population projections which have been made for the region, which forecast substantial growth. I don't remember the numbers off hand, but say we're going from 15 to 20 million people, and we won't challenge that assumption, what are the ways we can handle that?

We developed three scenarios. One scenario said that we're going to continue to grow like we've been growing. So we can just multiply the average amount of land that we consume as a function of the past population growth, and multiply that by the future population growth and assume that we're going to continue to sprawl out over the landscape. Another scenario is that we could say, in Maryland for example, we have this Smart Growth legislation that puts some restrictions on development. It says that the state government is going to direct its money to designated growth areas, and if you want to grow elsewhere you can pay for it yourself. The third scenario would be to really get serious about managing growth. We talked about ways where we could rebuild urban communities, provide incentives, have more restrictive zoning, and control growth by making it more compact; the same amount of people growing but we'll use less of the landscape.

So we looked at those three alternatives and it turns out that even if we did all the things that we need to, we will still have tremendous problems sustaining those gains. In other words, if we did all those things in agriculture, sewage treatment and atmospheric sources, but we didn't deal with land development and growth, we would at that point be losing ground and returning back to a degraded bay. So those solutions obviously have to be part of the mix. It's like the red queen in Alice in Wonderland; you always have to run faster to stay in one place. That's the challenge we face, because most people aren't arguing that we ought to take draconian steps. I don't know if we could, or if it's constitutionally feasible to take draconian steps to cap the population in the region. But if we are going to have this population growth, what does it take to stay in one place if we have to keep running faster?"

Kim Coble, Maryland Executive Director, Chesapeake Bay Foundation

Each year the Chesapeake Bay Foundation releases its State of the Bay Report, which uses a system of barometers to measure whether the bay is improving or becoming more impaired. I had the opportunity to meet with Kim Coble, Maryland Executive Director with the Foundation, to discuss the results of the 2006 report.

"It's the fall and while the bay is going into sort of a quiet phase with the cold weather and the changes in salinity and whatnot, our advocacy work is going into a very active mode. Legislative sessions are around the corner in January. We'll have a new governor, we'll have many new legislators, so we're trying to get ourselves organized and our new legislators educated, and hopefully, we'll be making some real progressive action for the bay. We're very hopeful. There's a lot of work that has to be done. The State of Maryland made a number of commitments to improving bay health and those commitments and goals are to be reached by 2010, as per the 2000 Chesapeake Bay Agreement. So this is the last group that can really help us get to those goals and get our commitments met. We're very hopeful that they're going to step up to the plate.

I think that there are a number of accomplishments that legislators can feel very proud about, steps in the right direction. The Chesapeake Bay Restoration Fund, the 'flush fee' or 'flush tax,' depending on which side of the isle you're on, was significant. It was a very creative solution to a problem for the bay. Under the Glendening administration the whole concept of 'smart growth' which was really outside of the box for the entire nation, quite frankly, made some great strides.

The problem is—and this is where we're hopeful that this group will do things a little bit differently—we need sustained leadership, sustained commitment. We need somebody to say 'I'm going to do what it takes to get the bay restored and keep it there,' rather than looking at a specific action and saying, 'ok, I did one thing; I've done my environmental deed for the term, or for my four years.' That's where I think that this particular group of legislators and the new governor (Martin O'Malley) and his administration will have an opportunity to truly be the heroes. It's been a long time since we've had a sustained commitment towards leadership for restoring the bay.

The irony of bay restoration is that we know what the problem is and we actually know what the solutions are. In some cases we might need to tweak this or tinker with that, but for the most part we know what to do. The roadmap has been laid. It's a matter of leadership in saying, 'yes, we are going to take this road, and, I'm not going to get out of the vehicle. I'm going to keep my foot on the gas peddle until we get there.' That kind of focus has not been around for decades.

Our population is no doubt increasing and the impact of that population will be exponential. It's going to be hard to keep even with that increase in population. 100,000: That's the number of people that are moving into the watershed every year. We're going to need to accelerate our efforts and our commitment in order to just stay even, let alone to make the progress we need to make.

While you can look out and say the bay looks pretty good and the environment's doing alright, it can be deceiving. There are a lot of things that occur underneath that water that are not healthy. I think if you ask our watermen and our scientists they'll be the first ones to tell you that underneath the surface things are not as good as we'd hoped. This year citizens experienced many more beach closures than we've had in years past. We have to go upstream, go up the tributaries, go into our own backyards and realize that the way we're living will not ensure a safe environment for our grandchildren."

A safe environment...can you talk about the correlation between human health issues and the local environment?

About what has been accomplished during the first 30 to 40 years of the Chesapeake Bay restoration effort?

"The nexus between our health and our environment is becoming ever more present all the time," said Kim. "The best case example we have is the power plants. All of us turn on a light everyday. All of us plug something in or use something that's plugged in everyday. We are all part of that problem. Those power plants generate the electricity that we use. In doing so they spew out a tremendous amount of pollutants and toxics that are harmful to our health, that are hurting citizens with asthma and other respiratory problems and are severely hurting our environment. We have nitrogen pollution going in the bay. We have mercury fish advisories for every tributary stream in Maryland. Power plants are a high level source of that mercury. So here we have a problem that's affecting our health and our environment. We're all part of that problem. How do we go about correcting it?

Last year in Maryland, we made progress by passing the Maryland Healthy Air Act. We have made some real strides over the last few decades. Our governors have gotten together and there have been several agreements between all the bay states. The first one was in 1987, and they all agreed to take specific actions in their states to improve the health of the bay. The most recent agreement was the Chesapeake 2000 Agreement. It was actually a very thorough, in-depth document. The Chesapeake Bay Program spearheaded authoring the agreement, but the stakeholders included hundreds and hundreds of people participating and discussing. I personally was involved in writing some of the commitments dealing with toxic chemicals. We spent hours and days sitting around the table trying to come up with commitments that would balance the needs of our society and community, the health of the bay and the environment. The document really is very well done, very aggressive. As we're approaching the year 2010 a lot of those commitments are due and those goals should be met. But we're far from meeting many of them.

Maybe a good analogy is if you're running a race and with each step you get further behind. Every day the price of technology that has to be implemented goes up. The number of people that are moving in goes up. The amount of pollution goes up. Every day it gets harder, and so everyday that we slow our pace down or don't meet these goals and commitments, we're just falling further behind."

Photo courtesy of Keith Campbell Foundation for
the Environment

Dr. Keith Campbell, Founder, Keith Campbell Foundation for the Environment

Keith Campbell is the founder and chairman of the Keith Campbell Foundation for the Environment. He's also the man that created Campbell & Company, a hugely successful investment advisory firm he founded 35 years ago. Keith has played a vital leadership role as investor in innovative programs designed to restore the Chesapeake Bay. Most recently he accepted the job as chairman of the board of trustees for the Chesapeake Bay Foundation. What gave Keith Campbell his drive to get involved in conservation and restoration issues? Keith grew up on Long Island, mucking around the edges of Long Island Sound. On his grandmother's nearby salt pond Keith and his father would venture out in their skiff in search of crabs.

"My dad and I would pole that boat around with two long-handled crab nets," he remembered. "We never used bait and we could net a bushel of crabs in less than two hours. That's when I was 10 years old and probably not a whole lot of help to my dad, between that, fishing, catching bait for fishing, and digging clams up out of the sand. Quahogs, they were called.

Scuba diving along the rocky coastline of Rhode Island was really a life changing experience for me. I got my first mask and fins and not too long after that I saw my first Jacques Cousteau type documentary.

My mother was a wonderful housewife and a wonderful mother. She was the greatest. I say 'was' because my parents are both deceased. I miss my mother and my father very much. My mother was a special person with a very warm heart, also very involved in the environment. In fact, when she died, the next morning I looked out of the French doors from my bedroom to a pool that's about 70 or 80 feet from the house.

The pool was built to look like a pond, and it does look like a pond. Standing on the edge of the pool was a blue heron. My mother's favorite bird. My wife and I have never seen a blue heron there before nor after that day. Now, I don't know what that all means, but to this day there is a Turner sculpture in that garden of a blue heron, my mother's favorite bird. Every day when I see it, it reminds me of my mother. That's a true story. So if you believe in the supernatural or a next life, I don't know if she came back in the form of a blue heron, but that blue heron spoke to me."

During his college years Keith studied marine biology with an emphasis on ichthyology but soon chose the more lucrative business he's still in. With success came the opportunity to give back. In 1998 he formed the Keith Campbell Foundation for the Environment.

"I founded Campbell and Company in 1972. It's grown substantially. We now have about 140 employees and we do business all over the world. We're actually one of the largest hedge funds. It took me about 20 years to really build it into something and then another 10 years to realize that I had built it into something that could be good for change.

While we don't do 100 percent environmental funding it's principally environmental; probably 90 to 95 percent. Essentially our mission is to finance and aid groups who are attempting to make change in the environment throughout the world.

I think it's important to realize that the Chesapeake Bay is an immense economic engine. It's not just because of what the bay produces, it's because of the lifestyle that is enabled by the bay. The cleaner the bay is and the more abundant it is, the better it is for the people who live on its shores or around it. Let me give you a perfect example of how valuable the Chesapeake is: In 1958 my father came down here to run the CBS affiliate WMAR-TV in Baltimore. That's how we moved here from New York. He had opportunities to manage television stations in Toledo, Ohio, Atlanta, Georgia, Houston, Texas and Dallas, Texas. He turned them all down because Bill Burton, who at the time was the outdoor editor at the Baltimore Sun, took him out on the Chesapeake Bay fishing. When Bill Burton got him out on the bay he said 'I'm coming to Baltimore, because of the Chesapeake.'

I started my business in California in 1972. I moved it here in the mid 70's because of the Chesapeake Bay, and the coastal bays and the beaches in the Mid-Atlantic. I came back here and I moved a business that today generates approximately 500 million dollars in gross revenue into the economy of the State of Maryland. We import most of that money. Half our business is U.S., half our business is international. That's driving other economic engines in this area and that adds to the quality of all of our lifestyles."

What kinds of projects and proposals do the Campbell Foundation for the Environment fund?

"The Foundation focuses again, where we can do it, on projects that are highly leveraged by the involvement of people at the grassroots level. So, if you've got a group of people who have a stream running through their backyard collectively, and the stream needs to be cleaned up, but they need $5,000 or $10,000 to get the 10 or 20 or 30 individuals equipped to deal with the stream, create buffers or clean the stream up, than we'll try to aid and abet them. A good example of that would be the Herring Run Watershed Association right here in Baltimore, under the direction of Mary Roby. They have done a terrific job. We've supported them for at least three or four years. Modest donation but a group that really works hard, has tremendous community involvement and is cleaning up Herring Run, which runs into the Back River, which runs into the Chesapeake Bay. It all starts in the head waters and it ends up in the bay, and it's not just what we put directly into the bay, but it's what we put into the tributaries to the bay.

One of the grants we made, in fact, was to build a state

of the art vessel which strangely enough is named after my wife, Patricia. It's plying the bay right now engaged virtually every day in planting oysters and building oyster reefs, which is what we really need to do. We need to find the substrate for oysters to set on naturally. Substrate for oysters normally has been oyster shell. The problem is that we've mined so much oyster shell and taken so much out of the bay, frankly, we've flattened the oyster reefs.

In the late 1800's Long Island was largely fished out of oysters. So the fishermen headed down this way and they found the Chesapeake Bay oysters abundant. But harvesting them when they're in 20 foot vertical reefs, that's how oysters used to grow, is not easy. So what they did was took basically their dredge equipment and their harvesting equipment, dragged it over the reefs and flattened them, so that number one they could harvest 'em then, but number two it would make future harvest easier. At one point they were taking 10 million bushels of oysters a year out of the Chesapeake Bay. As far back as 1900, a book was written called *The Oyster* by a fellow named Keith Brooks. It's a treatise on the oyster, biologically and in terms of harvest and in terms of its value in our ecosystem. The oyster as a single animal goes is probably the most valuable animal in the history of the ecosystem of the Chesapeake Bay. We don't have it anymore. The book pointed out that in 1900 we needed to regulate the harvest of oysters and change the way we take oysters or we wouldn't have an oyster industry.

The Chesapeake Bay oyster at one time accounted for between 15 and 20 percent of all of United States commerce in seafood. It also provided between 15 and 20 percent of the employment nationally of the entire seafood industry. Chesapeake Bay became famous for seafood because of oysters—not rockfish, not crabs, not eels, not anything else but oysters. The key to that was when they discovered how they could shuck and can oysters. That enabled them to ship them all over the country by rail. That's basically how the Chesapeake Bay got its fame for seafood, and that's also how the oyster got harvested into virtual extinction. We have to do something about that."

What do you see as the main hurdle to climb over, in order to get the Chesapeake Bay cleaned up and fully functioning once again?

"We need on the order of 20 billion dollars over a decade to clean up the bay. To get to between 60 and 80 percent of that we only need somewhere near eight billion dollars. We've just blown up the equivalent of almost two trillion dollars in Iraq, and this estuary is almost 200 miles long, drains a population of 16 million people from as far north as New York to West Virginia, includes seven distinct political entities, states and Washington, DC, 64,000 square miles—when you look at this, it's not too much to ask the states and the federal government to pony up over a 10 year period of time at least the eight billion. We've identified the problems, we know the technical solution to the problems. It means simply putting the money together to do it. It's peanuts!

We also must develop the political will to do it. The difficulties are that most politicians unfortunately look at what they do for their constituents on a very short term basis. The payoff here... I mean you can see the results of riparian buffers within one year of installation. I've seen it in six or seven years and it's a whole new ecosystem teaming with birds, animal and plant life and fish in the streams. The difficulty is that if a politician today says, 'ok I'm going to appropriate funding for this particular environmental need' the results generally won't be recognized until he's out of that particular office and onto something else.

I'm sure you're aware of Al Gore's effort on global warming and his book and movie *An Inconvenient Truth,* which I think is wonderfully done. The issue is how much are we contributing and what can we do to reverse it, how fast. But there are very, very important senior scientists with the government who have stated that we might have 10 or 15 years at most to turn it around. Otherwise what will happen is there'll be a compounding effect of the global warming that's going on now principally through warming of the seas, that will not be reversible in the foreseeable future. What does a one degree average temperature difference mean, or what does a degree and a half mean? Well, it means entire forests can be consumed by pests that didn't exist because of the temperatures that they can't tolerate. Jim Hansen of NASA is the foremost authority at the government level on global warming. He was told not to talk to the press about his opinions on global warming. He stated that publicly. He feels so strongly about it that he simply defied his superiors and went out and said, look, we have a problem here. Now I'm not an alarmist, but when people of that level with that education and that responsibility are willing to buck the federal government that employs them that really raises my antenna.

Energy policy has got to change. We have to find alternative energy sources. We have to change the ways we use energy from the kinds of cars we drive, from how the cars are powered, how we burn fossil fuels. We're not going to eliminate fossil fuels as an energy source, but when we do burn coal and when we do burn oil, when we burn all fossil fuels, we need to burn them efficiently. We have that technology now. The problem is that it's costly."

The Keith Campbell Foundation for the Environment has reached out beyond the Chesapeake Bay in their efforts to promote and support restoration and protection of the environment. Keith's love for surfing has him touring in search of the perfect wave. That journey has taken him to pristine environments which can be saved before they are damaged in the first place.

"We've done work as far away as the northwest Hawaiian Islands. The northwest Hawaiian Islands were declared a National Monument by President Bush. In spite of some things that I think he's done that are very, very negative to the environment, I must say that I think that was a good stroke. Eleven hundred miles of the most pristine coral reef ecosystem in the world and it was being fished at the time by eight commercial fishermen out of Honolulu, which will cease in five years. The Pew Foundation tried to buy the licenses but the fishermen wouldn't sell 'em. For the life of me I don't understand why. Nonetheless that's a done deal now and we put money and time and effort into that because of a strong belief not only in restoring the important bodies of water and protecting bodies of land and air, but also a very strong belief in protecting areas that are pristine and don't need restoration, they simply need protection in perpetuity.

We are, in my opinion, in the sweet spot in the next five to eight years. When I started the foundation I would have put the environment at number six on the political scene; it's now number three or four in the State of Maryland. Behind the normal health, education and welfare comes the environment. That's a big step in the right direction. I think that on the national level it's moved up at least one peg maybe from five to four, or six to five. Politically, people are now becoming aware of the environment—so politicians are now beginning to become aware of it."

Russell Train, Former Administrator, US Environmental Protection Agency

Russell Train is a Washington insider through and through. He grew up in the nation's capital during the 20's, the son of a U.S. Navy officer. "My father graduated from the Naval Academy in 1900," he told me. "His father graduated from the Naval Academy in 1865. This is home port, I guess, for me then!" *I spoke with Mr. Train at his home in Washington, D.C. back in the winter of 2004.*

"My father's father was the son of a Congressman from Massachusetts. Actually, he was elected to congress in 1858 as a Republican, just before the Civil War. That was the first year, I believe, the Republicans really fielded candidates around the country. So I guess my Republicanism goes back a long way. He served in Congress a couple of terms but he resigned in the middle of his second term to take a commission from President Lincoln as a Captain in the Army. He went out and his first battle was Antietam, which was probably the bloodiest of them all. He survived that and after the war he served nine times as Attorney General of Massachusetts.

I had lots of clergy on all sides of my family. I have at least three Baptist ministers in my background. I didn't grow up a Baptist; I grew up an Episcopalian. There was a big revival of religion back in the early 1800's. Some of my forbearers really got caught up in it. On my mother's side, the family here in Washington went back about five generations. I had a great, great grandfather Brown who came to Washington in 1807. He founded the first Baptist church in Washington. Then in the early 1830's he built a church down on 10th Street which later became Ford's Theatre, where Lincoln was assassinated. He was the minister there for many, many years until he died. In the meantime he was a very busy fella. Not only was he a minister in a fairly active church, but he was the Chief Clerk of the

Post Office Department, which was one of the most active departments in those days. He was the guy responsible for all of the contracts for carrying the mail around the country. He was one of the two founders of Columbian College, which later became George Washington University, which, of course, is still going strong in the city. He also was a member of the board of directors for one of our early banks here in Washington. He was Chaplain of the Senate and Chaplain of the House, not at the same time. But he had several terms in that regard. He was doing all these things at the same time. He and his wife ran a boarding house which was where most of the politicians lived. They didn't bring their families to Washington in those days. There was a lot of entertaining and socializing amongst the political figures. My great, great grandfather had the somewhat unusual name of Obadiah Braun Brown. He was sometimes described as a member of President Jackson's 'kitchen cabinet.'

Back in the late 20's my father was Captain of the battleship *Utah*. It was the oldest battleship in commission in our Navy in those days. When President Hoover was elected in 1928, Hoover and his wife made a goodwill trip around South America after their election and before they took office. In those days Presidents didn't get inaugurated until the following March. So he had plenty of time for a trip like that. My father was assigned the duty of taking his ship down to Uruguay and South American to Montevideo, the Capital of Uruguay, to pick the Hoovers up and bring them back to the United States. He did, and that was about a two week trip with stops here and there in Rio de Janeiro and elsewhere. Obviously, they got to know each other pretty well on that voyage. They became really good friends and respected each other. My father was always a huge admirer of Herbert Hoover. About a year later, my father was assigned as Hoover's Naval aid at the White House and he served there for maybe two to three years. He had a very close relationship with the Hoovers. He finally left the White House and was transferred to the Naval War College in Newport, Rhode Island. My mother was left to close the house here in Georgetown and the Hoovers very kindly invited me and my two older brothers to the White House for the night before we went up to join my dad. The idea was to get us out of the way of my mother so she could go ahead and close the house and do all the dirty work. So that was very thoughtful.

Of course, that was a fascinating time for the three of us. I remember very little about it. My two older brothers slept in the Andrew Jackson bedroom, as it's called. I slept in the small bedroom that opened into it. We had breakfast with the Hoovers. It was on the South Portico the next morning. I remember that because I sat next to the President and I had a huge glass of California orange juice in front of me. I don't think I had seen anything like that in my life. That's basically what I remember. I presume I had some kind of conversation with Hoover but I do not recall it. At that point I would have been maybe 11.

As a boy in my teen age years I had the fantastic good fortune of spending four summers in Europe because my closest friend here in Washington, who was named Alm Wilson, his father was a foreign service officer and stationed successively in Berlin, Prague, and then Brussels in Belgium. They wanted their son to come over for summers to stay with them. They'd been abroad for quite some while and hadn't seen him. They thought he needed some company so they very kindly invited me to come along on those trips, and I did. I had four extraordinary opportunities to see a lot of Europe at a really critical time. My last trip among those I've just described was from Brussels back home again and World War II broke out while we were on ship on the way back to the United States. So we saw a lot of what was building up in those days. We saw the tensions between the Germans and the Czechoslovaks. We saw a lot in Berlin, the burning of the Reichstag and the great mobs at that time. We were there when the Brown Shirts were attacked by the rest of the Nazis. There was a lot going on which I probably did not understand a great deal about, but at least I was exposed to it, and I've carried it with me to this time.

The Olympics were in 1936. We were in Prague that summer. My friend's mother Mrs. Wilson and my friend and I drove to Berlin from Prague, stopping at Dresden on the way to see one of the art galleries there. We went to the Olympics outside of Berlin. About all I remember of that was just being in the stadium with a vast crowd of about 100,000 all shouting, "Sieg heil, sieg heil, sieg heil!" with their raised arms as Hitler walked into the stadium. I could see him. He was across the way from us but I could see him quite clearly. My friend and I were then probably around 15 or 16, I'm not too sure. But we refused to stand up for Hitler. We remained seated with our hands in our pockets, a little curious about what the reaction of the people around us would be to that. They sort of looked at us, but paid no further attention to us. Of course, Jessie Owens was one of our great participants there in that Olympics. Great runner, I guess it was the 100-yard dash at that time, if I remember, and he won the gold medal and stood in front of the stand where Hitler was to receive his award, and Hitler turned his back instead of saluting the victors because Jessie Owens was, of course, black. Hitler, if he was anything, he was a racist. Those were interesting times."

To their father's dismay the sons decided against the Naval Academy and headed for Princeton (although they did enlist in the Navy during the war years).

"My two older brothers had gone to Princeton. They seemed to be having an awfully good time there and I decided I wanted to follow them. And that's what I did. After I went to college and after close to five years service in World War II in the field artillery I did have to make up my mind what I was going to do with the rest of my life. The law appealed to me. I always felt, and still do, that the law opens a lot of different possible avenues. Today you can be an environmental lawyer with an environmental organization and have a whole career in that direction. And you learn a lot of different things in a course on the law. Hopefully you learn how to use your mind in a logical and constructive way, which is useful no matter what you do.

   After studying law, I became a Congressional Clerk. They call it Chief of Staff now but in those days Clerk was the common term for all the congressional committees. Of course today you say you're the clerk and people probably think you're taking shorthand notes or something or other. Aileen and I met here in Washington when I was Clerk of the Ways and Mean Committee. We had a date or two and one thing led to another and in 1954 we got married. We've had a wonderful 50 years together. She's been a trustee of the Chesapeake Bay Foundation for nine years, I think, and loved every minute of it. I imagine she's going to keep pretty well associated there even though she may not be on the board.

   It was also a job that brought me in contact with an awful lot of people within the leadership on the hill, including not only the House but also on the Senate side, particularly when a tax bill would be in conference between the House and Senate. Eventually, after I went to the Treasury from the Capital, I served as head of their tax legal staff. But that was not for very long. That was during the Eisenhower Administration and when a vacancy appeared on the United States Tax Court I was nominated by President Eisenhower to be a judge. I was confirmed quite quickly because I knew all the players on the tax committees. That was no problem, and I served on the Tax Court for about eight years here in Washington."

   Judge Train's success on the bench meant that he was ripe for a promotion. Perhaps due to his family's early history as farmers and hunters, Russell Train was drawn into work as an environmental administrator.

   "I've just written a book called *Politics Pollution and Pandas*," he reminds us. "The pandas refer to the last 25 years or so that I've spend with the World Wildlife Fund as President, chairman and now chairman emeritus. The book is a memoir. It does purport to try to tell from my standpoint an important bit of history of environmental accomplishment in this country. I'd say the heart of the book is the eight years of the Nixon and Ford Administrations, where I had the privilege of serving variously as Under Secretary of the Interior Department, first chairman of the Council on Environmental Quality, and then for well over three years as Administrator of the Environmental Protection Agency under both Nixon and Ford. Landmark legislation in the form of the Clean Water and Clean Air Acts, among others, was pushed through during this time.

I had major legislative responsibilities in our government, as the Chairman of the Council on Environmental Quality in the White House and then as the Administrator of the EPA; we had to work with a lot of the Republican administration and the Congress which all through those years was controlled by the Democrats. Unless you worked with the other party, you never got anywhere. In consequence of that situation the two parties really worked closely together. I hardly remember any legislation, certainly in my field, that I would say was strictly a partisan matter at all.

One of my reactions today is that since bipartisanship seems to have vanished from the Congress you get a lot of extreme rhetoric but very little accomplished. Look at the legislative record of the last few years. There's very little done. There's an awful lot of sound and fury, a lot of hearings and what have you, people posturing, but very little concrete accomplishment. We got an awful lot accomplished in those days, certainly in the environmental area. And most of the legislation was enacted overwhelmingly. You built a real consensus. I think that's essential if you're really going to accomplish things.

Nixon was an enigma and he was strange in many ways, brilliant in many ways, effective in many ways and a disaster. He was his own worst enemy, certainly the whole Watergate fiasco was an example of that. When you're at the pinnacle, you're vulnerable. Maybe it's a good lesson for the rest of us. Nixon was certainly not an environmentalist. I've got to say, I don't think he understood many of the issues very well. However he knew one thing about it and that was that the people of this country were worried about the environment. I'm talking about the late 60's and the early 70's. The people of this country were worried. There were huge oil spills, there were rivers catching on fire, toxic chemical poisonings, a lot of things. It was very scary. There was rudimentary regulation; much of it was left to the states to handle. And it was plain that the federal government had to get more actively into the whole thing. Nixon seized on it. He made it a central effort of his administration, certainly in his first term. It was not only a political choice on his part, in that sense. It was a Democratic Congress whose environmental leader was Edmund Muskie. Nixon recognized Muskie as a potential Democratic candidate against him in 1972. Muskie's track record for the public was basically dealing with air and water pollution. Nixon made up his mind he was going to trump Muskie with his own issue, and I think he did. Hah—he 'stole his clothes!' I think somebody said that, and I think it's quite true.

Whatever the motivations were, Nixon grabbed the issue. He signed the National Environmental Policy Act into law on January 1, 1970 as his first official act of the decade. A few days later he sent his State of the Union message to the Congress, and at least a third of that message dealt with the environment. Rather a stark contrast with today when George W. Bush's recent State of the Union message does not have a word about the environment. If you want to talk about the George W. Bush Administration, I think as far as the environment is concerned it's a disaster, pure and simple. I don't think there's any interest in it, for one thing, except in a negative sense. There's nobody in the White House that has any background in the environment, any interest in the environment. The President has appointed key people in the resource agencies—Department of the Interior, Department of Agriculture, and EPA—with industry lobbyists. Particularly for extractive industries: timber, paper, pulp, mining, coal mining, oil and gas. These people are in key decision-making spots throughout the administration. I think that's wrong and I don't think that's really serving the best interests of the American people. It's serving the special interests, not the broader public. The other aspect of this which has absolutely appalled me is the fact that regulatory decisions at EPA seem to get made by the White House. The White House is forever injecting itself into regulatory decision-making by EPA, which is described in its statute as an independent agency. In the federal government I know it can't be strictly an independent agency. But it does not serve the public interest to have a political White House with no scientific capability, no environmental background, making the decisions that are now being made from a political standpoint. That is not in the best interest of the American people. I'd say the most important decisions at EPA do relate to health–auto emissions, the regulation of pesticides, herbicides and other agricultural chemicals, radiation, toxic chemicals–these are health problems and need to be dealt with in the best scientific way, taking into account, where appropriate, economic costs, and balancing these. But not from the standpoint of whether some special interest that's a big contributor gets special treatment. I think this is an outrage.

Energy has been a sharp interface with environmental statutes from the beginning, necessarily. Most energy production, if left uncontrolled in some way, tends to be quite highly polluting. At the same time energy people claim, sometimes with some justification, that environmental rules are restricting them from reasonable development and use of energy. There are intelligent middle grounds here. I remember an interview that President Ford gave some years back. He was asked about me as head of EPA and about Frank Zarb, who was head of the Federal Energy Agency at that time. He was asked how he got us to reach agreement on things. Well, he said very simply, he just told Train and Zarb to go into a room and sit and talk it out. That was a somewhat simplistic statement, I guess, but it conveys the idea. You do have to take both sides into account. This has been one of my major complaints about the so-called energy policy of this administration. Opening the Arctic Wildlife Range to oil development, for example, is an unhappy thing for most conservation-minded people. It's the last really enormous, pristine wilderness that belongs to the United States. You hate to see it cut up into oil patches and pipelines and spills and all that goes with it, even if a good job is done as I'm sure it probably would be. But as unhappy as I would be with that, if the administration at the same time had proposed and seriously intended to implement a balancing program for energy conservation and promotion of energy efficiency to save the oil that we squander in unregulated automobiles, that would put a different face on the whole thing, in my mind. It would be a balanced program. This administration doesn't seem to know what a balanced program is. It's one thing or the other, it's an extreme, and I don't like it."

Dr. Torrey Brown, Former Secretary, Maryland Department of Natural Resources

Dr. Torrey Brown received his doctorate from Johns Hopkins University, Baltimore, in 1961. Dr. Brown's education and career have come full circle more than once as he first became an Associate Professor and then Assistant Dean at the Johns Hopkins Medical School. He's a specialist in new biotechnology product development and currently Chairman of the Board of Intralytix, a Baltimore biotech company. Dr. Brown was elected as a Delegate to the Maryland legislature for 12 years (1971-1983) and served as Chairman of the Environmental Matters Committee before being chosen as Secretary of the Maryland Department of Natural Resources under Governor Hughes.

Governor Harry R. Hughes and Secretary Brown made an exceptional environmental team, accomplishing a great deal during the Hughes Administration. After spearheading the first Chesapeake Bay Agreement in 1983, Governor Hughes and Secretary Brown proposed a successful legislative and budgetary package of 15 initiatives designed to take vigorous action to restore and protect the Chesapeake Bay. Their accomplishments include the Chesapeake Bay Critical Areas law, a ban on phosphates that pollute the bay, the creation of the Chesapeake Bay Trust and license plate fund, and the rockfish moratorium. It's felt by many that these two men set the pace for the whole restoration movement. I met with Dr. Brown during the spring of 2007, at his office in a large restored warehouse building overlooking the Camden Yards Stadium, home to the Baltimore Orioles.

"I was in the Maryland State legislature for 12 years and got to know Governor Hughes because he was a senator, and then governor," Dr. Brown said. "He appointed me to be Department of Natural Resources Secretary. We spent a lot of time while I was in the Secretary's job finding ways to help improve the bay, and finding more money to support programs that helped improve the bay.

Harry Hughes was an absolutely fabulous governor. I mean, he instantly adopted the notion that the bay needed work and appointed a task force to do the work, to make the needed changes that were obvious at the time. He was very, very supportive of everything that affected the bay."

How did the Wye Island Group map out a vision of what needed to be done for the Chesapeake?

"We met down on Wye Island every Thursday for about eight months to say what each department–agriculture, natural resources, environment, planning, transportation–should do to work on the problem that they create. We put in nine bills that were to improve the bay and they all passed. Bills to decrease runoff from development, to improve sewage treatment plant operations, to decrease the contribution of runoff from agriculture... The legislature added one that prohibited detergents with phosphate. One of the problems for the bay is too much phosphate, too much nitrogen. That was well-known to be a problem and the legislature decided we should do that, so it passed.

We've come to better understand how harsh excess nitrogen is on the Chesapeake Bay, much of which results from runoff. Curtailing the use of phosphates in detergents was also very, very important, because it decreased the amount of phosphate that went into the bay. Later Pennsylvania and Virginia passed that. I think it was very important to have a victory and to have people realize that everybody causes part of the problem."

Tell us a little bit about how the Executive Committee came together with the heads of all the Chesapeake Bay states and the Mayor of Washington, D.C., and how they worked toward the first Chesapeake Bay Agreement.

"It was fascinating because the three states that affect the bay very much had never worked together in an organized way to improve the Chesapeake. Before they started to work together they were, I guess, less competitive than in a position to blame each other. Maryland would say the pollution came from Pennsylvania. Virginia would say the pollution came from Maryland and Pennsylvania. No one had really documented the relationship between the bay and what each state contributed. At that time the varying interests also acted like it was somebody else's fault. The watermen would say it was industry's fault or the city's fault. The cities would say it's not our sewage problem, its industry's toxic chemicals. So everybody blamed each other. Nobody really knew the contribution of each segment. Once it was obvious that everybody had an effect–developers, industries, cities, farms, watermen, sports fishermen—that everybody all together was the problem—then we could start talking about how to improve the behavior of each group.

There was defensiveness on everybody's part until the bay studies showed that everybody contributed. The cities and developed areas contributed excess sewage, untreated. Agriculture contributed fertilizer and runoff, sediment. Developers realized that they contributed runoff. Watermen realized that they took too many fish. Once the data was in, then everybody said we've got to all work together. We all have to solve the problem we're creating."

What were your feelings when you went to Governor Hughes with the idea of placing a moratorium on fishing for rockfish, striped bass, in the Chesapeake Bay.

"Rockfish were going down for decades, I guess. Everybody tried to do something less than final to decrease the catch of rockfish. The old law of many, many years before the moratorium was that you could catch rockfish everyday of the year all day and night and keep as many as you wanted, because they were so plentiful no one thought they could be hurt by over-fishing. But they were reproducing less and less. The idea of the moratorium was that you can not make a mistake if you just stop catching them. There are a lot of reasons for fish species to be hurt. One of them is man taking them, or killing them, and you couldn't make a mistake if you just stopped that. I used to illustrate it by saying that we were killing all the calves. If you had a herd of cattle and you harvested or killed the calves you'd never have a continuing source of supply to continue having a herd. So we put a moratorium on catching any rockfish until enough of them had grown up and spawned that the progeny would be left to sustain the population.

I had no idea how long it was going to take. Nobody did. But it worked, and they repopulated the bay. Now the idea is to protect them while they're spawning and all the rules and regulations aim at saying every fish gets a chance to spawn at least once."

How did people feel about the rockfish moratorium? Was there a huge outcry of opposition?

"Oh, some of them were wildly opposed, violently opposed. The Natural Resources Police said I shouldn't go on the Eastern Shore without a protection unit because the watermen were so violently opposed. Now they're appreciative of what everybody did. But the general public was phenomenally supportive in that they really abided by the moratorium. I remember the first year I think we checked 14,000 boats who were out fishing during the time when you weren't supposed to be catching rockfish. Only two or three had rockfish. But it was a very rigid rule. You couldn't catch 'em, you couldn't target 'em, even to throw 'em back. You couldn't own any even if you caught them in Virginia. You couldn't bring them into Maryland. Obviously it happened, but it was not allowed to happen. You can't prevent a rockfish from getting on a hook but nobody could keep them and nobody could catch them for fun."

How did you find the courage to make such an unpopu-

lar decision that affected so many people, people who weren't used to what we call 'managing species,' who believe perhaps that what's found in nature is the property of whomever who finds it?

"You just got to say, 'I think this is right and I'm expecting it will work, and it's the only safe thing to do'. And the Governor was very, very supportive. He said, 'If you think that's right, do it.'"

Governor Harry R. Hughes, Former Governor of Maryland

Governor Harry R. Hughes's Administration proved that public opinion does matter, and that environmental problems can be dealt with when leaders focus on the importance of the problems at hand. This three-term governor provided such leadership, while searching for solutions to the Chesapeake Bay's problems. I interviewed Governor Hughes on his front porch overlooking the upper Choptank River, in his boyhood hometown of Denton, on Maryland's Eastern Shore.

"The way we got into the restoration was Senator Mathias had put in a bill for the congress to do a study of the bay. The staff brought it to me and said, 'Let's do something about it this time, instead of just putting it on the shelf like all the ones before it.' We formed a little group we called the Bay Group, or the Wye Island Group. Torrey Brown and other deputies and secretaries spent a lot of time down there, one day at a time, working up the program. We went with it, and we spent a lot of time trying to sell it to groups around the state, and newspapers, before the session started.

The bay was popular, very popular, and by the time we were in session we had built up a pretty good head of steam to support for what we were proposing. We said, 'We've got to stop talking about it and we've got to do something. We've got to control the growth around the bay. We've got to stop having them put things in the bay that harm it, such as phosphates in the detergents, nitrogen...' We didn't do much about nitrogen. Nobody thought that was a problem at the time. That was something that cropped up later. They're doing something about it now.

Improving the sewage treatment systems... we did all kinds of things. And it was very difficult because of increases in population that we were having in Maryland. There weren't the great predictions of increases at that point, as we're having now. The dramatic increase in population was not forecast back more than 20 years ago."

What was the climate like at that first Chesapeake Bay summit meeting, which brought all the members of the Executive Committee together in Virginia back in 1983?

"We got Governor Robb from Virginia and Governor Thornburg from Pennsylvania, the mayor of Washington and William Ruckelshouse, a good man who was the head of the EPA, they all came down to sign the agreement. It was a very basic agreement to start with, but it got the thing going. It said that we'd get together and make every effort to clean up the bay and continue the effort. We kept telling people, 'Don't expect results overnight. It took 200 years or so to get the bay in the condition it's in and we're not going to turn it around overnight.' But we really did think that we'd make better progress than has been made. It's been 20 years now and we thought 10 years.

The bay forms the character of Maryland. It was a very popular issue. Had it not been we would have never gotten things like the Critical Areas Legislation through. They're having difficulty now on some land use stuff they can't get through because of the strong local control.

One of the things you have to remember is that Maryland has a very long and strong tradition of local control of land use. Very strong. To get something passed like Critical Areas was unheard of. Critical Areas was preventing the development of anything within 1,000 feet of the shoreline of the bay or the navigable rivers, with some few exceptions. Not much. It wasn't easy to pass. We would have never gotten it through if there weren't all the work that had been done in advance, and had it not been for the support from the public of Maryland. In parades, people would yell, 'Save the bay! Save the bay!' It's a very popular issue."

How did you respond when Torrey Brown came to you

suggesting that there should be no fishing for rockfish, Maryland's signature fish species in the Chesapeake Bay, for an unknown number of years?

"Rockfish were disappearing. Torrey Brown and his people came in to see me about it and I think I shocked him. He said, 'You know, what we should really do is put a moratorium on rockfish'. I said, 'Ok.' Hah—I thought Torrey would jump out of the chair. He said, 'Ok, Governor!' I'm paraphrasing a little bit but basically that's what happened. And there wasn't the revolution that we might have expected. There was obviously some disappointment and objections to it, but there wasn't any Civil War. And I guess it worked."

Bernie Fowler, Former Maryland State Senator

The story of Bernie Fowler clearly demonstrates that there is more than one way to becoming a successful leader in life. His rise in politics and as an environmental leader may in some aspects be similar to that of others, but is decidedly different than most. While Judge Train was dining as a child with the President, for example, Bernie Fowler was earning his stripes on the little peninsula known as Broomes Island, Maryland.

"I tell people quite often when you drive from Brooms Island to Annapolis, it only takes you about an hour and ten minutes," he said. "But when you're a little boy with raggedy knickers on Brooms Island, growing up in a very poor community (and my family was very poor), when you go from there to the Capital of the State of Maryland, it's a long journey...a long journey.

I grew up in the little, water-oriented community of Brooms Island. I think, as a boy there were about 150 homes there. Probably about 75 boats altogether. These were people that worked the water. Brooms Island was a wonderful place to grow up as a child. Very laid back, very friendly, at least among the islanders. Sometimes if you came from somewhere else maybe you would interpret it as being not quite so friendly. But we had strong family ties there.

My family on Brooms Island goes back, as far as I know, to my grandmother and grandfather. That would be Peter and Emma Dove. My dad was born over in, they called it that time Walville; it's really St. Leonards, on Maple Road. In fact, his dad's farm was adjacent to the Jefferson Patterson Park and Museum property. Five hundred and twelve acres of land there, a mile and half of waterfront. Grandpop Fowler had a little farm right next to that.

Brooms Island itself, it was always referred to as an island, but it was more of a peninsula. There's no bridge there to get across to it. Everybody there in my early days as a little boy and young adult, depended on the water industry mainly to make a living. Some of them that managed their finances well did quite well on the water, because back in those days, aquatic life was very abundant. Back from the time I can remember, up until the early 70's, that's when there was a real noticeable decline in the water quality and the absence of aquatic life.

I did a recent windshield survey of the island. I went down there because I didn't want to trust my memory. I started right at the very end of the island, and I remembered a fellow there by the name of Captain Jim Rogers who was a farmer and a waterman. I started counting the people that oystered for a living and I ended up with about 60 boats that went out of either Grapevine Cove or Island Creek, which runs around the peninsula into the river. About 60 boats went out of there all the time during the oyster season. Not uncommon for two men and a culler—a culler is a younger person usually that separates the oysters and the shells, puts the sizable, good oysters in the hold of the boat. The rest is raked over the side off of what they call a culling board.

We had oysters that was much longer than my hand. I don't know if we have any shells to substantiate that, but it was unbelievable some of the oysters. They had several very productive bars, right across the end of the island being one. It was not uncommon for two men and a culler to catch as many 40 bushels of oysters in one day. And I've seen them sell for as low as 25 cents a bushel.

At one time the oyster house that's recently been demolished, Warren Denton and Company, was owned by two brothers and a man named Rogers. My uncle, John Denton, decided in the early 30's that he wanted to do something else besides being in the packing house business, so his brother and Mr. Rogers bought him out. He went doing something else. But it was probably the most productive oyster shucking house anywhere you'll find on the East Coast. They had all the contracts for Superfresh, it was A&P store in those days. And they shipped all around—Cleveland, Chicago, out west. Some of it was shipped by train, but much of the deliveries were made by the trucks they had there. There was never a train there. If oysters were going, say, way out west somewhere, they could unload those oysters on a freight train, refrigerator cars, and sent them on forever. But most of the oysters they shucked and delivered from Broomes Island were delivered by their own truck drivers and trucks.

It was a marketplace to begin with. They bought crabs, oysters, fish, you name it, and they processed all of them there. Oyster house, I guess was the most appropriate name for it. It certainly turned out to be the biggest entity they had in the business. They did quite well from the standpoint of revenue. They also served a very important community function because the people didn't have to go far to sell the oysters.

There were two places down there. Mr. Clarence Sewell had a place, and he handled quite a bit of, particularly fish. He didn't do any shucking that I know of there. But Warren Denton and Company was the biggest as far as seafood was concerned. I worked in there just doing menial things, like helping to wash down, or moving some of the skimmer cans, you know, where they dump the oysters in. The shuckers would come in; they had about a 135 shuckers at one time at that oyster house.

One of the things I remember so vividly when I was growing up, when I was in high school; I started to high school in 1936. When I'd come home in the afternoon, I walked from where the post office is up there now, that was where the bus stopped. It was about a mile from there to my house, where mom and dad lived. So we'd go down there and I'd go in and check in with her after I dropped my books off. The next place I'd hit would be the oyster house, because by that time of the day, the shuckers were growing tired. They were getting ready to knock off, go home. There was never an afternoon I can remember of going down there that someone didn't start singing. They would sing some of the old Negro spirituals (they called them that in those days) or gospel songs, you name it.

One would start, then another one, then another one, and by the time they finished up, that whole oyster house was just inundated with melody and harmony that you wouldn't believe. I just wished so many times that we'd captured that. But we didn't have the technology we have today. I don't think they even had recording machines then, if they did I wasn't aware of it. What a beautiful, beautiful sound. How I've often longed to hear that just one more time. But that's gone. That part of history will never, never surface again.

Let me go back a little bit and tell you a little more about that, and then you'll understand why so many of us have such an affection and such an addiction to the river. During that windshield survey, you'll recall I told you that we determined there were about 60 oyster boats going out there every day that the weather was fit. We also had 12 commercial seine crews. They call them haul sailors, five men in a crew. They made some wonderful catches down there, particularly with the croakers. I've seen one captain down there, I think was Vivian Pitcher, caught 700 boxes—that's 100 pound of fish in each box—700 boxes of hardheads in one haul! It was unusual to catch that many, but not unusual to catch as many as 200 or 300 or 400 boxes. I think his 780 boxes was probably the largest catch they ever had down there. I was involved with that with three different captains. Captain Norman Dove was one, all seine fishing with him. All seine with Captain Lionel Parks. And the third one was Captain Lowrey, who had the clam place down there. I worked with him. It was hard work while you were doing it, but, you know, you made a lot of money sometimes in 48 to 72 hours, depending on the size the catch. 'Cause you had to get all those fish to the packing house, they had to ice 'em down, put 'em on a truck. They'd drive those trucks up to Baltimore and back around the clock until you got all those fish out of the net and got them sold. We saw a lot of good things.

I was down there just last week again and as far as I can determine, I can't find one active oystermen on Brooms Island. Not one. No haul seine crews at all. There's no nets left at all that belong to any of the Brooms Islanders. Someone in the area may have one, you know, from the Eastern Shore to haul the river occasionally. Not to my knowledge. I guess that's the price you pay for progress. And when you look at the way that Southern Maryland has grown—population, industry, and everything—it's just booming, houses all over the place. In fact, I don't know whether I'll live to see it, but I suspect before too many more years it'll be megalopolis all the way from New York to Florida. I think there won't be much left that don't have bricks and mortar on top of it.

That was a part of life that was meaningful and so enjoyable for me. And not just me, I mean, this was a way of life there. There was no concern for drugs, and no concern for the crime. It just didn't happen. They'd have a little fistfight once in a while, kind of liven up things, but no one ever got shot. No one ever got robbed. There was none of that.

Our great activity on the weekends was having an oyster scald. What you do is you get the oysters, and we'd usually do that on a Saturday, the young boys would, the young men. All of the boats when they'd come in and put out their catch on Friday (very few of them oystered on Saturday) they'd always have some oysters left over. Because when they unloaded they took a tub, drop it down into the boat from the block and fall, and then the men in the boat, they'd fill that oyster tub up. They called "oyster tub up" and then they'd hoist it, put it in a wheelbarrow, take it on in, dump it in the plant there. Well, at the very end of that it was rare occasions where they'd come out exact even. So there was always a little bit of oysters, maybe a peck to two, left. So we'd go around, nobody minded us doing it, and we'd take the shovel and we'd take oysters from all the boats around.

We'd have eight or 10 or 12 of us get together. Somebody'd buy the crackers, somebody else would buy the vinegar, the salt and pepper. We'd have an oyster scald. They usually had a small crock they could put that in. You'd always put a couple bricks or something on the bottom of it and throw the oysters in then. And you didn't boil them, you actually steamed them. They'd shrivel right up and when they'd shrivel up, the oyster would open up also. So you could just crack 'em open, shuck 'em, and stick 'em in a bowl there with your vinegar and all. That's what we did for a pastime. That was our fun. Then chose up sides and play a little ball. No televisions then, no electricity, no plumbing.

I graduated from high school when I was only 16, in June 1940. Then I headed off to the big city, went to the Navy Yard after I was accepted, spent about 28 months there. Then I enlisted in the Navy in World War II. Soon as the war was over and we got back, I came back home. I couldn't stand the city any longer then. It was fun when I first went up, but it was getting kind of dangerous, and I didn't spend a whole lot of time at the bars and stuff, so I enjoyed being back home with, you know, my family and the crowd I grew up with.

From there, I went into business in 1947, built a little snack bar down on the shore there. We were not a big operation. I started up on a shoestring. I had to borrow money to make sure I could make change for the customers the first weekend I opened up. Had some rowboats, I had a couple inboard boats, outboard motors, I had a snack bar there. See, people would come and rent a boat from you. In those days, you'd rent a rowboat for eight hours for two dollars. Fishing was good. If you didn't catch fish, it was because you were not a very good fisherman. There were plenty of fish there to catch.

My wife's mother and father used to come down. They were my regular customers. Every Sunday during the fishing season, without fail, it's so strange because her mother would come in, and I didn't have a pay telephone. Weren't that sophisticated in those days. So she'd come in and she'd say, 'Bernie, may I use your phone to call my baby?' I'd say, 'Sure, go ahead.' So I'd open the little compartment I had there, she'd go in the room to use the phone. Then one Sunday afternoon, maybe three years after that, they drove up and I was taking out the Coke cases. In those days you didn't have throwaways, it was all glass bottles, wooden cases. If you had missing bottles, you had to pay for it. So I'd very carefully stack 'em all up and then I'd put 'em outside, because we'd do a big business on the weekends and I may have 20, 30 cases of empty Coke bottles sitting out there. It was tiring, but I'd get that done early, before I got real tired on Sunday afternoon, because I rarely ever went to bed on Friday night and Saturday night. Folks were going and coming all night long.

So the car drove up, and her mom got out, and I see this real pretty little girl getting out of the car. And her mom says to me, she says, 'Have you got a minute, Bernie?' And I said, 'Oh, I'll take it, yes.' So she said, 'Well, I want you to meet my baby.' And that's what started it all. And this September, the ninth, will be 55 years of as good a marriage as you could hope for. We've had some times where we had to really get down and work hard to make ends meet, but always had a strong faith in our creator. The Lord's been good to us—good to us, good to my family. We've had a wonderful life. And I guess there are things I would change if I had it to live over again, but right now I can't think of too many. It just worked real good.

After I sold my place, I still had a hankering and a hunger for the water. I had a little boat and I'd go fishing quite often. Then it got to the point where you couldn't see the bottom, you couldn't catch any crabs. The bottom got so cloudy, you couldn't see hardly a foot below the surface. In 1940, I could see wading in water up to my chest, crystal clear. The bottom looked like Silver Spring, Florida. It was just as clear as it could be, unless you had a storm or turbulence that created some muck there. It was absolutely astonishing the clarity of the water. The seaweed, which went out a couple hundred yards offshore, that helped to provide habitat, feed small aquatic life, and also it helped the sediment and it would produce a lot of oxygen. We didn't have the algae bloom that you have now.

In 1963, we had three million gallons of effluent from waste water treatment plants going into the Patuxent River. There never was any discharge through Southern Maryland counties, never sewer plants up against the Patuxent River.

Today, there's about 50 million gallons a day. In the not too distant future, they predict as much as 80 million gallons. I've been arguing for years now that there's a saturation point; there's a point of no return. The river's only so resilient, it only tolerates so much. But with the enrichment from wastewater treatment plants, the urban run off, sedimentation... you know as well as I do the causes of it. We're educated. We know the problem. But we have not mustered enough political courage or enough money to clean it up. Most of the reason for the conditions we have today, it's really because of greed. It's driven by capital, by development, by building...by ignoring the signs.

In 1979 we got Governor Hughes down for a trip on the river. That was following the law suits we had in court. The three Southern Maryland counties at one time sued the federal government and the State of Maryland, and we won all three cases in the federal court of the District of Columbia. In all three cases the judges issued an order there'd be no more federal funds flowing into the Patuxent watershed until they come up with a plan to clean that river up. We spent about three, four days up in Marriotsville in Howard County. After selling my place down there, and seeing the river going downhill, it was a very sad day. There were people like Dixie Buck, who was an extraordinary crabber. She caught crabs when no body else could. She caught as many as 25 dozen soft shell crabs in one day by herself. Sold them for a penny a piece, 12 cents a dozen. When you see all of that leaving, and if you have any real heart at all, you feel like you want to do something.

As Bernie Fowler playing Bernie Fowler, nobody would listen to me. But I figured if I got into the public eye, and get an audience, I might be able to do something about it. So after serving on the school board for six years, I ran for county commissioner and was elected in 1970—sworn into office December the 4th, 1970, as president of the board of county commissioners. I served in that office for nine of the 12 years that I served as a county commissioner. And during that period of time I was able to solicit the help of other two counties and hundreds of other people to support the cause of, 'Hey, we have just as much right to a clean river down here as they do to use that for a receptacle for waste.'

We tried everything. We went to the governor's office at that time, went to the Attorney General's office. We talked with the Secretary of Department of Natural Resources, which was the Water Resources department then. We got fairly cordial responses, but when you looked behind, nothing was happening. We were getting a lot of talk, but that was all. So in desperation, when I was keynote speaker for the Tri-County Council Annual Meeting over at Shorters' in 1975, I did the best I could to convince them that if we didn't do something a little more dramatic, we were gonna lose the river. I recommended that we put up taxpayers' money into a pool, hire environmental attorneys, and let them research to see if there was anyway that we could stop it. The attorney was successful. The three counties couldn't have worked better. County commissioners, a very diverse group, but they all were bonded by this anxiety of trying to get that river cleaned up. We made headway once the judge dropped the hammer on them. We got the attention of the high officials in the state and we started to making some headway.

And really back in the early 90's the river was getting much better. The clarity of the water was so much better, the seaweed was coming back. There's still some down there, but not like it was there. It wasn't until about, I guess, maybe '96, '97 something like that, I began to notice that the transparency of the water was beginning to change, you know, it was getting muddier, harder to see. Grass was leaving. Crabs were very, very scarce. Still are today. Although we've had some good hand line fishing and all, there's never been any abundance of fish that, you know, was worthy of people investing in a seine boat and all of that to make a living at it.

After I served 12 years in the county commissioner's office, I thought I'd done about all I could at that point, and it was either out or up. So I decided to run for the senate. I was elected to the senate in 1982, was very successful all three terms that I ran. Retired in 1994. Got complacent. Figured, you know, we had everything in place. We had all the major waste-water treatment plants cleaning their act up. We figured things were going good, at least I did. And I just got a little bit...well... I fell asleep at the switch, really. We were almost there. I mean, the water was clearing up, everything was looking good, and then we lost it and it started downhill. Right now, as we speak, it's still going downhill.

You know, if we can't clean the Patuxent River up...it's all within the boundary of Maryland. There are no other jurisdictions involved in the decision making. We call the shots on the Patuxent River. It's unique, absolutely, and it is a microcosm of the Chesapeake Bay. If we can't pull together and clean the Patuxent River up, we're fooling the public that we'll ever clean the Chesapeake Bay up. That's a small project to demonstrate. I forget the exact square miles, but the Chesapeake Bay has got something like 64,000 miles of watershed, and if we can't clean that river up, if that is not symbolic of what we can accomplish, it's sheer folly to think we'll ever get the whole bay cleaned up. So I'm hoping that this is not Custer's last stand. It may sound like it, and I hope our faith won't be like Custer's. I hope we'll be successful. Because with all that's going on, and with all the bursting in the economy and lots of money around and everything...you know, you can ride the big cars, you can have the big home, you can have the largest bank account, but in the final analysis, when you are closer to the sunset of your life, if you aren't able to, you know, look yourself in the face and eyes and say, 'I've done the best I could to make this world a better place,' then I think it's a cardinal sin, it's a shame on all of our parts. So that's what keeps me motivated. That's what keeps me going."

The Legacy of Senator Bernie Fowler keeps us all going in our efforts to restore the bay and to insure a safe and healthy environment for generations to come. He stood up for all of us in demanding clean air and clean water for his community. He dedicated his life's work to the possibility of seeing environmental and social changes come to fruition in his own lifetime.

There is still time. But it's clear that current policies and priorities must shift away from squandering our national endowment and hard-earned tax revenue—we need to focus more on cleaning up the dangerous and deadly messes we have here at home. We must put our own house in order. Simply stated, we can do it. As American citizens we come together in times of war and in times of economic and environmental crisis. The way we comport ourselves in periods of environmental and economic decline in large part defines us as a healthy and wise society. And in the end, these issues and challenges are not about Democrats and Republicans, or rich and poor. They are about protecting the health and well-being of all American citizens, and our common way of life.

The greatest wealth and resource we have in the Chesapeake Bay region is the people. Many of the people interviewed in this book are professionals dealing with issues relating to the health of the Chesapeake Bay, and the rest are directly invested in the success of those efforts. It is my hope, and the hope of everyone involved in the Voices *project, that you will hear these voices, and become inspired to preserve and protect the Chesapeake Bay.*

Afterward

Beginning of the Voices of the Chesapeake Bay Project

Early Travels

As a 16 year old teenager I dropped out of high school in favor of hitchhiking across the country, a trip which lasted for eight years. Like so many other kids of my day I rejected traditional schooling to focus on gaining life experience out on the open road. During those wandering years I traveled through all 48 continental states, talking along the way to people from various walks of life, and simply taking a look around. I never left school or suburban life to escape. The age of tune-in, turn-on and drop-out was already fading into the distance. I was running toward knowledge and experience, not away from it. This was the beginning of my quest for lifelong learning.

In 1999 I relocated to Maryland from Philadelphia, working a day job at the new flagship Borders Books & Music at White Flint Mall in Rockville. My plan was to work a mindless job, allowing time to fulfill my desire to write. Like all the other mindless retail jobs I'd taken the one at Borders consumed me, evolving from clerk into store manager. My book-writing plans fluttered out the window. But there in the large and warmly carpeted Borders Music store, I offered a series of interactive public discussion groups in the spirit of Benjamin Franklin's Junta, and New England town meetings. Each week I'd bring in experts to discus various new releases from the 100,000 titles offered by that gargantuan music store. My appetite for music was voracious.

Throughout my life and travels I have absorbed every type of music. As a child I was introduced to folk music and Broadway show tunes; in my early teens I was a student of the Top 40, as heard through a pocket-sized transistor radio. The Top 40 was a veritable goldmine of every musical style imaginable. In the early 70's I was swept up into the psychedelic world of The Beatles, Stones, and my favorite, the Jefferson Airplane. There were two boys in my suburban Chicago neighborhood that let me tag along downtown into the Chicago blues clubs to see the many originators of the form. We lived and breathed music as kids of the 70's. Music was unstoppable, and packed a powerful message of love and peace. I never let go of the idealism. The listening sessions I presented at Borders were a continuation of that spirit, and an understanding that the arts are transformative.

Radio Waves

The final Borders Music listening party was entitled "Rock and Roll Grows Up: Is There a Need for an Adult Rock Radio Format in the Washington, DC Region?" It seemed to me that WHFS, the original progressive rock radio channel in DC, had turned away from its roots and was only playing music geared for teenyboppers. Fair enough for the kids' sake, but I thought there should be another station, one for the older listeners who wanted to hear the new stuff plus classic rock artists mixed with other styles such as blues, folk, reggae, and world music, in a single radio mix. The panel I put together for this discussion had representatives from the old station, concert promoters from Wolf Trap and the Birchmere, and Washington deejays who presented blues shows and folk hours. In setting up the event I searched out Jake Einstein, the founder of WHFS, to ask if he would attend the panel.

Einstein, a former Eastern Shore newspaper man, was a maverick. He had the vision to develop one of the nation's finest progressive radio stations during the early 70's at the dawn of FM radio. I was told I could find him in Annapolis, where he was busy trying to recreate the free-form, DJ-driven radio style at WXZL, a local station.

I arrived in Annapolis that day in June of 1994 with a manifesto. I had been attending street festivals and passing around a leaflet called "Radio Revolution: Rock and Roll Grows Up." Along with this written demand for a return to progressive radio in Washington, DC, I brought Jake a laundry list of superb performers, new and old, who were not getting any radio airplay.

After I had railed on for a half hour about the need for better radio, Mr. Einstein looked me in the eye and said, "You know, you should have a radio show."

I was ecstatic. I had access to a seemingly unlimited supply of music and could bring it to the public through this radio format called "free-form," where the deejays choose the music. And I've been doing so ever since on The Sunday Brunch (originally The Sunday Morning Show) on 103.1 WRNR. The Sunday Brunch has garnered four Best of Baltimore awards, and, thanks to the listeners and the folks at WRNR, the show began its 14th successful year in July of 2007.

The Sunday Brunch is all about seamlessly blending musical styles and showing connections between older music and the new stuff. I have played every type of music you can imagine on The Sunday Brunch, and I've tried to make each show unique, edifying, enchanting, perhaps even spiritual, while always thoroughly entertaining. But the journey didn't stop there.

Early *Voices*

In 1999 I was introduced to an imaginative environmental educator named Jennifer Hicks, who worked at the Chesapeake Bay Foundation. Jen had woven an environmental ethic into her lifestyle and I felt a kinship with her, understanding that the environment is an important component in the larger context of our lives. She and I tossed around the idea of having a special hour devoted to presenting various ideas and conversations about the Chesapeake Bay as part of my radio show. I thought that a spoken element would fit in nicely with the music, create a good feeling in the community, and perhaps bring back some middle-aged music lovers who years ago had given up on music radio and become talk radio listeners.

Sometime near the end of 1999, I met Claudia Donegan and Robin Jung Brown, who helped transform this idea into reality. Claudia was an Annapolis local. Her late father was a ship's captain, a bay pilot from Baltimore, who helped foreign vessels navigate the shallow Chesapeake Bay waters. Claudia was educated as a geologist and had also worked for the Chesapeake Bay Foundation. A true environmental activist, Claudia has devoted her life to preserving and protecting the Chesapeake Bay.

Voices of the Chesapeake Bay creators Robin Jung Brown, Michael Buckley, Claudia Donegan

Robin was a trained biologist who moved to Annapolis in 1998 to work for the U.S. Geological Survey Patuxent Wildlife Research Center in Laurel, Maryland. She joined the local Sierra Club and answered an ad in The Chesapeake, the club's newsletter, to work on an environmental radio project called Watershed Radio with fellow Sierra Club members Chris Bedford, Andy Roberts, and Janice Oppelt. They wrote and recorded more than 300 one-minute environmental spots dealing with the Chesapeake Bay, which were broadcast on many radio stations. I met Robin when she was delivering the first demo of Watershed Radio to WRNR. She told me about the program and I told her about the idea that would eventually become *Voices of the Chesapeake Bay.*

We had some initial meetings to discuss possible guests for the show, and I decided on a series of 10 hour-long shows over 10 weeks, to be presented annually. I don't think the folks at WRNR fully comprehended how these segments would fit into the all-music format, but I convinced the station managers that this would be good public service programming and that each *Chesapeake* segment would have a musical element.

The initial concept was to present a feature interview with somebody who would talk about their interaction with the bay, plus a secondary interview and a "creature feature" highlighting various plants, animals, and marine species each week. The hour would be rounded out with a couple of songs about the bay.

Little did I realize that, beyond Natty Boh jingles from Baltimore's Brewers' Hill, there were few recorded songs about the Chesapeake Bay. I managed to unearth a few contemporary tunes that mentioned the Chesapeake and Maryland; found a bluegrass song about the great Baltimore Fire, a Chesapeake folk song by Jonathan Edwards, plus an instrumental called *Chesapeake* by the brilliant acoustic guitarist Al Petteway. Claudia knew of an older African-American waterman, Earl White, who picked and sang blues songs while working on oyster boats. There was a captain in the lower bay named Davy

Crockett who performed Jimmy Buffett songs, adding some extra words, reflecting on his life on the Chesapeake Bay. And we found Tom McHugh, a traveling musician who used American blues music to teach American culture in Turkey. He was a member of a performing group called *Chesapeake Scenes,* which had developed a show of Chesapeake songs and stories.

The three of us, Claudia, Robin and myself, met many times to discuss guests we would feature on the first series. I think it was around this time that Robin suggested the series title *Voices of the Chesapeake Bay.*

Project Beginnings

As the producer of the radio show and of the *Voices of the Chesapeake Bay* series, I decided it would be best to have Claudia and Robin do some of the first interviews without me present. It was my plan to let them learn to record in the field, without Mr. Radio Guy looking over their shoulder. Just as Jake Einstein sensed a certain talent in me, I believed Claudia and Robin had the talent and sensitivity to be great interviewers.

Our initial choices for interview subjects were not organized in a linear fashion. I do not remember us ever mapping out a strategy for how to tell the story of the Chesapeake Bay from beginning to end. We just tried to think of people who had good stories to tell. For better or worse, I am a true believer in variety, surprise, spontaneity, instincts, and intuition.

The preferred method for recording *Voices* interviews was out in the field. We brought in Richard Breed, a field audio technician who worked at the White House, and John Calahan, an audio engineer who freelanced at NPR. They brought a sack of loaner equipment to our first meeting, including a portable DAT recorder (digital audio tape) and studio-quality handheld microphones. Medford Canby later helped us make the leap to recorded CDs, a new phenomenon at the time.

After the initial series of segments, the *Voices of the Chesapeake Bay* project went into a brief hiatus. Claudia and

Robin were a bit road weary and decided to cheer the project on as consultants. Among the many other contributors to this project was writer Paula Anne Delve Phillips. For three years Paula assisted me as a researcher, interviewer, events planner, and publicist. She shared my vision for the work and helped me take it to another level, seeing opportunities in the many challenges that arose. I am grateful for the encouragement and assistance offered by Claudia, Robin, John Rodenhausen, Scott Weiss and Paula Phillips, among others.

Radio sponsorships for the original *Voices* series came from a group of local Annapolis real estate agents. Carroll's Creek and the Wild Orchid restaurants became show sponsors for the second and third round of *Voices* segments. When an exclusive *Voices* sponsorship opportunity became available the Boatyard Bar and Grill answered the call, and they have been with us ever since. The Boatyard, led by owner Dick Franyo, is at the forefront of businesses that contribute to Chesapeake Bay restoration efforts.

Dick Franyo, owner of the Boatyard Bar & Grill and *Voices* project supporter

In 2004, I joined forces with the Boatyard Bar and Grill to create the *Songs of the Chesapeake Bay* CD. Dick Franyo acted as Executive Producer for the project and with the generosity of all the musicians and artists who participated the CD has thus far raised $5,000 for a handful of deserving organizations, including the Chesapeake Bay Trust, Chesapeake Bay Foundation, Living Classrooms Foundation of Baltimore, the Maryland Watermen's Association, and the *Voices of the Chesapeake Bay* project.

Rams Head On Stage provided a place for two *Voices of the Chesapeake Bay* concerts. The shows included families of actual watermen and others singing songs and spinning yarns on a stage framed by Chesapeake Bay artifacts, including an osprey nest built by students from the Key School of Annapolis, and other artifacts lent to us by the Chesapeake Bay Foundation, the Oyster Recovery Partnership, and Blacks of the Chesapeake Foundation. The concerts also included an exquisite slide show of Chesapeake Bay art and photography by 12 artists from the region. One of those artists was David Harp.

Out of the 250 plus *Voices* interviews recorded so far, one of my favorites was with David Harp and author Tom Horton. When I was told just a few months before the completion of this manuscript that Dave was interested in working on the *Voices* book I was elated. With generous assistance from the Keith Campbell Foundation for the Environment, led by Keith Campbell and Verna Harrison, the beautiful photos by David Harp that you will see throughout this book were shot over a three-week period—in the hottest part of the summer, I might add.

The *Voices* radio series continues on 103.1 WRNR Annapolis each Sunday morning, and is available worldwide at WRNR.com. You can find more information about the project at www.VoicesoftheChesapeakeBay.org.

Resource Guide

Alex Haley, *Roots* (Seattle, WA, Vanguard Press, 2007)
Alex Haley Foundation, Inc.   kintehaley.org

Alice Jane & Robert L. Lippson,
Life in the Chesapeake Bay
(Johns Hopkins University Press, 1984, 1997)   press.jhu.edu

An Inconvenient Truth   aninconvenienttruth.co.uk

Aspen Institute   aspeninstitute.org/

Atlantic States Marine Fisheries Commission   asmfc.org

Beltsville Area Agricultural Research Service   ars.usda.gov

Blacks of the Chesapeake Foundation   blackschesapeake.org

Blackwater Wildlife Refuge   friendsofblackwater.org

Boatyard Bar & Grill   boatyardbarandgrill.com

Calvert Cliffs National Park   baygateways.net

Calvert Marine Museum   calvertmarinemuseum.com

Carole C. Baldwin and Julie H. Mounts,
One Fish Two Fish Crawfish Blue Fish:
Smithsonian Sustainable Seafood Cookbook
(Smithsonian, 2003) mnh.si.edu/seafood/

Caroline Historical Society–Poplar Grove carolinehistory.org

Chesapeake Bay Foundation CBF.org

Chesapeake Bay Foundation Student Action Network cbf.org

Chesapeake Bay Futures chesapeake.org/stac/futreport

Chesapeake Bay Gateways Network BayGateways.net

Chesapeake Bay Maritime Museum cbmm.org

Chesapeake Bay Program ChesapeakeBay.net

Chesapeake Bay Trust cbtrust.org

Chesapeake Climate Action Network chesapeakeclimate.org

Coastal Heritage Alliance coastalheritage.org

Conservation Fund, the ConservationFund.org

David C. Holly, *Tidewater by Steamboat*
(The Johns Hopkins University Press, 2000) press.jhu.edu

David W. Harp and Tom Horton,
Water's Way: Life Along the Chesapeake
The Great Marsh: An Intimate Journey into a Chesapeake
Wetland Bay Country
(The Johns Hopkins University Press, 2000, 1994) press.jhu.edu

Dinosaur Fund, the glue.umd.edu/~gdouglas/dfund

Eastern Shore Land Conservancy eslc.org

Friends of Calvert Cliffs State Park dnr.state.md.us/publiclands/
southern/calvertcliffs

Gary Jobson, ed., *An America's Cup Treasury*
(Norfolk, VA, Mariner's Museum, 2000)   mariner.org

Gary Jobson, *Fighting Finish: The Volvo Ocean Race*
(Nomad Press, 2002)   nomadpress.net

Harrison's Chesapeake House   chesapeakehouse.com

Harry R. Hughes Center for Agro-Ecology   agroecol.umd.edu

Harry R. Hughes with John Frece,
My Unexpected Journey: The Autobiography
of Harry Roe Hughes
(The History Press, 2006)   msa.md.gov/msa/stagser/
                                                          s1259/151/pubsonline

Hartge Yacht Yard   hartgeyard.com

Historic St. Mary's City   stmaryscity.org

H.M. Krentz   oystercatcher.com

Hutchinson Racing   hutchinsonracing.org

Intralytix   intralytix.com

James Michener, *Chesapeake: A Novel*
(Random House Trade Paperbacks, 2003)   randomhouse.com

Jefferson Patterson Park & Museum   jefpat.org

J. Brooks Flippen, *Conservative Conservationist*
(Louisiana State University Press, 2006)   lsu.edu/lsupress

Jimmy Cantler's Riverside Inn   cantlers.com

John Cronin and Robert F. Kennedy, Jr., *The Riverkeepers*
(New York, Touchstone, 1999)   touchstone.
                                        co.uk/group/Media-And-Publishing

John Page Williams, Jr.,
Exploring the Chesapeake in Small Boats
(Cornell Maritime Press, 1992)   cmptp.com

John Page Williams, Jr.,
*Chesapeake Almanac: Following the Bay
Through the Seasons* (Cornell Maritime Press, 1993)   cmptp.com

John R. Wennersten,
The Chesapeake: An Environmental Biography
(Maryland Historical Society, 2001)   mdhs.org

John R. Wennersten, *Oyster Wars of Chesapeake Bay,
Maryland's Eastern Shore: A Journey in Time and Place,*
(Tidewater Publishers, 1981, 1992)   cmptp.com

Keith Campbell Foundation for the Environment   campbellfoundation.com

Lenny Rudow, *Rudow's Guide to Fishing the Chesapeake,
Rudow's Guide to Rockfish* (Tidewater Publishers, 2005,
Geared Up Publications, 2007)   geareduppublications.com

Lucia St Clair Robson
Mary's Land (iUniverse, Inc., 2003)   luciastclairrobson.com

Marine Stewardship Council   msc.org

MD Dept. of Economic and Business Development   choosemaryland.org

MD Dept. of Natural Resources   dnr.state.md.us

MD DNR Tributary Strategies Teams   dnr.state.md.us

MD Historical Trust   marylandhistoricaltrust.net

MD Watermen's Association   marylandwatermen.com

Mick Blackistone,
Dancing with the Tide: Watermen of the Chesapeake
(Tidewater Publishers, 2001)   cmptp.com

Mike Tidwell, *Bayou Farewell: The Rich Life and Tragic
Death of Louisiana's Cajun Coast* (Vintage, 2004)   randomhouse.com

Mortimer Adler   wikipedia.org/wiki/Mortimer_Adler

Muskrat Lovely   muskratlovely.com

National Geographic Society   Nationalgeographic.com

National Marine Manufacturers Association   nmma.org

National Oceanic and Atmospheric Administration   noaa.gov

National Outdoor Show
nationaloutdoorshow.com

National Trust for Historic Preservation   nationaltrust.org

Natural Resources Defense Council   nrdc.org

Naval Academy Museum   usna.edu/Museum

Old Dominion Sailing   odusports.cstv.com/sports/c-sail

Oyster Recovery Partnership   oysterrecovery.org

Patuxent Wildlife Research Center   pwrc.usgs.gov

Pat Vojtech,
Chesapeake Wildlife: Stories of Survival and Loss
Chesapeake Bay Skipjacks
(Tidewater Publishers, 2001, 1993)   cmptp.com

Piscataway Canoy   tuscaroras.com

Pleasant Plains Farm   pleasantplainsfarm.com

Robert H. Burgess, William Fox, ed.,
Chesapeake Sailing Craft: Recollections of
Robert H. Burgess (Tidewater Publishers, 2007)   cmptp.com

Russell Train, *Politics, Pollution and Pandas*
(Island Press 2003)   islandpress.org

Sandy Point State Park   dnr.state.md.us/publiclands/

Skipjack Restoration Program   cbmm.org
Smithsonian Environmental Research Center   serc.si.edu

Smithsonian National Museum of Natural History   mnh.si.edu

Smith Island, Maryland   smithisland.org

South River Federation   southriverfederation.net

Tangier Island, Virginia   tangierisland-va.com

Tilghman Island, Maryland   tilghmanisland.com

Tom Horton, *Turning the Tide:*
Saving the Chesapeake Bay (Island Press, 2003)   islandpress.org

Tom Horton, *An Island Out of Time:*
A Memoir of Smith Island in the Chesapeake
(Vintage Books, 1997)
                                                            http://somd.com/
                                                            Detailed/3023.php

Underground Railroad   nationalgeographic.com

University of MD Center for Environmental Science,
Horn Point Laboratory   hpl.umces.edu

University of MD Center for Marine Biotechnology   umbi.umd.edu

University of Maryland Chesapeake Biological Laboratory   cbl.umces.edu

U.S. Department of Agriculture   usda.gov

Vincent O. Leggett, *Chesapeake Bay through Ebony Eyes*
(Bay Media.com, 1999)   blackschesapeake.org

Virginia Institute of Marine Science   vims.edu

Volvo Ocean Race   volvooceanrace.org

Waterkeeper Alliance   waterkeeper.org

Weems & Plath   weems-plath.com

West River Sailing Club   westriversc.org

William W. Warner, *Beautiful Swimmer*
(Back Bay Books/Little, Brown & Company, 1976/1994)
                                                            bluecrab.info/resources.htm